Saving Long Island

The David-and-Goliath Battle to Preserve the Pine Barrens

Richard Amper

New Netherland Press
Schenectady, NY

ISBN: 978-0-937666-68-5

Published by
New Netherlands Press
Pine Bush Historic Preservation Project
Schenectady, New York

Table of Contents

Preface

"Never doubt that a small group of thoughtful, committed citizens can change the world; indeed, it is the only thing that ever has."—Margaret Mead

Thirty years after becoming an "official" environmentalist, and upon the urging of literally scores of enthusiasts of the Pine Barrens Preservation Initiative, I've set out to write the story of how a small group of dedicated people preserved Long Island's premier ecosystem. It is a story of persistence and strategy.

I don't present this book as a historical compendium of every citizen action or government proclamation or task force. Instead, I mean it to be a first-hand, personal account of the things individuals did and didn't do to protect drinking water and preserve habitat for past, present and future generations.

What many have called "Long Island's finest achievement" and New York Governor George Pataki called "a model for the state and the nation," the preservation of the Pine Barrens deserves to be documented for the important environmental, political and social achievement that it represents. The environmental effort has been widely acclaimed, honored by the United States Environmental Protection Administration, the New York State Bar Association, and the Sierra Club and it received a Caldor Conservation Award from The Conservation Fund.

But more important, how it was accomplished, against great odds and with enormous social consequences, may motivate and aid others to pursue other environmental or social objectives, be they of greater, equal or lesser importance.

This book will document the earliest interest in Pine Barrens preservation and note the milestones along the way. (As you might expect in an endeavor of this magnitude, it took many people to accomplish the goal.) It will acknowledge the contributions of ecologists, government officials and just plain citizens who helped make preservation real, while it identifies those who paid lip service to environmentalism but either stood in the way or worked to prevent permanent protection of the Pine Barrens. As the old saying from Count Ciano goes, "Victory has a hundred fathers, but defeat is an orphan."

Ironically, those who developed the Pine Barrens Preservation Initiative employed, as a basic strategy, giving credit to anyone who could be moved to help our effort in any way. "You are uniquely positioned to help advance this cause," we told governors, senators, assembly members and local officials at every turn. Now, many of them view their involvement in Pine Barrens preservation as among their greatest life achievements.

With all of these contributions, large and small, it is this book's position that without the effort of one particular group, the Pine Barrens would not have been saved. Landmark litigation was needed, and one group brought it. Historic legislation was needed, and one group led the drive. Administrative leadership was needed, and one group demanded it.

That group was the Long Island Pine Barrens Society, begun in 1977 by three prescient students, John Cryan, Bob McGrath and John Turner. They were joined along the way by others who brought essential skills to the task. I was lucky enough, or crazy enough, to have been attracted to their crusade in 1989. The Society came to be supported by more than 125 other environmental and civic groups, over the years, and eventually by hundreds of elected officials. Ultimately, the overwhelming majority of nearly three million Long Islanders supported and invested in the cause.

Despite their critical importance to drinking water protection and habitat preservation, by 1989 the Pine Barrens were being lost at a rate of 5,000 acres per year, with 234 development projects, valued at $11.2 billion, pending before local town boards and planning boards as the 1990s dawned. Powerful real estate developers and their friends in public office were vigorously paving over Long Island from west to east. Despite all odds, the Long Island Pine Barrens Society halted the onslaught, won the hundreds of millions of dollars needed to acquire the land, and preserved the ecosystem it championed. In so doing, it also demonstrated what intelligence, persistence and dedication can do to improve the world, or at least the place we call home.

Others will write about this remarkable endeavor from their own perspectives. The subject is worthy of thorough analysis. I, however, was truly uniquely positioned to view history in the making. As Executive Director of the Pine Barrens Society for more than 30 years, I had the opportunity to see how the direction of this effort and of public policy was changed. I was there for the five straight years of 80-hour work weeks; helped design the winning strategy; begged for donations; fought with politicians; appeared on television, radio and in the press; faced the threats; knew the players; and ultimately celebrated the victory with the most value-conscious group of individuals I ever met. I am writing this story to celebrate this heroic endeavor and to encourage others.

Acknowledgements

First, I want to thank my wife, Robin, for putting up with everything associated with the Pine Barrens Preservation Initiative. Through difficult economic times, endless days and nights and extraordinary personal pressure, she supported and encouraged my efforts.

My family was very understanding of my neglect during the "War of the Woods." My brother, Tom, was helpful with communications during the campaign and later with this book.

Enormous assistance in writing this book came from three women who, at one time or another, worked for the Society. Carrie Meek Gallagher, who had written on this subject earlier, collaborated with me, interviewing many of those who played a role in preservation. Christine Chase and Jill Lewis spent countless hours researching background and details and checking facts. They were enthusiastic and invaluable.

Thanks too, to the thousands of volunteers and supporters who were very much a part of the crusade and to the scores of environmental and civic organizations which collaborated in the process. I especially salute the individuals who stuck their necks out for this cause, from the individual petitioners on the lawsuit, to the researchers and organizers who came out time after time with persistence and perseverance to attain our goal. To the Long Island leaders, in and out of government, who understood the importance of Pine Barrens preservation, my heartfelt appreciation. Two Long Islanders deserve credit for the cover photos, Jennifer Clements and John Cryan.

The co-founders of the Long Island Pine Barrens Society, John Cryan, Bob McGrath and John Turner changed my life forever. There were times when I was ready to kill them for all the work, pressure and frequent frustration that dominated my life for three decades. But their understanding of environmentalism in general and commitment to Pine Barrens preservation in particular was at once inspiring and motivating. They shared their lofty values and goals with me, and I was the beneficiary. Thanks, too, to those who served on the Society's Board of Directors over the years. They all helped us get where we wanted to go. All those associated with this remarkable endeavor should be very proud of their accomplishments. Tom Casey, a dedicated environmentalist and literary thinker, provided excellent editing help and encouraged me to finally finish this book as did Nina Leonhardt. I'm truly grateful.

Finally, for all the many great contributions from many great people who helped bring about this historic achievement, there were two, without whose dedication and devotion the Pine Barrens would not have been saved. Michael Deering and Jennifer Miller toiled tirelessly and relentlessly, mostly behind the scenes, inspiring and helping me, especially during the most difficult times. Their intelligence and caring made the difference between winning and losing.

Getting Involved

"I like to see a man proud of the place in which he lives. I like to see a man live so that his place will be proud of him."—Abraham Lincoln

One day/evening shortly before Thanksgiving in 1986, Gayle Brovetto came knocking at my door. We were neighbors in the little hamlet of Lake Panamoka, near Riverhead, Long Island. Her face was white and she waved her hands frantically as she started to talk. It seemed that a large development project in our neighborhood had quietly been approved by town government.

She ranted about how some son-of-a-town-councilman had won approval from Brookhaven, Long Island's geographically largest town, to build 24 town-house-type homes on the only undeveloped portion of Lake Panamoka's perimeter. There was no environmental review, she asserted, just a railroaded green light. Gayle's family had lived in the neighborhood for ages, and she was a model of civic commitment. She knew and loved the lake's rich history, collected Native American artifacts and truly cared about the community.

I was not a naturalist but I understood that the lake was certainly vulnerable.

Lake Panamoka, the Island's third largest freshwater lake, is fragile -- about 60 acres in size. It is what geologists call a "kettle pond," a depression carved out by the last glacier and a surface expression of Long Island's water table rising and falling in sync with the table. In the late 1930s, second-home developers began selling off mostly half-acre tracts to city-dwellers who began throwing up small log cabins for summer occupancy.

Over the years, however, many of the summer homes were sold to year-round residents and hundreds more built for full-time residents of the larger hamlet of Ridge, creating a classic example of over-development: an area of just 400 acres containing more than 600 modest houses built around one small lake. The length of the development gestation insured an eclectic mix of residents, from vacation homeowners earning huge salaries to a permanent population of 10-15 percent on public assistance, with every level in between. My wife and I moved there in 1972 and also had an apartment in the city, convenient for our work.

What almost all Lake Panamokans have plenty of, however, is a keen appreciation of the natural resource that brings them together. Through the Lake Panamoka Civic Association, founded in 1949, the residents prohibited motor boats on the lake. They discouraged the use of fertilizers and pesticides and taught neighbors to walk their dogs away from the lake shore.

At the time Gayle came to call, I was a checkbook environmentalist. You know, the kind who knows the environment is important, but is "too busy" to get involved directly, so he does his part by sending contributions to this environmental organization or that.

It's only natural. I grew up in the 1950s in Great Neck, where our parents had brought us for a better life. I encountered nature mostly in terms of lawns. I attended the University of Missouri, attracted by the first journalism school in the country. Then I came back to New York, just in time to land a job with the creation of WCBS Newsradio 88. After that I worked at a Long Island-based radio station and then at a film company back in the city.

Next, I went to work handling communications in the not-for-profit sector. I worked for the Association for Retarded Children on Long Island and the Muscular Dystrophy Association in New York. I learned a great deal about promoting non-profit organizations and served as Associate Producer of the Jerry Lewis Labor Day Telethon, where I focused on communicating about the organization's programs of research and patient care.

In 1980, I started my own Manhattan communications design firm, involving institutional identity, positioning, marketing and public relations (now Richard Amper Associates).

Now, here I was sitting at my dining room table, listening to Gayle's tirade—not very receptively. To me her complaint sounded like NIMBYism—Not in My Back Yard—the protest of neighborhoods satisfied that once they were living in a good place, nobody else was welcome. I told her that I was "too busy" to get involved in this fight, that the "fix" she alleged was probably exaggerated and that I had done enough for my community during my stint as civic association president from 1976-1977. She argued that contamination of this lakefront property would imperil the lake as a whole. "Let me think about it," I replied. She went away.

But she came back. And she came armed with environmental information indicating that the property to be developed had remained undeveloped precisely because its development threatened the ecology of the lake. Groundwater flow, she had discovered, would wash pollutants directly into the lake, killing it. Rare plants and animals would be destroyed and drinking water quality compromised. As for the political chicanery, her story turned out to be absolutely true. I'm not sure whether it was concern about the environment or anger over the political abuse that convinced me, but any notion that I was "too busy" or had already done my bit, disappeared. I didn't know what had to be done, but I promised Gayle I would figure it out and help do it. I shook my head saying, "I can't believe I'm doing this." "It sounds like the call of destiny," my wife, Robin, joked.

As Gayle left the house smiling, I scratched my head. Anchored as I was in New York City, I'm embarrassed to admit that I didn't really understand the structure of local government, didn't know who my local elected officials were, and didn't know the area's environment or the laws that protect natural resources. That was about to change.

The next day an earnest young man arrived on my doorstep. We had never met before. He walked in and was very polite and personable. I didn't suspect it at the time, but he would change my life. Somehow, John Turner, co-founder of the Pine Barrens Society and at the time Director of the Division of Natural Resources for the Suffolk County Parks Department, had found out about the proposal and wanted to help stop it. John is a positive fellow, friendly and understated. A native Long Islander, he is possessed of a quiet, "aw shucks" quality that helps him sell his ardent commitment to the environment in general and the Pine Barrens in particular. His scientific knowledge and enthusiasm for his subject confirmed my decision to fight the development. What's more, he understood the legal process by which development parcels are properly approved. He suggested, not subtly, that this one hadn't enjoyed it. By this time, John had us both on the same page.

The battle was joined. Gayle gathered a small corps of neighbors to mount an opposition. They were ready, willing, and clueless. I approached the challenge as I would any communications design project for any client. First, we needed research. We needed to find out quickly what our options were, how much time we had to apply them and what resources were necessary to stop "Shadow Oaks," as the proposed development was called. Robin took this task on herself. Next, we needed community organization. It was clear we would have to reach out to our neighbors and organize them for effective, compelling action. An energetic young woman with small children, Kathy Lindahl, agreed to take on this part. I agreed to work on mass communication and fundraising.

Within days we had information on New York's State Environmental Quality Review Act from a knowledgeable Suffolk County environmentalist, Louise Harrison. We located a bright environmental attorney, Christopher Kelley of the respected East End law firm, Twomey, Latham, Shea and Kelley, who agreed that a legal challenge would be necessary to overturn the project's approval. And we learned that the fight was going to take a lot of money and a lot of time—neither of which we had.

The holiday season was a blur of activity. Working through the Lake Panamoka Civic Association and its ailing President Danny O'Connell, we wrote to our neighbors, soliciting contributions and volunteers. A community of extremely limited means set out to raise $20,000 for legal fees and mailings. Later, these same neighbors responded with letters, postcards and attendance at key town and county meetings. Our neighbors' response was inspiring.
The statute of limitations on our legal challenge to the preliminary subdivision approval was 30 days. We rushed, filing what is called an Article 78 proceeding, just two days before the developers, Robert Reid, Jr., the former Town Councilman's son, and his partner, Thomas Scionti, planned to bulldoze the site.

I went to visit Brookhaven Town Supervisor Henrietta Acampora, whose grandmotherly appearance belied a sharp tongue, salty language and allegations of corruption. She assured us that no favors had been done, no environmental injustice had been committed, and no remedy would be forthcoming. Her bright, fast-talking deputy, a red-headed young man named Peter Scully (who in the years to come would help out positively in more than one environmental struggle) asked what we planned to do. "We'll fight in court, and we'll also fight in the court of public opinion," I warned.

"If I had a dime for everyone who promised they'd expose me in *Newsday* [the Long Island newspaper], I'd be a rich woman," Acampora responded, and abruptly motioned me out. She would get her rendezvous with *Newsday*, but that would come later.

The lawsuit filed, it was time to "go public." It's an old saying that in struggles for government attention, it's the squeaky wheel that gets the grease. The Town had approved a major subdivision on the shores of a freshwater lake without requiring an environmental review. The implications for surface and drinking water and rare and endangered species, coupled with the relationship between the developers and a former town official, made this issue ripe for intensive press coverage.

We decided to ask neighborhood children (many of them too young to be trusted with scissors) to tie green ribbons around hundreds of trees ringing the lake—an image tailor made for Long Island's newest media venture, News 12 Long Island, the first regional all-news cable network on television, pioneered by Charles Dolan of Oyster Bay, Long Island. His son Pat was its News Director. We pitched them a story on the contrast between holiday celebration and the desperation of one small community--an easy sell.

We prepared press releases and background materials, but the green ribbon campaign ran into a snag. The local florist, Patricia Van Deinse, could supply unlimited quantities of red ribbon at no cost to the community if we weren't wedded to green. We weren't. We made the edit on the computer and faxed the press releases: "The red ribbons tied around the trees at Lake Panamoka are not holiday decorations," the press release read. "They're symbols of protest." On December 19, 1986 the struggle to "Save the Lake" was on the air.

Pat Dolan assigned the story to a young, smart, News 12 reporter, Mary Mucci. (Years later, she married him.) She came to the lake, then headed directly for Brookhaven Town Hall. Ah, the power of the press! The next day, the town put out a statement. "New information," they said, had been received by the town from the New York State Department of Environmental Conservation. The information suggested "the need for further review," of the project. Acampora's bright deputy Scully showed up on television to assure everyone in Lake Panamoka that, "It appears that preliminary approval will be rescinded . . . based on the new information we've gotten from the D.E.C. Clearly, the town is as concerned about its natural resources as any of those residents over there. Their action to protect their community is healthy and one that we welcome."

Of course, Scully simultaneously appeared on tens of thousands of other television screens across Long Island. One of them was being watched in Medford by a 28-year-old environmental educator and Pine Barrens Society co-founder, Robert McGrath. He phoned the next day and asked if he could meet with me during the school break between Christmas and New Year's. He was reticent, almost secretive, in his request, but said he thought he could be helpful. I welcomed his input.

Early on Christmas Eve, a lone cameraman without reporter arrived for a brief "sound bite." Obviously, News 12 wanted to promote their new network just when we needed publicity for our protest. My nine-word "News 12 certainly made a difference for Lake Panamoka" led a 30-second promotion that was followed by clips of television coverage of the Lake Panamoka story over a voice track that said, "On December 19 at five o'clock, News 12 Long Island broke the story of a town divided over a lake. The Lake Panamoka Civic Association was embroiled in a dispute with town officials over a planned housing development. Permission to build had been granted before an environmental impact study was conducted. Following our report, town officials called to say the development had been stopped and promised a thorough investigation. If you think news doesn't make a difference, watch News 12 Long Island. We make a difference." We gave them the sound bite, essentially promoting their network, and in return we got our story playing all through the holiday weekend, to the delight of the neighborhood and to the consternation of Brookhaven and the state Department of Environmental Conservation.

The day after Christmas, the *Newsday* I retrieved from my driveway included an article by reporter Mitchell Freedman which began, "Town officials are taking a second look at a controversial plan to build 24 homes on Lake Panamoka." It went on, "But, no matter what they see, the decision is likely to create problems." Now we had the town's concern over the newspaper coverage to add to News 12's.

Bob McGrath arrived with confirmation, the next day. After solicitous introductions, the clean, crew-cut teacher/administrator offered heartfelt congratulations but warned that the early success was no guarantee of victory. Where Turner was friendly and wanted to have a discussion, Bob cut to the chase. "Land is not preserved until it's purchased," he said simply. He urged an immediate refocus on all available funding resources for acquisition of the 19-acre parcel, including those of the state, county and town. Where Turner was focused on promoting the need for preservation, Bob was focused on what we needed to do to obtain it. Together, they made a great team.

He was right. In January, 1987, I returned to Brookhaven Town Hall to press for acquisition. Our plan was to ask very nicely and then go out and turn up the heat. Peter Scully met me at Supervisor Acampora's door. I had been told that Supervisor Acampora appreciated a good joke and I had one at hand. "Okay, now what do you want?" she asked.

"Madame Supervisor," I began, "did you ever hear the story about the greedy developer who dies and heads to heaven?" I asked. "Go ahead," she replied, cautiously.

"Well," I continued, "he is met at the Pearly Gates by Saint Peter" (a line not lost on the Supervisor's quick-witted deputy) "and is advised that he has pressed the wrong elevator button and instead has a reservation below."

"`There must be some mistake,' said the developer. `Surely God decides who gets into heaven and who doesn't.'

"'Ordinarily, that's true,' said Saint Peter. 'However, only when weighing between good and evil, and you're one of the very few to arrive here who's never done anything good.'"

The Supervisor seemed to be enjoying the story but couldn't figure out where it was going.

"Showing the developer the book that God keeps on each of us," I continued, "Saint Peter challenged the developer to find one thing he had ever done to offset his numerous sins. Sure enough, there on page 19 of a 2,100-page tome was a hand-written note scrawled in the margin indicating that he had donated ten cents to the March of Dimes when he was in second grade."

By this time, even Scully looked puzzled. I continued, "'You've got me on a technicality,' Saint Peter admitted, 'I'll have to take the matter to God.'"

"Returning in seconds, St. Peter was asked by the developer, 'Well, what did she say?'

"Saint Peter replied, 'She said, "Give him his dime back and tell him to go to hell!"'" The joke ended. I quickly added, "And that's precisely what we want you to do with Bob Reid's son. Scully and Acampora understood immediately that I was asking that the development be rejected, and the land purchased. I got up and left. The seeds of acquisition of the property had been sown.

Later in January, Panamoka residents sent thousands of letters to state, county and town officials. In February, the Society recruited other groups to press for preservation, including the Ridge, Yaphank, and Rocky Point Civic Associations, the Longwood Alliance, the Brookhaven Land Resources Council (precursor to the Open Space Council) and other environmental and civic groups. March brought helpful warnings from the New York State Natural Heritage Program and The Nature Conservancy of the threats represented by development of the parcel.

March also brought a cold, late night visit to an adjacent pond. A suspicious neighbor called me and said, "there's this guy splashing around a pond by the lake." I went to check it out and discovered a rugged wader-clad guy with a light on his head. I talked to him, learned that he was Dr. Robert Johnson, a biologist. He wouldn't tell me what creature he was searching for. I watched his tight-lipped exploration from the shore.

So, what was he looking for? I couldn't begin to guess. But, I thought, the Pine Barrens experts would know or have a pretty good guess. I talked to them, and they quickly figured it out. "Well," Turner said, "he's not working with us so he must be looking for something that would help the developer. It must be a rare plant or animal." It turned that Turner knew this pond pretty well. "There are no threatened plants in that pond," Turner said, "so it must be an animal species." He paused for a moment—then his eyes lit up. "It's got to be the Eastern Tiger Salamander—rare and endangered." Turner smiled, "if it is a tiger salamander the developers have a serious problem on their hands." Turner went on to explain that it was difficult to obtain a development permit immediately adjacent to an endangered species habitat. So, "Shadow Oaks" had one more problem than the residents of Lake Panamoka. That's why Johnson didn't have much to say about that to me.

It was for a state endangered species that breeds in the vernal ponds surrounding Lake Panamoka that Dr. Johnson, a consultant for the developers, had been searching for that frigid March evening as I stood shivering by the pond. Not surprisingly, he hadn't found them, but he didn't want to. If salamanders were not on the property, then the developer could move ahead with their project. Unfortunately for the developer, we found one.

We began poking around to find out if anyone had seen the elusive amphibian. Highly unlikely, I surmised. I was wrong. A local school child had chanced upon him during a rare moment when he had emerged from underground, perhaps in search of warmth himself or merely to raise a red flag. It turned out that Mike Malloy and his family, who lived in the area, had enjoyed his company briefly. "I named the salamander Tony, as in Tony the Tiger salamander," Mike explained.

The Pine Barrens Society leaders were ebullient. They planned to add Mike's experience to testimony before the Brookhaven Town Planning Board in June. We decided to keep the find under wraps until then.

We visited elected officials in April to press for acquisition, visited the Suffolk County Legislature on May 10 seeking preservation funds, and prepared for a showdown in front of the Brookhaven Town Planning Board on June 15.

We knew we were playing for the ship. To get the Planning Board to turn down a development project advanced by a local politician was going to require a big, buttoned-up pitch for preservation, if Lake Panamoka were to block "Shadow Oaks."

We needed a big turnout—not a few whiners—four busloads of angry Panamokans. We knew we'd need a slick slide show so we went out and shot two dozen pictures of Lake Panamoka and the plants and animals that lived there. We needed impassioned speakers; they ranged from concerned neighbors, animal lovers, and supportive public officials from outside of the town. We knew we'd need colorful signs and badges – creative neighbor Kathy Lindahl took the lead on that one. We needed a variety of speakers mixing environmental science with civic pride with righteous indignation. We were still painting signs the night before the big meeting. We were worrying about things like how many people will actually show up, whether the speeches will come together and what the reaction will be.

The next day, Lake Panamoka was ready. Gayle Brovetto, Kathy Lindahl, new LPCA president Robert Gelbach, and 250 other neighbors piled onto four chartered buses loaded with sandwiches, drinks, hand-made felt badges in the shape of stop signs, and plenty of posters reading, "Save the Lake: Stop Shadow Oaks."

It came off perfectly. The entire Panamoka community had collectively decided to march on town hall to demand protection of a preciously-guarded natural resource. The speakers hit all the right notes as they raised legitimate environmental concerns, with a healthy dose of civic pride and righteous indignation thrown in for good measure. The slide show won oohs and ahhs as pictures flashed on the screen of a Great Blue Heron swooping over the lake, a hummingbird at a neighbor's flower pot, and, finally, "Tony," the Tiger Salamander, our trump card.

It was a great day for Lake Panamoka and a great day for "Tony" and his family. Our star performer, Mike Malloy, the ten-year-old Panamoka school child, told the planning board, "How can the builders say there is no Tiger Salamander?" Malloy asked, "I had one as a pet last fall, but I let him go so he could be where he belongs. I hope the Town won't let them kill Tony and his friends."

It was a knock-out. The press and the Brookhaven Planning board were wowed by the presentation. The "Save the Lake" campaign had taken a giant leap for protection of Lake Panamoka.

"They came. They saw. And if they didn't conquer, at least they impressed," Mitchell Freedman wrote in the June 18 *Newsday*. Brookhaven Planning Board Chairman Jack Luchsinger said, "We've had many presentations since I've sat on this side of the table, and I don't know of any that was done any better." The teeter had tottered.

We had a powerful ally. Suffolk County Legislator Gregory Blass, the presiding officer of that body, called for joint town/county acquisition of the property during the hearing, and News 12's Mary Mucci, staying with the story she broke, reported, "This time, they were not a voice in the wilderness. Residents who have been fighting to preserve the wilds of Lake Panamoka have organized and enlisted the support of some influential Suffolk leaders." Long-time News 12 and New York City anchorwoman Melba Toliver concluded the story, saying, "Brookhaven officials told residents they were impressed by their arguments and that they would give serious consideration to them."

The presentation got us unparalleled notice and credibility. That led to more public support— from politicians and the media. The presentation and its media coverage turned the tables on Shadow Oaks.

The successful presentation helped win the July 1987 State Supreme Court position in the hands-on Justice Thomas M. Stark ruled for the Lake Panamoka Civic Association and against Brookhaven Town, officially overturning the town's approval.

Two hundred Panamokans turned out for a rally at the local community pavilion seeking state, county and town funds for permanent preservation. State Senator Kenneth P. LaValle and Assemblyman Joseph Sawicki, Jr. encouraged the crowd but offered nothing in the way of state funding. By autumn the town had approved $400,000 and the county $800,000 to buy the environmentally-sensitive tract for permanent preservation. Ultimately, Suffolk County picked up the tab, the first purchase under its Drinking Water Protection Program, using a quarter-cent fund created by Suffolk voters.

On June 4, 1988, we organized a family-friendly lakeside ceremony featuring a Dixieland band playing "Happy Days Are Here Again." Neighbors celebrated the hard-fought victory with an old-fashioned beach barbecue at a ceremony marking the first use of the popularly-supported fund for Pine Barrens preservation. Local artist Liz Weidner created a five-foot-long tiger salamander. Suffolk County Executive Patrick Halpin and Brookhaven Supervisor Henrietta Acampora, Legislator Steven Englebright, U.S. Congressman George Hockbrueckner and County Clerk Edward Romaine joined in the festivities.

Long Islanders could now regard preservation as an important accomplishment. So, the party was not merely a neighborhood celebration. It occurred shortly after the creation of the Suffolk County Drinking Water Protection Program, which subsequently was responsible for nearly $3 billion in water quality and land preservation.

As County Executive Halpin walked to his car, he turned to John Turner and me and said, "Twenty acres today ... what tomorrow?"

"Twenty thousand tomorrow," Turner responded and smiled.

I shrugged and returned to my business in New York City. For me, it was the end--or so I thought.

In the Beginning

"Think of our life in nature—daily to be shown matter, to come in contact with—rocks, trees, wind on our cheeks! the solid earth! the actual world!"—Henry David Thoreau

When I told Halpin and Turner that the Panamoka victory represented a job well done and that I could now return to my real job, I believed it. The next week I returned to my Manhattan commute on the Long Island Railroad thinking that my excursion into environmentalism was over. But the experience had changed me more than I realized.

The train ride from Ronkonkoma to Penn Station provided a solid eighty-minute block of time to think and plan. But as I thought about my business clients and their projects, my mind kept switching tracks. Turner's dream of saving 20,000 acres of pine barrens ran through my head. That would be a cool thing to do. And then a further thought: that would be a cool thing for *me* to do. Could our efforts be scaled up for a bigger battle? What would it involve?

Part of me wasn't sure. Me an environmentalist? I thought of them as tree-huggers. Their hearts were in the right place, but they rarely seemed to accomplish anything. Okay, but then maybe someone like me is what they need.

Perhaps the environmentalists were thinking something similar. Pine Barrens Society founders John Turner and Bob McGrath, who had advised me during the "Save the Lake" battle, stayed in touch. Both were working to preserve the Oak Brush Plains in Edgewood and other areas threatened by development, and from time to time one or the other would drop by for a chat— mostly about their efforts. I got the impression it was part of a plan to make me a full-time environmentalist. I also heard from the more reserved, third founder, John Cryan, who preferred calling me from his New York office.

McGrath and Turner, now in their early thirties, grew up together in the town of Smithtown in central Suffolk, eight houses apart. Cryan, a few years older, lived in Commack, the hamlet next door. As tweeners in the late 1960s, McGrath and Turner explored local "woods" together, riding many miles on their bicycles. Cryan often rode his bike down Commack Road to the Oak Brush Plains.

At age six Cryan fell in love—with the rare, endangered Karner blue butterfly. His parents went out and bought him a butterfly kit (but kept the "killing fluid" out). "I caught them, then lay on my belly watching them for hours," the shy, bespectacled naturalist recalls. Soon he began drawing them and joined the Junior Entomologists Society, which was created by the American Museum of Natural History staff. His interest never waned, but he did drop out for a time at puberty, until, as he said, he "got over being embarrassed about chasing butterflies in front of girls."

When McGrath was 12, he began volunteering during the summer at Hoyt Farm Nature Preserve in Commack, under the supervision of the Park Ranger, Bob Giffen. It was here that he first met Cryan, then 16. "John would come to Hoyt, which was near his home," McGrath recalls, "and enjoyed volunteering for Giffen. Giffen mentored us in many aspects of natural history. He gave us focus and inspired us to study further."

A few summers later McGrath introduced Turner to Hoyt Farm and to Cryan and Giffen. Giffen took an immediate liking to the ardent but self-composed Turner and hired him full-time. From this point forward Hoyt Farm was central to the three of them and became a home base where they would meet and discuss all aspects of natural history. It was here that Cryan started studying the Pine Barrens scientifically, moving the group's interest beyond hiking in the woods.

The young men began exploring the Pine Barrens and the East End in earnest, using Hagstrom maps and the U.S. Geologic Survey to identify undeveloped areas, bushwhacking brush when necessary, as many areas did not have cut trails. "We were visiting not merely token preserves but vast expanses of open space, learning more and more and having the time of our lives," McGrath recalls. Urged by Park Ranger Giffen, the young men read books about the pinelands by nineteenth and early twentieth century naturalists, such as Timothy Dwight's *Travels in New England and New York* (Vol. 3, 1821), and Roland M. Harper's, "The Natural Vegetation of Western Long Island South of the Terminal Moraine," *Torreya* 17:1 (January, 1917:1-13). The boys also treasured Winslow C. Watson's, *The Plains of Long Island* (Albany, NY, 1860).

The boys' enjoyment of the woods grew into a deep, informed appreciation, leading them to form a group that organized hikes with discussions afterward about what they had observed. They put together a slide show with pictures taken on their hikes. In 1977, when Cryan was 20 and Turner and McGrath 17, they along with Mike Deering, Kevin McDonald and other local friends who would become important to Long Island's environmental preservation, launched a more formal organization: the Long Island Pine Barrens Society. The Society was initially oriented to raising awareness and appreciation of the pine barrens. The boys, now college-age men, began touring the Island, giving their slide presentations at libraries and club meetings, educating listeners about areas that most residents took for granted. The Society promoted scientific research as well, and in 1980 began publishing *The Heath Hen*, a professional journal with a mailing list of 500 respected environmentalists. The group also worked to turn out pro-preservationists for public meetings involving Pine Barrens protection efforts.

When I met them in the mid-1980s, they were members of the workforce. McGrath was an outdoor environmental educator for the Western Suffolk Board of Cooperative Education Services (BOCES), Turner worked for Suffolk County Parks, and Cryan worked for the New York State Department of Environmental Conservation. In the year after "Save the Lake," they encouraged my interest, taking me for hikes in choice areas of the region and passing on the books that had inspired them. I had grown up on Long Island and lived the past twenty years in the pine barrens regions, but only now discovered what an extraordinary place it was.

Long Island's pine barrens, formed during the most recent period of glaciation more than 12,000 years ago, once covered fully a quarter of the one million acres that comprise Long Island. They encompassed the Hempstead Plains in central Nassau County, and the Oak Brush Plains in western Suffolk; the South Setauket Woods near Stony Brook on the north shore and the globally-rare Dwarf Pine Plains in Westhampton. The 105,000-acre Central Pine Barrens area, which includes the now-protected 53,000-acre Core Preservation Area, stretches from Rocky Point in the northwest to Hampton Bays in the southeast.

Pine Barrens are ecological communities built on dry sandy soil and dominated by grasses, low shrubs and smaller-sized pine trees, such as pitch pine and jack pine. They exist only in the Northeastern United States, where they comprise less than two percent of the land area. Long Island's is second only to the New Jersey Pinelands' one million acres, one-fifth the land mass of the state, and declared by Congress a National Reserve in 1978. Third in size is the Plymouth County/Cape Cod Barrens in eastern Massachusetts (45,000 acres). The Albany Pine Bush (2,000 acres) and the Shawangunk Pine Barrens near New Paltz (about 4,000 acres) are the largest of the half-dozen or so other pine barrens in New York State.

Archaeological finds reveal that Native Americans hunted in the pine barrens and fished the rivers and lakes for centuries, before English "settlers" arrived in the early 1600s. The English, looking for land where they could grow what they grew in England, and finding the porous, nutrient-poor soils inhospitable, dubbed the region "barren." George Washington cursed "those ill-thriven pines."

Other visitors found more to appreciate. Walt Whitman, while granting that the wide tracts of pine and scrub-oak could be "monotonous and sterile," nevertheless spent "many a good day or half-day . . . wandering through those solitary cross-roads, inhaling the peculiar and wild aroma," and catching from the swamp-cedars on at least one occasion the heart-piercing song of "the unrivalled hermit thrush."

In fact, the ecosystem is home to the greatest diversity of plants and animals anywhere in New York State—thousands of species, many of them endangered or threatened. There are more than 100 bird species, many of which are disappearing elsewhere; an outstanding population of butterflies and moths; and extraordinary plant communities, some of them globally rare. No wonder that The Nature Conservancy designated the Long Island Pine Barrens among its first dozen "Last Great Places" in the entire Western Hemisphere. Dominated by spindly pitch pines and scrub oak in its dry uplands, the barrens support taller pines and tree oaks in moister areas. They also contain a diverse range of wetland communities, including marshes, heath bogs, red maple swamps, rare Atlantic white cedar swamps and remarkable examples of coastal plain ponds. As I read the books that Turner, McGrath, and Cryan recommended, and started hiking with them, I was dumbfounded. Here was a natural treasure that matched Long Island's storied oceanfront, and I, like most people who lived here, hardly knew of it.

A succession of naturalists studied the Pine Barrens and called for preservation. During the 1930s, '40s and '50s, ecologists such as Roy Latham, Leroy Wilcox ("the Birdman of Speonk") and Robert Cushman Murphy studied and wrote about the region and its flora and fauna. In *Fish-Shape Paumanok* Murphy wrote in 1964, "There should be a Pine Barrens State Park and it should be a good big one." In the '70s a new wave of environmentalists, including Dennis Puleston, Gil Raynor and Paul Stoutenberg studied and wrote about the Pine Barrens, Naturalists like Fred Schlauch and John Cryan began exploring first the Oak Brush Plains and the Smithtown Pine Barrens.

To this point consideration of the Pine Barrens was largely an academic matter, with papers written in scholarly journals. In the Seventies Cryan, Turner and McGrath used their slide lectures to bring the wonders of the barrens to a widening circle of Long Islanders. Then in July 1977 *Newsday* ran a long article, "The Pine Barrens: Our Forgotten Responsibility," in its Sunday "Long Island Magazine" section. The story, with attractive photos and a map of the region, exposed the public to the riches of the Pine Barrens for the first time in the general circulation press. What had been widely regarded as wasteland was now winning recognition as a true natural treasure--one needing protection. "Much of the Barrens has been lost forever," wrote the article's author, Fred Schlauch, "and every enduring acre should be considered endangered. If we do not act wisely in the near future, the Pine Barrens will follow the Hempstead Plains into oblivion."

Besides being wondrous, the Pine Barrens is critically important. Its porous, sandy soil recharges an average of 150 million gallons of rainwater per day, which percolate into Long Island's Long Island's largest aquifer—the natural reservoir that provides pure drinking water to nearly three million Long Islanders.

But this precious resource was being threatened. As the population surged eastward, development kept carving away more and more of the pine barrens recharge area. When Cryan, McGrath, and Turner founded the Pine Barrens Society in 1977, only half of the original quarter-million acres remained. By the time I joined the fight, we had lost 25,000 acres more.

It was more than the loss of acreage that was a threat; it was the piecemeal way the region was hacked apart, one development here and the next over there, without meaningful planning. By 1967 Harvard's famed entomologist Edward O. Wilson and Princeton mathematical ecologist Robert MacArthur had presented their findings on ecosystem viability—how each species requires a certain amount of space to survive, that is, contiguous space. As a habitat "island" decreases in size, species die off, first the rarer and more endangered species—the ones that require the greatest minimum space—then others. The loss of diversity then threatens the ecosystem itself. Pine Barrens ecologists had begun to worry about what minimum contiguous area must be preserved if the barrens were to survive.

There is a related problem. The barrens are what is known as a fire climax ecosystem, meaning that they require periodic wildfire for regeneration. The soils are droughty, nutrient poor and acidic. The barrens of today probably developed between 5,000 and 2,500 years ago during a very dry period. Lightning strikes brought periodic burning, and when they didn't, Native Americans set fires themselves. The fire destroys competing plant communities, but not the pitch pines. Their flaky bark, filled with insulating air pockets, allows them to survive and send out new growth after the fire. Plus the fire opens up the pine cones which now drop seeds onto a newly-exposed forest floor, where the thinned canopy permits sunlight to regenerate native vegetation. Scrub oaks, too, are fire-adapted, with up to 90 percent of their biomass underground, ready to create new shoots after a fire. These natural processes are most effective in contiguous areas.

In 1995 there were two gigantic simultaneous fires over 5,000 acres -- in Rocky Point and the Hamptons-- that attracted national attention. Scientists realized that years of fire suppression near developed areas had allowed too much accumulation of plant litter on the forest floor. The result: when fire came it was unusually large and hot, damaging some areas of the Pine Barrens and threatening adjacent communities. The experts now recommend that land-managing agencies conduct limited and controlled "prescribed" burning where fire has been absent for too long— just as Native Americans had done. That's a real problem if you have a checkerboard of development—you're always going to have homes or businesses right near where you need to have fires.

Of greatest danger is the threat to the Island's water. Less open space means a smaller recharge area, while more human activity means more contamination—from household sewage, industrial and chemical wastes, fertilizers, pesticides and other toxins—all of which compromise the water in the aquifer and surface waters as well.

Preservation got its start in the late 1970s, in Rocky Point and Riverhead, where the Radio Corporation of America had accumulated 7,200 acres of Pine Barrens to contain huge trans-Atlantic radio transmitting and receiving arrays. More modern technology rendered the arrays obsolete, so in 1978 RCA sold the land to the New York State Department of Environmental Conservation for one dollar—relieving themselves in the process, of course, of millions of dollars in property taxes.

The acquisition of the land presented a novel problem to the D.E.C., which was now responsible for the "care, custody and control" of the property, but had no personnel to provide it. D.E.C Commissioner Peter Berle and its Regional Director Donald Middleton realized there should be a dedicated entity responsible for the job and in 1978 created the Pine Barrens Task Force, a group within the D.E.C. Although it lacked any statutory power, it nonetheless served as a forum for advancing the Pine Barrens as a priority, especially within government circles. Berle and Middleton were true public servants, committed to making government for the public interest. Commissioner Berle himself attended the first meeting of the Task Force, although he was on Long Island principally to negotiate the RCA property acquisition. When the RCA negotiations ran late and the Task Force meeting began, he and Middleton shuttled up and down the halls, determined to keep both on track. Berle went on to head the National Audubon Society and was senior partner at the Manhattan law firm that years later handled the Pine Barrens Society's appellate work.

One predictable result of this attempt to do something constructive was a fuss raised by Suffolk County Planning Commissioner Lee Koppleman. Of course, he would have objected to any plan not his own. Koppleman intended to be the Big Kahuna in LI planning. The coming years would show again and again that he was better at, and more interested in, fighting turf wars than preserving land. On this occasion his complaints never gained traction.

At this point, and for the next decade, preservation on Long Island could hardly be called a movement: it was a series of actions by a collection of committed individuals. They often joined forces but did not form a united group, nor did they have a defined set of goals or a set of plans to achieve them. Rather they were responding as best they could to the specific threats that came up.

Suburban sprawl had marched west-to-east across the Island for more than half a century, and by the 1980s it was rampant in Suffolk County. You couldn't swing a cat without hitting a developer who had found some parcel of land to build McMansions on and make a killing.

Thanks to Long Island's tradition of home rule, environmentalists found themselves in a giant game of whack-a-mole. Suffolk alone had ten townships, each empowered to approve land use within its borders. Some, like Brookhaven (popularly referred to as Crookhaven) were perennially corrupt, with one administration after another brought down by scandal. Other towns practiced a more familiar kind of coziness. Elected officials weren't necessarily against environmental protection if it didn't interfere with real estate development (for they did believe, erroneously, that new residential development was good for the local economy). They just did what pols do—whatever is best for them. In practice that meant that in the absence of a vocal opposition to a building proposal (the usual case), they were happy to accommodate an influential citizen, and likely campaign donor.

At any time there were dozens of proposals in play. Environmentalists had to choose their battles —without the benefit of an overall vision or strategy to guide their decisions. Often, how big a campaign was mounted depended on who lived in or had a personal attachment to an area. The Pine Barrens Society's founders, for example, led the campaign to preserve the Oak Brush Plains, where they used to hike as kids, and Stony Brook geologist Steven Englebright led the fight in Manorville, the site of some of his research. Efforts to block projects and preserve land had a leg up on the east end, especially on the south fork, thanks to the resources and connections of their well-heeled residents.

Englebright was a Professor at Stony Brook University and an ardent environmentalist. An enthusiastic bear of a man with a mustache and a broad smile, he favored old, comfortable clothes which fit him well or indifferently at various weight levels and weatherproof shoes for his often-spontaneous forays into the woods. Steve saw politics as a means for achieving his pro-environment agenda, not an end in itself, as it is for too many politicians. His entry into politics came about in an interesting way.

In the early 80's, Lynn Buck, Co-President of a volunteer group, Save Good Groundwater, set out to preserve the Red Creek section of the pine barrens in Hampton Bays. This was a pristine area, among the first of the large parcels that environmentalists sought to protect. When the preservation plan came before the Suffolk County Legislature, it lost by a single vote. The Legislator from Englebright's neighborhood, Ferdinand Giese, had voted *No*, and Englebright was furious. "I'll get you for this," Englebright promised him. He did. He ran against Giese in 1983, defeated him and began his political career with preservation at the core of his platform. His anger brought into the legislature a powerful advocate for the environment, a strong influence on his colleagues. His leadership brought Suffolk County government to a new level of commitment to land and water protection. He played a key role in making the drinking water program a reality and in winning legislation preserving key Pine Barrens land.

Englebright was a force for environmental protection well before he ran for office. He often teamed up with Lorna Salzman, a resident of East Quogue, and mid-Atlantic representative of Friends of the Earth. She was recognized as a smart, relentless, campaigner, "aggressive" or "pugnacious," according to one's point of view. She was involved in the drive to shut down the Shoreham nuclear power plant and co-founded what later became known as the Green Party.

Englebright and Salzman's efforts in the late 70s and early 80s exemplified the dedication of Long Island's early crusaders, and also showed the difficulties and limitations that preservationists faced in a decidedly unequal war. They faced a foe with enormous resources, a ruthless attitude that fair play was for weaklings.

Even when battles were won, they came with unacceptable losses, as was the case in Westhampton, the gateway to Long Island's posh south fork. There lies Gabreski airport, a small facility lightly used by the Air National Guard and private aviation, surrounded by the Dwarf Pine Plains, a unique ecosystem frequented by uncommon wildlife species such as black-throated green warbler, American kestrels, marsh hawks, screech owls, northern saw-whet, and long-eared owls. In 1978 Suffolk County Executive John V.N. Klein, in a bid to boost the local economy, proposed to build an industrial complex there to make it an International Economic Development Free Trade Zone. Materials could be flown into the airport from all over, assembled, and flown out without customs inspections and without taxes. It was a decent idea— except for the location.

When they learned of the airport plan, environmentalists went bonkers. Englebright and Salzman organized opposition to the project, supported by, among others, local civic groups concerned about what expansion of the airport would do to the Hamptons vibe. The groups retained a bright new lawyer, Steven Latham, whose law firm went on to play a critical role in ongoing efforts to protect Long Island's environment. In weekly Sunday meetings they mapped an ambitious strategy to fight the scheme.

Pushback from the public would be the key, but getting media coverage would be a challenge. The dominant outlet on the Island, *Newsday*, was going through a heavily pro-development period and had recently completed a series, "Long Island at the Crossroads," calling for major infrastructure development. *Newsday* backed Klein's proposal, and it was not long before a significant list of elected officials, right on up to Governor Hugh Carey, were endorsing the plan.

Englebright and Salzman focused their plans around a public hearing to be held in June. They planned to mobilize a swarm of opponents to show up at the event, led by respected environmental experts. While at Cornell, Cryan worked with vegetation science professor R. H. Whittaker and his Ph.D. student Linda Olsvig. Cryan encouraged them to research the rare and endangered flora in the airport vicinity. At the time of the hearing, they were nearby. Englebright knew that the strength of their expert testimony would be powerful. They insisted that Whittaker and Olsvig testify at the hearing. Making public hearings into media events would become a standard tactic of ours—starting with our campaign in Lake Panamoka.

The commissioners, representing the U. S. Commerce Department, the Treasury and the Army, were crisscrossing the country for these EDZ hearings, which usually attracted a handful of people. This one was different. When the commissioners arrived at the County Legislature's auditorium in Hauppauge, they found it packed with angry citizens and world class scientists. The experts attacked the location of the proposed Zone, described the rare and fragile pygmy pine community, and insisted that the complex be located instead at MacArthur Airport in Islip. The opponents succeeded in creating "more controversy," said the commission chairman, than any similar meeting he had attended.

The presentation was effective, and the developers knew it. They saw that their project was in danger, and placed the blame on the pygmy pines.

Leroy Wilcox, "the Birdman of Speonk," ornithologist, local historian, naturalist, writer, and Long Island duck farmer, began banding birds to study their movements in 1927, and in the course of his life banded over 132,000 of them. On Friday, August 11, he was walking the dwarf pine area, checking up on "his" birds, when he encountered a view like none he had ever seen. A giant tract, some 20 acres, had been bulldozed. Plowed under. Gone. Without warning and without remorse. It was the act of the depraved mindset that says, if you want something you take it, regardless of anything or anyone else. (We would see it at work repeatedly.) Apoplectic, Roy rushed everywhere to raise the alarm. When he got to environmentalist Steve Brown, he was ranting and raving, "with a face as white as his hair," as Brown relayed to Englebright at the time. "You can't believe how terrible he looks." On Sunday, Roy died of a heart attack. Nobody who recalls the episode doubts what caused it.

On Monday, environmentalists arranged a news conference at Westhampton Airport. Despite the chilly rain, people turned up. Southampton Supervisor Martin Lang, the most prominent opponent of the project, spoke out. Mitch Martin Bouvier, a relative of Jacqueline Bouvier

Kennedy Onassis, was there with many of his Hamptons neighbors. Until now, *Newsday*, as expected, had largely ignored the protests, but at this point Salzman had had enough. When the paper's East End reporter Bob Wacker appeared, she stormed up to him, and two inches from his nose, shouted, "When is *Newsday* going to cover this f--ing story?"

"Today," Wacker replied.

His story appeared the next day, and reaction was fierce. Donald Middleton, regional director of the D.E.C was quoted as saying, "I can't think of an action better designed to galvanize the opposition. They have acted against an idea whose time has come, and they will probably regret it." But County Executive Klein dug in his heels, insisting that environmental concerns must be subordinated to economic needs. Lee Koppelman of the Long Island Regional Planning Board chimed in. Regarding those responsible for the bulldozing, he said, "I'm not going to say those guys are evil. They are doing precisely what the county and town had indicated are good for economic development." What county and town politicians said was always good enough for Koppelman.

The bulldozing, the press conference, and the *Newsday* coverage had their effect. Public opinion formed quickly and one-sidedly. In the weeks that followed, politicians who had backed the project one by one swung their boats over the side, explaining why they could no longer support it. Klein's explanation, when he finally caved, was one of the cutest. He told the *Southampton Press* that the project was "one of those things [that is] hard enough to make go if everybody is on the same side. It's impossible if local government is against it." His point was that under home rule, the opposition of the Southampton Supervisor was sufficient to block the project. That was true, but Supervisor Lang had announced his opposition at the outset. What was new was that as other politicos bailed in the face of public opinion, any chance that Klein could roll Lang had dropped to nil.

The battle ended with a partial victory. The plan for a free trade zone around the airport died, the campaign against it raised awareness and support for the cause of Pine Barrens preservation, and the Dwarf Pine Plains were saved. But 20 acres were lost. And so was a beloved champion of the region, Roy Wilcox.

A similar story began the following year, when developers proposed to build two private golf courses that would threaten the freshwater wetlands surrounding Swan Pond in Calverton. An environmental consultant for the developers testified—falsely as was later proven—that the pond was not a natural lake, but one artificially created by the cranberry industry. Middleton, the D.E.C. regional director initially supported the project, and tree-cutting permits had been advocated by a regional administrator, Anthony Taormina, but had not been issued. The developers proceeded without them—all too common practice in those days. John Burnley, who worked for Englebright for a short time at the university, took a field trip to the area and came back visibly shaking, with tears in his eyes. "They're bulldozing wetlands at Swan Pond," he told Englebright. Englebright, being a geologist, knew that Swan Pond was a natural lake, based on topography. He went to Stony Brook University's library archives and located a map from the Library of Congress dated 1836, clearly showing Swan Pond as an existing natural body. He testified and proved the consultant wrong.

As at Westhampton, the visible and wanton destruction struck people hard. At this point the tide turned on environmental preservation. Lang secured a stop-work order. D.E.C. Commissioner Berle blocked the second golf course. Middleton's position changed, too. Englebright recalls taking him out near the Pond, climbing a wooden fire tower with him and letting him see the treasure that was at stake. Other politicians, including Klein, placed a new value on preservation. Suffolk County and The Nature Conservancy that preserved 5,000 acres near the airport. The remaining property became a Suffolk's first natural park. It was named for Robert Cushman Murphy.

Even so, as I learned about later efforts, it always felt like two steps forward, one step back. And the proposed developments just kept coming and coming. The environmentalists didn't have the resources to conduct this kind of war. And while they fought the projects they could, so much land would be gobbled up there wouldn't be enough to preserve. The warriors in the arena at the time were so deep in the struggle, saving what they could, it was hard to keep the big picture in mind. Nature preserves were great, but we needed to preserve a whole *ecosystem*. It became clear to me that we needed a comprehensive approach, a strategy to preserve *the* Pine Barrens. We had to take on development, not individual developers. (Actually. we never used the word "development" either—always "overdevelopment.") And we had to take on the political establishment that bowed to developers' wishes.

But how to fight them all at once was a problem. Legally, you can only challenge a project once it is proposed, and they were proposed one at a time, each in its own town. Local residents could file suit, because the development affected them personally. But those not directly affected lacked "standing" to sue. However, Cryan believed he had an answer. In college at Cornell University he had worked with professors studying buck moths, which made their home in the Albany Pine Bush. An Albany environmental group, also called the Albany Pine Bush, was already locked in a battle to preserve the land. They argued that their organization, because it was dedicated to protecting the Pine Bush, would be harmed "in a manner or degree different from the public at large" and thus had standing to sue. The Pine Barrens Society, Cryan told me in one of his frequent phone calls, could make the same argument and in that way would be able to sue to block projects across the Island. One suit could block all of them at once, if we could come up with a reason—a viable one—that would apply to all the projects. That was still a huge *if*, but at least we had a place to start.

The commute to the city was becoming more and more annoying. My PR work was a bore relative to saving the pine barrens: the jobs not important enough, big enough, or difficult enough. My thoughts turned to what the job would involve. In the ten years of its existence the Pine Barrens Society had done much. They had successfully campaigned to get 700 acres of Oak Brush Plains transferred from the Department of Health to the Department of Environmental

Conservation for creating a preserve. It went on to fight for additional land near Brentwood. It also worked to prevent the auctioning of Pine Barrens parcels obtained by tax default, helped beat back a proposal to build a 20-mile "scenic highway," that would have cut through the South Fork Pine Barrens, and worked to prevent the extension of County Road 111 through the Pine Barrens in Manorville. In 1985 the Society helped create the Suffolk County Pine Barrens Review Commission. In practice, this committee made generally good recommendations on development projects, but unfortunately it lacked the power to enforce its recommendations. The Commission supported legislation to halt development along the Peconic and Nissequogue Rivers, which were not protected by any previous laws, and campaigned to get funding for land acquisition included in the 1986 New York State Environmental Quality Bond Act.

It was good work, important work, enormous work. Yet it would not be near enough to get the Society where it wanted to go. What had been done so far was what Englebright later described as the "first half" of the Pine Barrens war. The next half would require a new strategy on a whole new scale.

On the train I tried to assess what the job would actually require. How much land—and *which* land—would have to be preserved? What would we need to file the lawsuit? How much money would it cost? Once it was filed, what would be the public fallout from stopping all development on Long Island, and how could we deal with it? How many projects were we talking about? How many volunteers would we need to gather information on them? How many to organize and join demonstrations? What would the media campaign look like? How would we raise all the money?

At this point I should have known that my decision had been made, but in my mind I was still debating it. If we moved to stop development across Suffolk County, it would mean war—the biggest, most acrimonious war Long Island had ever seen. Could we win it?

I'm no Don Quixote. I wasn't about to give my blood, sweat, and tears for a cause that couldn't be won.

The developers had money, and lawyers, and political influence, and big bucks for incentive. They could win support from politicians with generous campaign contributions, something that not-for-profit environmental groups were not permitted to do. Add to this, a tradition of home rule that worked against regional planning--and which politicians would fight to maintain because it gave them power and with it, consideration and sometimes money.

Against all that, I pondered, what could we bring? That would have to be the people of Long Island. We would need the overwhelming majority of them to take up pine barrens preservation as their cause. This place that people were hardly aware of had to become people's passion. Convincing them that preserving the land would not be enough. Not nearly enough. We had to get them concerned enough—or mad enough—to make them demand it. To overcome the incredible inertia of "the way things are" and turn large numbers of them into activists. It would be a war for hearts and minds that would take a wildly ambitious advocacy effort.

I wouldn't be starting from nowhere. Those already in the fight had done much to raise awareness of the problem of overdevelopment. God knows there was plenty of antipathy to the scourge of constant traffic, the blight of strip malls, the horror of seeing Long Island's woods and ponds and farmland paved over for tacky McMansions.

Yes, I thought, we could tap that. Build on it—you should pardon the expression. That could be done, and it was right in my wheelhouse. I'd always loved my work—using my communications skills to advance a cause more often than a product. Many of my clients were non-profit, public service groups and I had had years of experience serving organizations like the Association for the Help of Retarded Children and the Muscular Dystrophy Association. I was good at print, radio, television and direct mail (the Internet wasn't available yet). My mind raced. No, there was no movement to save our vanishing woodlands, but there were ways to change that paradigm.

I was also plain angry—the way developers would just destroy precious woodlands and pay no price for it; the way politicians would fall in with developers. I alone could not fix it but seeing what they were doing boiled my blood. I couldn't watch it and not do my part to stop it. And what was my part?

Throughout this time, of course, the pine barrens had become a growing part of our day-to-day lives—Robin's and mine. Robin and I had often talked about and my growing involvement in the movement and my thoughts of devoting myself to it fulltime. She was, as she never for a moment ceased to be in our fifty-five years together, enthusiastic and supportive.

One Sunday morning in December, cold but sunny, Turner appeared at my door without notice. "Get away from this office right now and come with me," he said. Off we went to Cranberry Bog in the Eastern Pine Barrens. John marveled over the plants, the birds and the ponds. I had come to the environment only as a means to protect Lake Panamoka and the community in which I lived. In fact, I thought of many environmentalists as well-intentioned ideologues-- without a clue. But John's wonderment and appreciation of this ecosystem was real--and contagious. I'd never been in a more beautiful part of Long Island. The sounds, the scents and the surroundings created an oasis in the midst of suburban sprawl. "It would be a shame to lose all of this, huh?" Turner said. What he meant was, "It's time for you to sign onto this, Dick. Come on."

A few nights later, sitting by the fireplace after dinner, Robin and I had the last of our should-we-or-shouldn't-we conversations. Were we really prepared to do what this would take? It would mean twelve-hour days, seven days a week—for years. That didn't deter me too much, or Robin either. She knew what I was like, and she lived it with me, from "Save the Lake" last year, all the way back to the summer decades before when I coached Little League, and it was baseball 24/7, and she was a more zealous fan than any of the parents. I reminded her that the Pine Barrens Society would not be in a position to pay me a salary—for at least a couple of years. "We can make it on my salary," she said. "You want to do this, Dick. And you *can* do it. So you should. Think what an accomplishment it will be."

Creating a Village for Fun & Profit

"Life's greatest gift is the opportunity to work hard at work worth doing."—Teddy Roosevelt

On the afternoon in June 1988 when we celebrated the success of the Save the Lake campaign, Englebright and I were walking off the beach chatting casually about what might come next. And as we shook hands, I said, the way one would, "If there's any way I can help on something down the road, let me know." He did.

About a month later he called me in the middle of the night. There was, he said, "a very big problem—no, challenge—in the very heart of the Pine Barrens." He couldn't discuss it on the phone, was sorry for sounding so mysterious, wanted me to meet him the next day. "This is very big," he said and hung up. I knew saving the Pine Barrens was going to get very intense, but I wasn't expecting this.

The next day, a Saturday, I met him for breakfast in Setauket. Enthusiastic as he is, Englebright is also a careful, ponderous thinker and speaker. Do not plan to have a five-minute conversation with a geologist. Then there was his seeming paranoia, evidenced by his low, urgent voice and frequent, rapid looks around the room. If I didn't know better, I'd have thought he was a nut job.

The tale he spun made Gayle Brovetto's Lake Panamoka conspiracy story seem mild. A year earlier, he said, a small cabal of real estate developers and speculators had renewed a previously failed effort to incorporate a village at the mouth of the Peconic River, adjacent to Wildwood Lake. The sole purpose of the incorporation was to establish a legal entity that could approve development projects. In this case, mega-projects that even permissive town governments would have laughed at.

The Village was a scant 3.2 square miles in size—a crooked, horseshoe-shaped land assemblage that included the Peconic River waterfront and what Englebright termed "the right aorta of the heart of the Pine Barrens." The incorporation scheme was the brainchild of eccentric architect and developer Leonard Sheldon, backed by powerful, unnamed real estate interests who believed that hyperdeveloping environmentally sensitive land on Long Island was a good investment. "We're talking marinas, convention centers, amphitheaters and the largest subdivision ever to be proposed in the Town of Southampton," Englebright said. "With a goddam monorail to connect everything together." Huge sums of money were being promised, private investigators were being paid to check out pro-environment opponents and closed-door meetings were going on nightly.

I rolled my eyes. "It's true, all of it," Englebright assured me. "Go, find out for yourself." He completed the yarn by identifying "two white knights" who were courageously battling this monster but were "hopelessly confused about what they should do and nearly exhausted from the effort."

"Your mission," Englebright concluded, "is to go to Pine Valley, find the white knights, and show them how to expose the evil forces and rescue the Pine Barrens." Mercifully, he did not add, "If you or any member of your forces are captured or killed, this Legislator will disavow any knowledge of your activities." That might just have deterred me.

Instead, I got into my car, armed only with a Hagstrom's street map, and headed for the center of Pine Valley, Wildwood Lake. The highway turned to suburban road, then to one lane country road, then to a rutted dirt road. I bounced along in my low-to-the-ground Miata until the path ended abruptly at the Pine Barrens forest, next to a small house with a solar array, windmill generator and, inside, a pot belly stove that heated the entire house. "Environmentalists," I muttered as I alighted from the car and stretched my back, checking the car for structural damage.

A round-faced, round-bodied man bounced from the side door of the house, a look of relief and welcome on his face. "Steve said to expect you," he said. "Thank you for coming. I'm Joe Colao. Come on in."

"I guess they graded your road recently," I said.

"I doubt it," Colao replied.

"Oh no, they definitely graded it. They gave it an "F."

Colao laughed heartily, then introduced me to his smiling wife, Joan; the other white knight, former cop Vincent Scandole; and Sheila McCauley, a wisp of a woman with "disapproval" written all over her face.

For the next four hours, Colao and Scandole rolled out maps, produced stacks of documents and told unbelievable stories about the goings-on in Pine Valley. They had bits of evidence but not a stitch of proof of anything like the conspiracy they and Englebright alleged. Sheila sat in the corner and glowered. Joan served an unending stream of food and drinks.

The year before, Colao and Scandole told me, Leonard Sheldon and his son Christopher, a law student, had gone to the working class community and promised the 800 residents lower taxes and control of their own destiny. On August 11, 1987, voters approved the new village by a vote of 154-46.

Formal incorporation took months. Colao and Scandole had challenged the move in court, losing in March 1988. On April 20 voters elected four trustees with Mary Petrazewski, a homemaker and school bus driver, as Mayor. The senior Sheldon volunteered to serve as unpaid consultant to the Mayor. The "knights" then pressed successfully for a 90-day moratorium on construction, until the Village could put a zoning code in place. Vinny ran in November. He was elected. He drove them crazy,

Colao and Scandole used legal and parliamentary maneuvering and downright disruption to time and again block progress on the project. They persuaded contractor Peter Batalias to go public with his charge that Leonard Sheldon inflated the price of land Batalias wanted for a garbage recycling plant in the Pine Barrens. He reported that Sheldon had guaranteed that village trustees would approve a required zoning change, but demanded an $80,000-a-year job for his son at the new facility. Sheldon shouted his denials. The Suffolk District Attorney promised an investigation.

Colao also went public, charging Sheldon with back-room negotiations with a major real estate developer and hiring a private investigator to "dig up dirt" on him and his wife.

The two paralyzed government for months. Meetings held at town hall or in people's houses regularly erupted into angry denunciations, charges and countercharges, often reported in the local press. At one meeting, punches were exchanged, and Chris Sheldon threatened to sue Scandole for assault.

Michael LoGrande, the former Suffolk County Executive, was director of the Association for a Better Long Island, a developers' organization, from 1988 to 1990, and had sought the job of Pine Valley's village planner. He withdrew in the face of the turmoil and bad press. An experienced politician and respected planner, he didn't want to be associated with the stories coming out of Pine Valley.

Bringing me up to the present, Vinnie explained that the week before, the Southampton Town Planning Board had held a public hearing on Sheldon's proposal and quickly approved key parts of it. Now all the developer needed was final approval from the Village, which they would get as soon as the zoning code was finished, and the two white knights were running out of ways to stall. "What can we do?" Vinnie asked.

I thought for a moment. "How many residents in the village?"

"800," Joe replied.

"How many voted in the last election?"

"About 200."

"What if you just take over the village? All you'd need is a couple hundred votes or so, and *Voila!*, you're on the Village Board!"

"Then Vinny and I could legally control the village with just the Mayor or one supportive Trustee. We could kill bad projects or even disband the village. It's brilliant!" Colao exclaimed.

"Let's get a couple pictures of you guys in environmental settings, get the details on your backgrounds and qualifications, and put together a campaign.

"Right now?" Scandole asked. "Just like that?"

"Hell, yes!" said Joe.

There were too many of us to ride in one car, so we decided to take two. Glowering Sheila buttonholed me outside and invited me to drive with her. It meant one less trip for my poor little car down that rutted road. I had no idea how many times I would travel it in the weeks and months ahead.

Vinny and the Colaos went ahead in Joan's Bronco. Sheila said she knew where to meet them. The moment they disappeared from sight, she put the car in park. Glaring at me and poking her right index finger repeatedly into my chest, she began a five-minute-long harangue.

"What's your angle?" she shouted, "What's in this for you? How dare you come out of nowhere and try to hoodwink these good men who are standing up for every decent person in this community with your P.R. line and phony offer to help. Who really sent you, who's paying your salary, and how dumb do you think we are to fall for your whole line of crap?"

I was dumbstruck. The little woman had a big chip. Then I thought for a moment. Professional communicator though I was, I had not thought to consider the healthy skepticism of people who had regularly been taken advantage of by self-serving special interests and the government that serves them. Joe and Vinny hadn't thought to question my involvement, they were too desperate.

"Who sent me is Englebright," I told her. "Who's paying me is nobody." And as far as how dumb you are, how smart is it to turn down free help?" She didn't have an answer but she wasn't convinced. Sheila gradually faded away. Joe and Vinny christened her favorite chair, the "harrumph seat."

The campaign was nothing if not well organized. The white knights and their friends laid out maps showing all the streets in the Village. They scheduled Joe and Vinny to visit each house at least once before Election Day. They learned to identify those they visited as "saints," or avowed supporters of our campaign, and "sinners," or avowed opponents. A third category represented "undecideds."

I urged them to enroll unregistered supporters and not to waste time trying to dissuade opponents of their position, but true believer that he was, Colao could never stick to this plan. He'd wander home after 11 pm having spent 30 and 40 minutes a pop trying to talk closet developers into becoming tree-huggers.

Results of the house visits were turned over to Joan or the Colao's neighbor, Mitzi Byrne, to be developed into get-out-the-vote telephone lists for election time.

Joe and Vinny worked with me on campaign materials, mostly basic flyers. I tried to get them to focus on the current administration's absence of progress in reducing taxes or improving government services, and to avoid the "Giant Conspiracy Theory." In home visits they did just fine, but the campaign literature was filled with charges about how Sheldon and his cronies were going to pave over the community on behalf of big-time real estate developers. If nothing else, these attacks kept the opposition on the defensive.

Their opponents were no less than Chris Sheldon himself and an ally, Barbara Kreshon, who aimed to fill the two vacancies and thus maintain a majority on the Village Council. Sheldon turned out an endless stream of flyers explaining why "developing the tax base" was the only way to reduce taxes.

Because it was difficult to debunk outright lies—and there were many—we tried to preempt them by addressing issues first. A former college student of mine, Adriana Brako, an avid environmentalist with a keen interest in sustainability issues, was looking for a project. We suggested that she go to the Sheldon campaign and volunteer. She did, and to our delight, they took her on. While the campaign did not share with her any of their dealings with developers, she was able to get us virtually every piece of campaign material they designed. We would quickly craft messages that undercut theirs, and rush ours out ahead of them. Adriana enjoyed telling her friends that she had become a "spy." On Election Day, when campaigns scurry to distribute their final get-out-the-vote message, she went dark.

We suspected that the controversy would increase turnout. From the house visits, we calculated that as many as 400 would vote. We also guessed that some among the "saints" were merely sounding supportive to avoid confrontation with "the mad men" or to get them out of their houses quickly. So, we steadily worked to secure 250 likely votes to ensure victory.

About a week before the March 19 election, with 700 of the 800 homes having been visited and 200 "likely" votes promised, I arrived at Colao's house at 6:30 P.M., about 45 minutes before they were to commence the night's "evening house visits." The candidates were in a funk.

Colao sat bundled in a sweater and what looked like a horse blanket. He wore big woolen gloves and had a stocking cap pulled down over his ears. Joan was feeding him soup. Vinny sat dejected in the harrumph seat. Neither spoke as I came in. It was obvious that Joe was really sick, but it was equally clear that we'd hit a serious down point in the long campaign. Joe and Vinny were plain worn out.

I walked immediately to the phone and called home. "Robin," I said, "don't expect me home at all tonight. Joe and Vinny are apparently so confident of victory, they've decided to take the rest of the campaign off." Joe burst out laughing, sending a spray of soup across the room.

"Amper, you son-of-a-bitch, you know exactly what to say to make even a guy on his deathbed feel guilty." Then he added, "Give me an hour and I'll go out and try for pneumonia." Vinny laughed, too, and the scary moment had passed.

As Election Day approached, Joe and Vinny were turning out daily flyers. The big-builders-come-to-pave-our-village theme was front and center. The charges had a true ring to them, but the denials kept coming, and there was no "smoking gun" to prove their case. I kept feeding what I knew to a *Newsday* reporter, Steve Wick (who later wrote the seminal book on East End farming, *Heaven on Earth*). He kept telling me he was looking into it.

The Saturday before the vote, Joe finished "the last campaign literature," he said. We had arranged for all his friends to hit the streets on Sunday, when everyone would be home, to hand deliver the final appeal to save Pine Valley.

That night I slept in the Colao's basement guest room, and the next morning Joe came in and woke me at 6:00 A.M. He was grinning from ear to ear. "Amper, you're not going to believe this!"

Jubilantly, he handed Sunday *Newsday* across the bed. There, on the front page was a banner headline which read, "VILLAGES FOR SALE?" And below it, "Islandia, Pine Valley Roll Out Red Carpet for Developers."

In an extensive, multi-page investigative story with sidebars, *Newsday* confirmed all of the dark deeds in Pine Valley that Colao and Scandole had been saying the whole time. That developers had poured money into the town to buy support. That Sheldon planned a mammoth development complete with hotels, amphitheater, cultural center – and monorail. That Sheldon and a buddy had indeed hired a private detective to get dirt on Colao. *Newsday* had supplied enough "smoking guns" to shoot up the town—and shoot down the village.

The story also identified AQN Associates of Glen Cove as the proposed developers of the 25-acre riverfront parcel, which local attorney Robert Tooker admitted he had contracted to sell to AQN. The firm was controlled by ink and newspaper mogul Karl V. Anton, Jr., and John Quinn, a Glen Cove developer who had been charged with 21 misdemeanor and felony counts in connection with an abandoned condominium project. He later pleaded guilty to two misdemeanors. The third partner, Stuart Cornelius "Neil" Fisher, came from a Washington, D.C. real estate investment trust. A public relations consultant for the project was Edwin "Buzz" Schwenk, the former Suffolk County Republican Party Leader who was convicted in 1981 and served two months for tax evasion. Interestingly, Schwenk had consulted for the Teamsters while they were trying to develop their 1,600-acres of Pine Barrens, previous to the Hampton Hills proposal. Schwenk also served as Executive Director of the Long Island Builders Institute, a 570-member, pro-development trade group that would become a principal adversary of the Pine Barrens Preservation Initiative.

Allen Smith, an attorney for AQN, admitted that the company had agreed to build a village hall for Pine Valley as an incentive for approval of their development plans. And, in order to acquire the property on which a local church sat, AQN promised to build the congregation a new one "anywhere in the village they want."

Joe and Vinny quickly decided to replace their last campaign flyer with a copy of the newspaper. They hit every newsstand, drug store and diner within miles for as many copies of the paper as the businesses would part with. When the volunteers arrived for flyer distribution, they were reassigned to "highlighting." Using yellow magic markers, we highlighted key revelations in the big story. Joan made little stick-on notes which read, "Read it and weep. Then vote Tuesday for Joe Colao and Vinny Scandole." Volunteers distributed more than 200 copies of the newspaper, mostly to "saints" and "undecideds."

Throughout Tuesday, the Colao/Scandole "Get Out the Vote" machine chugged along. Likely supporters and swing voters were called at their homes, then checked off the list by poll watchers as they cast their ballots. Walkie-talkies connected the poll watchers to the phone call makers, and "sinner" voters were tracked to gauge voter turnout for the Sheldon campaign. A van was on standby to deliver rides to the polls, along with a squad of baby-sitters to watch people's kids while they voted. A "saint" could probably have had their grocery shopping done for them that day, had anyone asked.

There was a brief run on the polls around 7:00 P.M. as residents returned from work or dinner. As the 9:00 P.M. deadline approached for polls to close, there were still 17 "prospects" who had not cast their ballots. We pressed Joan and Mitzi for one more round of calls. "This will be the third call to each of these people," Joan protested. "They said they'd vote, and they're getting testy."

"One guy told me if I called again, he'd vote for Chris Sheldon," Mitzi added.

"Apologize to them tomorrow," I persisted. "Get them to the polls tonight."

With the election going to the top two finishers, Joe ended up with 158 votes, Vinnie 157, and Chris Sheldon 150. A few newspapers or phone calls less and the result might have been different.

At the first village meeting after the election, one of the incumbent trustees and the village attorney quit because they had lost control of the village. Also, the board voted to hire Daniel Karpen, an eccentric environmentalist, to devise a master plan for the village. Karpen wrote official correspondence from the point of view of, and signed by an alter ego, a character he invented -- Hippity Hop the Frog. Habitually disheveled, he would attend meetings of the County Legislature in his trademark wooden shoes, at least once with a live duck under his arm.

The next week Mayor Petrazewski resigned when residents of a mobile home park accused her of siding with builders who wanted to develop the site. A Colao friend, Michael Illardi, was named to the vacant Trustee seat, assuring control of the village by the "good guys." A gracious woman, Edwina Borders, then a village trustee, was named Mayor. She promptly filled her trustee vacancy with Chris Sheldon, for the sake of "village unity," she explained. The result was the opposite: continued spectacles at village board meetings for months to come.

In the spring of 1989 the Suffolk County Pine Barrens Review Commission came out against development of Hampton Hills, and the village called on Suffolk County Executive Patrick Halpin to buy the property for permanent preservation. He did, and the Hampton Hills subdivision was dead.

Next Colao and Scandole put in place tough new zoning that would prevent large-scale development of the waterfront. Then they went for the knockout: a voter referendum to dissolve the village itself. Sheldon still had considerable support and waged a fierce battle. On election day the resolution squeaked by, 165-142. On December 31, 1990, the Incorporated Village of Pine Valley was no more,

Joe and Vinny immediately joined the Board of Directors of the Pine Barrens Society.

Dreaming It Up & Making It Happen

"You see things; and you say `Why?' But I dream things that never were;
and I say `Why Not?"—George Bernard Shaw

I was now committed to joining the effort to save the Pine Barrens. It would have to be a full-time commitment; anything less would guarantee failure. The first step was to come up with and understand the goals.

In the early months of 1989, the three Pine Barrens founders and I had numerous conversations about how to proceed. They knew that they wanted to preserve the Pine Barrens. I knew we needed to develop a strategy. We agreed that Goal One was to stop development in the Pine Barrens – we were losing 5,000 acres a year to rampant over-development in the towns of Brookhaven, Riverhead and Southampton. Next, we would need a strategy to preserve the land from future development—an undertaking virtually unprecedented.

As I pondered how to stop development, I reflected on the discussions I had with Cryan, who had been active in the effort to protect the Albany Pine Bush and seen it done. He explained how litigation over proposed development had led to legislative action to preserve the area. He not only understood the arguments made in the landmark case, he knew the lawyer who made them, Lewis Oliver.

I recalled that this case established that an organization such as the Albany Pine Bush has standing to sue in order to block projects that could harm the environment. Once they got their day in court, the organization advanced another new and powerful argument: that the environmental impact studies of projects could not be prepared individually—as was currently required—but the combined impact of all proposed projects in the region must be determined before any of them could be approved. Environmentally, the argument made sense. The whole purpose for requiring an Environmental Impact Statement is to reveal the potential harm that could be done. One project may not hurt the environment much, while all of them together might be devastating.

Cryan and Oliver's argument was effective and persuaded the courts at one level after another. At last, in a landmark 1985 ruling, New York's highest court decreed that the New York State Environmental Quality Review Act, required "lead agencies" (in this case, government bodies that review land use applications) to consider cumulative impacts when reviewing the Albany developers' applications. In the end, more than 3,000 acres of the Albany Pine Bush were preserved.

The Pine Barrens Society could use this ruling, suing to halt development across all the three towns until a cumulative study was completed. That would give us time to build public opinion and pressure politicians for preservation. It was a great plan, but a gargantuan task. There were hundreds of projects across 100,000 acres of pine barrens, with more on the way. Every proposed project had to be identified and challenged in court within a month of its approval. This meant filing new lawsuits every month for more than a year. We would need a dozen volunteers to gather information on every project and forward the information to our land use attorney.

That was just the beginning. The whole project would be very big and very complicated. The goal was to preserve pine barrens land, but how much land did we need? How much could we get? What and where were the most important areas? What would it all cost?

Government would have to get involved. We'd need to win support from state, county and town politicians. We'd need to coax or pressure them to raise enormous sums of money, for goals that many of their coziest supporters would oppose.

Ultimately, to only way for us to influence the politicians was to galvanize massive public demand for preservation—a huge challenge. At the time, fewer than 3% of Long Islanders knew what the pine barrens were or where they were located. Preservation would take tons of public money—in a region where taxes were already sky-high. The developers could be counted on to pound the drum about taxes, about needing construction to power Long Island's economy, and so on.

We had solid arguments on our side, but they had the money and connections to get their story heard over and over. Without an advertising budget or the time for a traditional educational program, we would be largely dependent for success on public relations and "earned media"— that is, news coverage (in print, radio and television). We would need a steady stream of activities and events that would make news. That would mean organizing rallies at public meetings, protests at development sites, and on and on.

I was confident I could do it, but I also knew how much effort, man-and-womanpower and money it would take. As I worked it all out, I paused. I was looking at an endeavor way bigger than the scale the Pine Barrens Society had ever operated on.

McGrath, Turner, and the new president of the Society, Michael Deering, had asked me to outline a plan for preserving the Pine Barrens. I knew for sure they were not prepared for anything like this. What could I say to convince them that all of what I was proposing was critical to success? And assure them that it was all actually doable?

On a bitterly cold night in March 1989, we gathered at the home of Michael Deering in Smithtown. I spent fifteen minutes walking them through the project as I envisioned it, describing all that went into it and what it would cost. They sat silently, their faces taking on blank expressions. When I told them that it would take four years and $400,000 (this was in 1989 dollars), they stood up simultaneously without a word. McGrath and Turner picked up their backpacks and headed for the door.

I obviously needed to spend a couple of minutes talking them down. I suggested that the Society consider "a new set of givens." They reacted thoughtfully, were still thinking clearly, strategically. The normal sequence, they said would be first to build the Society institutionally, then launch the Initiative. But the Pine Barrens were being lost at such a rate that the ecosystem would be lost if we didn't do at once everything that had to be done. This was a new way of thinking for the Society's leadership. It was encouraging that they were thinking this way, but I wasn't convinced they were ready to take the project on.

They adjourned to Michael's kitchen for an "executive session," but I could clearly hear fragments of their conversation.

"Let's be realistic."

"There's no way we can put together that much money."

And finally, "What have we got to lose?"

They returned to the living room, and Deering made the offer. "If you can raise the money, you have the job!"

It was the strangest job offer I ever received. At that moment, I had absolutely no idea how we were going to raise any of the money we would need to wage the battle, let alone pay me a fair wage. "You've got a deal," I said. We used the remaining portion of the meeting to agree on individual assignments and help identify needed resources. The Pine Barrens Preservation Initiative was underway.

I initially worried that I might indeed be involving myself with a group of unrealistic environmental extremists. As a businessperson, surely, I could help bridge the gap between such environmentalists and practical, no-nonsense developers, who could at least be counted on to do what selfishly benefited them. A needless fear and a false premise, respectively.
The Society's Board was comprised of the most honorably-motivated people I have ever met. They were unassuming, down-to-earth pragmatists who had no fantasies about either what needed to be protected or what could be. Logically, scientifically, they analyzed the landscape: 100,000 acres, hundreds of proposed projects pending, and few resources available to advance an agenda.

The Board decided early on that if we were to depend on Wilson and MacArthur's *Theory of Island Biogeography*, we would need to establish the minimum area of contiguous Pine Barrens that must be preserved to keep it a viable ecosystem, given species ranges, fire dependency and other factors. The correct way to determine this was to conduct a Generic Environmental Impact Statement for the entire Central Pine Barrens, including a study of the cumulative impacts of the more than 200 projects currently pending before the Towns of Brookhaven, Riverhead and Southampton. The towns and county steadfastly refused to conduct such a study. Most experts thought a properly conducted study would determine that at least 35,000 acres would be necessary to keep the Pine Barrens viable. We privately adopted that figure, while continuing to press for a proper study.

I was assigned three major jobs: managing the lawsuit, prodding the government to acquire and preserve pine barrens land, and persuading the public to support preservation. The founders concentrated on what they knew best – identifying the primary targets for preservation.

Litigation was job one if the Pine Barrens were to be spared. It sounded simple. It wasn't. To halt development, I recognized that a lawsuit would have to challenge every subdivision, site plan and zoning change application before the Town Boards, the Town Planning Boards and the Zoning Boards of Appeal in Brookhaven, Riverhead and Southampton about once every 30 days as the individual projects were approved separately. The "Pine Barrens Suit," as it became known collectively, actually consisted of some 22 separate lawsuits over two-and-a-half years, making the same cumulative impact claim but based on the changing specifics of each application and approval. And, we discovered, there were 234 of them!

It was a staggering challenge—"the mother of all environmental lawsuits," Turner quipped. Indeed, it was the largest environmental lawsuit ever brought in New York State. The main petition was a hefty 1,200 pages.

A key benefit of the legal strategy was the provision under land use law that the granting of permits for subdivisions is "stayed" while the matter is before the court. Given that more than three-fourths of the 234 building proposals were for subdivisions, we were effectively watching the first cessation of Pine Barrens destruction in history. This would allow us time to advance the public education and expedited acquisition strategies.

A major public education campaign was needed immediately. And given how little people knew about the pine barrens, and the enormous cost of preserving them, it would be a tough, tough job.

To the inevitable question, "Why should we do this?" we needed a powerful, an irresistible, answer. I met regularly with Cryan, McGrath and Turner to strategize on how to frame the issue.

The founders were ecological purists – focused on preserving the ecosystem and its flora and fauna. I remember John Turner warming to the prospect of educating Long Islanders on the denizens of Long Island's Pine Barrens. Englebright, geologist that he was, focused on the danger to ground and surface water.

At times the debate got lively. McGrath admitted, "We were young, idealistic, and maybe a little arrogant, I guess. We really felt strongly that the flora and the fauna were worthy of preservation for their own sake." Englebright gave as good as he got during their debates. As Cryan remembered, "Steve had a temper. He was known to throw things!"

I was fine with a full-throated discussion, with everyone having their say, because this was a decision we had to get right. The decision couldn't be based on philosophy, but what would influence Long Islanders. My public relations instincts gave me doubts about stressing biodiversity. I also resisted of pushing both issues together, as was suggested at one point. We would need hordes of people to leave their houses and storm public meetings, thousands to call political figures and write letters to editors. To get that kind of response would take one big thing, simple and threatening.

The payoff came one night at a meeting in my living room. It was getting late, and we were all winding down when McGrath said casually, "What about *drinking* water? Long Island's aquifer, underneath the pine barrens, was the first federally designated "Sole-Source Aquifer"—meaning it's not feasible for us to get our water from anywhere else." He continued, just as casually, "New York State has designated Long Island's pine barrens as one of nine "Special Groundwater Protection Areas"—vulnerable areas needing protection. In fact, it's larger than all the other eight SGPA's combined."

I jumped out of my chair, realizing how obvious the solution was! Bingo! It's not "biodiversity." It's not "groundwater." It's *drinking* water!

That was it! What message could be simpler? We *had* to save the pine barrens—our drinking water depended on it. "The Pine Barrens overlie and protect Long Island's largest source of pure fresh drinking water" became our mantra included in everything we disseminated.

The drinking water issue enabled us to go on the attack, something we knew we had to do. With no advertising budget, the only way we could get our message out was through press coverage —"earned media" to use the industry term. To get coverage you need controversy. We knew the lawsuit would generate opposition—the developers would scream bloody murder about construction being shut down across the Island. Our point would be simple: with Long Island's drinking water at stake, it only made sense to determine the impact of all the proposed development before we went ahead. This would paint developers as unreasonable, and selfish, determined to make their buck first, no matter the harm to our water supply.

At every forum we would pound out the message: "First find out what we need to preserve to protect our drinking water. Build only if and where it is safe to do so."

As a public relations man, I knew the public would be concerned about their drinking water. But how could we protect the Pine Barrens? After much thought, I had an "Aha" moment. There already existed a program to purchase watershed-sensitive land – the Drinking Water Protection Program! This program called for using 1/4 cent of Suffolk's sales tax to buy-up such parcels. The program had passed by referenda in 1987 and 1988, both times by 84% margins. I asked, what if we equated the Pine Barrens Preservation Initiative with protection of the Island's largest and purest groundwater supply, ensuring the hundreds of millions of dollars that would ultimately be required to purchase the acres deemed necessary to protect the Pine Barrens?

"That would be beautiful," Michael Deering observed. We planned to target unresponsive politicians as well as developers, painting the politicians as even worse. "We expect developers to put their pocketbooks first," we planned to say, "but the politicians' job is to put the public interest first."

My brother, Tom, helped design the overall communications language, outlining approaches for use of print, radio and television, and supplying specific language for op-ed pieces, letters to the editor, editorial replies and copy for brochures, speeches and press kits. He and I agreed to position the Society as comprised of no-nonsense, reasonable people who were perfectly willing to be "in your face" if necessary, to ensure that government did not do favors for "builders with big bucks" or "the development-at-any-cost crowd" at the expense of "drinking water for our children and grandchildren."

A long-time friend, Alan Singer, a successful video editor, advised us on the use of television. He suggested that the little Society would come to be seen as a formidable opponent once the lawsuit was announced, and he urged that we define our strength by the wisdom of our position and the number of people who were certain to support it: "The public interest versus the special interests," as he described it. Alan would later join the Board and, later still, serve as president.

Then there was the matter of money. Up to this point, the only remotely serious fundraising was the November 1988 anniversary dinner for the Society, which I attended as a guest. Volunteer-activist Sherry Johnson produced it at the Rock Hill Country Club in Manorville. Previous dinners had been potluck affairs at someone's house or a park or other public place, with an average take of $500. This one raked in a record high, $3,500. Suffolk County Legislator Steve Englebright was the honoree, although no one thought to get him a plaque or anything. In 1995 we honored him again, plaque included.

We agreed that, even though financing was going to be one beastly challenge, we would decline contributions from any group or individual who could compromise the integrity of our campaign. We would be trading only on our reputation for integrity. This would require scrupulous avoidance of even the appearance of impropriety or the capacity to affect our policy through financial assistance. And we vowed that need would dictate how much fundraising we did, rather than available funding dictating the program. This was easier said than done.

The Society raised most of its money from grassroots organizing. Most of our supporters were blue collar, everyday people, who gave an average of $23 a year. The transition into the first "high end" support came with the donation of a 1973 Cadillac convertible. One day, we got a call from a rich guy with a misbehaving car on his hands who appreciated our crusade. "Fix it, sell it and I'll write it off on my tax return," he declared.

We had a mechanically-knowledgeable volunteer assess the car's condition and make $258 worth of repairs, and, after we tooled around in it for a week and a half— and after rejecting John

Cryan's offer to "take it off your hands for $1,000 cash"—sold it for the largest donation in the Society's history thus far: a Blue Book-certified $3,700.

Once we became visible, though, some high-profile East-enders came forward and made our fundraising a whole lot easier. Writer and advocate Sherrye Henry recruited renowned public relations mogul John Scanlon and Manhattan radio personality Joan Hamburg to throw events at their remarkable Hampton homes. Ted Conklin, an enthusiastic supporter who ran the exquisite American Hotel in Sag Harbor, hosted several fundraising events for us. Donations came from luminaries including Alan Alda, Chevy Chase, Martha Stewart, Peter Mathieson, E.L. Doctorow and Jerry Della Femina. It was a major breakthrough for the Society.

But this high level of support followed years of low volume donations, support that rang true to our drinking water-for-everyone constituency. At our first annual benefit gala—a $150 per ticket affair honoring those who had made important contributions to environmental protection—we provided free tickets to those willing to generate an equivalent amount by selling advertising in our souvenir program or obtaining items of similar worth for our "silent auction." We found ways to be inclusive at every turn.

I talked to media resources, planned a membership campaign, estimated administrative and fundraising expense. I identified more than 100 environmental and civic organizations which would have to be recruited. We would need their members in order to build the critical mass of active supporters necessary to win the war.

The Society's image itself needed a make-over. Its slogan at the time was "Dedicated to the protection and preservation of Long Island's pitch pine/scrub oak woodlands." Whew! We proposed it be changed to, "We Mean Business About the Environment!"

The Society's logo bore the image of a state-threatened species, the Buck Moth, and its publication was actually named after an extinct bird, the heath hen. The new logo showed the public where the Pine Barrens were—the spot of green yet to be saved on an outline of over-developed Long Island. Our newsletter became "The Pine Line."

In the weeks ahead, we launched the community organization required to get the work started. We prepared mission statements, outreach to other environmental and civic groups, solicitation of volunteers, a press kit and a brochure.

I recognized from the outset that we had to shape perceptions. To be successful the Society would have to be perceived as honest and trustworthy, strong and capable. And to be perceived that way we would have to *be* that way.

First, we always had to be truthful. With no name recognition, no advertising budget and plenty of powerful opposition, we had to be careful to speak only the truth, check facts and claims before issuing a public statement, and not mischaracterize what was going on. We had to resist the temptation to make public inferences about the unsavory relationship between some developers and local government, even when tempted by this Brookhaven land use scandal or that. We wanted to position ourselves as a dependable, reliable news source that could be counted on to tell the truth, even if a bit more candidly than our opponents appreciated. As a result, reporters routinely turned to us to tell a story they knew to be true, couldn't say themselves, and couldn't get any political or establishment type to say on the record.

A second principle was that we never promise or threaten anything we couldn't deliver. This, too, was a matter of credibility. If we didn't deliver, we would be indistinguishable from the mass of demanding but impotent community groups who are routinely laughed away by hard-boiled politicians. In fact, even though we never failed to follow through on a pledged consequence, it still took years before our adversaries recognized that when we threatened to do something, we did it.

Third, not knowing how much work would be required to attain our ambitious agenda, we had to do as much as we possibly could. There was no procrastination. Even if we couldn't finish a task, we could start it. Our word processors were full of works in progress. A corollary of this was that everything written that could be modified for another purpose, was. We would convert a letter to an elected official into a news release on the subject, talking points and public information sheets. Then we would modify it for the Society's newsletter, which was published religiously every three months. We were in constant communication with our supporters.

I realized that every step of the effort would require meticulous preparation. Whether preparing for negotiation, a televised debate or a major policy announcement, we thought through every detail of our immediate and long-term objectives and how they could best be advanced by the present opportunity. We rehearsed our roles and practiced our presentations, then constructively critiqued our performance to refine our techniques.

We recruited a large base of support, from both organizations and individuals. We did not require them to adopt our strategy and tactics, but merely to support our objectives. We committed to holding regular meetings throughout the process to keep the most interested and useful groups fully informed and to obtain their input. Any time another group could deliver our message, especially in the media, we referred reporters to them. The public expected the Pine Barrens Society to support Pine Barrens preservation, so we used other friendly messengers every time we could. We also tried not to say anything in public with which less than 75 percent of the population could be expected to agree. In short, we reinforced existing public perceptions rather than attempting wholesale re-education. We worked to be simple, direct, consistent and purposeful in our communication, distilling the essence of our position and using every opportunity afforded us.

We needed to be proactive, setting the agenda whenever possible, sticking to game plans even while constantly re-evaluating the wisdom of the strategy at every point. Throughout the process, we made up our minds to set the terms of the debate and provide leadership. Mike Deering remembers that in forum after forum—meetings, public hearings, even the tense negotiations, "Participants were always reacting to our documents." We had fewer resources, and the labor was back-breaking, but by drafting agendas, writing proposals and working documents, even designing the proposed cumulative impact study and the legislation itself, we were always negotiating from our position, not from that of our adversaries. "The team that comes with paper always wins the day," Deering regularly reminded.

We recognized that to be accepted by the power brokers, we had at least to appear powerful. We figured that the filing of the lawsuit and its impacts on our opponents would have that effect, but we also needed to convince Long Island's leaders we had the resources and influence to get the job done. We required board members, who basically lived in L.L. Bean garb, to appear in coats and ties or suits or dresses. We knew that the builders, bankers and other business Neanderthals would try to stereotype us as hippies and dreamers; we were determined not to let that happen.

We knew we had to respect others encountered during the crusade. We vowed not to hate anybody or to carry the fight beyond the forum of public advocacy. This was a challenge to our discipline, but it allowed us to behave civilly, even cordially, to our adversaries, be they developers or government officials. We could criticize their conduct and policies as bad for drinking water protection and habitat preservation but could not personally malign them or carry the hostilities into non-public policy areas. As a result, we maintained unusual out-of-court, off-the-battlefield relationships that may not have been warm but at least were not mean-spirited. The developers did not understand this capacity and did not very often exhibit it themselves.

We reached out to valuable resources, especially skilled or knowledgeable people whose help we needed. As a result, we obtained support from some of the brightest legal, scientific and civic minds. Even though it sometimes cost us money we didn't think we could afford, we never compromised with essential resources.

We were constantly accounting for egos. Especially in the world of politics and power, self-importance factored into every strategic and tactical decision. However right our objective, however obvious the means of obtaining it, we had to consider the egos of those whose support we needed. We were constantly adjusting our message for the individual whose support we sought or whose opposition we needed to minimize. However, we never "went along to get along" with politicians' positions which were inconsistent with Pine Barrens preservation.

Finally, we treated our volunteers and fellow crusaders with enormous respect and deference; we served food and drink during work sessions, recognized and thanked them for their efforts and celebrated victories with them. Most of all, we knew that determination and perseverance were going to win the day, so we spent little time loftily philosophizing on the nobility of our goals and even less on ideology or theory. Instead, we were determined that we could win simply, as Alan Singer put it, "by working longer and harder, trying to think smart, and not thinking we would win just because our cause was good."

Suing the Bastards

"To love what you do and feel that it matters—
how could anything be more fun?"—Katherine Graham

Having arrived at a strategy and sense of direction, we had to pull together resources to achieve our identified objectives. We knew the campaign would be costly, the number of volunteers needed and the amount of time it was likely to take. A daunting task!

Before we could begin our work, we needed to protect the volunteers from potential attacks from our opponents. Sherry Johnson resigned from her position as Vice-President of the Society. Her husband, Roy, did work for various government agencies, and he wanted her to have no part in the litigation. In fact, the litigation scared everyone. Many of us transferred ownership of our homes, cars and other valuables to our spouses, obtained umbrella insurance policies and were scrupulous about what we said and did, avoiding anything slanderous, even while we harshly criticized the developers and government.

The Society had standing to sue, because their members could demonstrate potential harm on the part of the developers. But we wanted to strengthen our standing by recruiting residents of the pine barrens to join the suit. Many who supported the suit shied away from direct involvement because developers had a history of suing and litigation scared everyone.

New York has a decent law which prohibits Strategic Lawsuits Against Public Participation, or SLAPP suits. It is an outgrowth of the formerly common practice of developers to sue anyone who opposed their projects. The threat of the suit alone often discouraged groups or individuals from challenging land use applications. The SLAPP law provides for treble damages if the developer fails to demonstrate that the group was motivated by actual malice, not a legitimate concern. Interestingly, our opponents did not raise the standing issue until later litigation on other matters. -

Still, as we searched for individual plaintiffs to strengthen the Society's "standing" to bring the case, we sought those who had proximity to a proposed development. Direct impact on one's own drinking water is another example of an injury that might be strong enough to confer "standing."

When Johnson left, we recruited Joe Colao and Vinny Scandole of Pine Valley fame for the Society's Board and to join the suit. They quickly recruited Michael Illardi and his wife, Maureen Dolan; Betsy Lytle and Rose Zahler, neighbors and activists who lived in the Pine Barrens, agreed to be individual petitioners. Betty Brown, president of the North Fork Environmental Council and civic activist Don Seubert, the president of the Medford Civic Association, who with his wife actively fought land use abuses in Brookhaven, signed on along with a caring local mother of four, Dawn Pinto, who "just wanted to make sure this special place isn't ruined for my kids and others." The Society's new Secretary, Nina Leonhardt, who was environmental chair for the Lake Panamoka Civic Association during the Save the Lake campaign, and I signed on as individual petitioners as well, because the law grants associational standing to an organization if its members have individual standing.

Our lawyer, Lewis B. Oliver, who had argued and won the Albany Pine Bush case, was an enormous, eccentric attorney with an irascibility that was at once annoying and useful. He drove us crazy, but he drove our adversaries even crazier. We understood from the outset that such a sweeping claim with such staggering consequences for the development industry would not likely be resolved by the lowest court. In New York, that is, strangely, the Supreme Court, with the Appellate Division the next higher level and the Court of Appeals the ultimate arbiter of state law.

The Supreme Court in Suffolk was populated mostly by former politicians who had been rewarded for their years of service to government and more important, loyalty to the party. Most of them were Republicans. We did not hold out much hope that we would succeed there. However, the Appellate Division's Second Department, having jurisdiction over Long Island, is based in Brooklyn and was mostly comprised of jurists from New York City who were more often Democrats. While at the time registered Democrats on Long Island were not much more environmental than registered Republicans, Republican politicians' allegiances to business interests have often made them less supportive of environmental efforts. Our Board was comprised of both, and our policies were strictly non-partisan. We called ourselves "equal opportunity offenders," happy to criticize miscreant politicians on both sides of the aisle.

In the spring of 1989, Lew Oliver drove down from Albany to meet the board and get started on the litigation. He declined our offer of an airplane ticket, possibly because he'd have had trouble fitting into a single seat. He wanted $20,000 "up front and more later." In the first of what seemed like an endless series of loans made by Society Board Members and friends, Joe and Vinny, who were business partners, advanced the money, and we quickly retained Oliver. Because Lew was not based on Long Island, and to control costs, we wanted to have as much of the work as possible done by volunteers.

Oliver needed a lot of information. He wanted all the pertinent facts on each of the 234 pending projects in the Pine Barrens, including type of application (subdivision, site plan or change of zone), what was proposed on how many acres, what environmental attributes and threats were involved, whether the towns or county had required an environmental impact statement, and where the project was relative to all of the others. The research was staggering.

We fielded three teams of volunteers, one each for Brookhaven, Riverhead and Southampton. With more than two-thirds of the proposals in Brookhaven, that team was the largest. Six volunteers took turns filing Freedom of Information Law forms required to get access to government records on the building projects. Then they would painstakingly review each project's file, some of them many inches thick, searching for the needed information, including comments from other agencies and individuals on the environmental problems with the project as proposed.

Volunteers like Debbie Kuhlman, Nancy Holmes, Joe Colao, Steve Mallory, Lorna Saltzman, Dorothy Czensack, Robin's friend Helen Fogarassy, Janet Smith (who stayed on as a volunteer for more than a decade) and college professors Liliane and Norman Thurau, spent unending hours at the offices of the Brookhaven Town Planning Board working at a card table they brought with them each day. Town officials were suspicious about their motives, but eventually, as their weeks there turned into months, the officials said they could leave the card table as a permanent fixture.

They copied relevant documents at 25 cents a page and transmitted them via overnight mail to Oliver in Albany for incorporation into the petition. They sent more than 5,000 documents, each screened, indexed and mapped by an ardent Society Board Member and jovial flake named Karen Blumer. She held a series of environment-related freelance jobs and was working on a book, *Native Plantings*, which discouraged conventional suburban landscaping in favor of using plants indigenous to Long Island.

The work done by the volunteers at the town planning departments began to pile up at Karen's. To entreaty after entreaty, she replied that she was only days away from completing her book and would then return to the task. Weeks went by. After a while, she stopped taking my calls. I pleaded with the board to intervene, to no avail. "Give her a chance to finish her book," Turner admonished. (Later I learned that he was writing his own book, *Exploring the Other Island: A Seasonal Nature Guide to Long Island*, about Long Island's natural treasures and where to find them at different times of the year.)

Finally, one night Turner and his wife Georgia joined me in an unscheduled visit to Karen's house in Brookhaven. There we discovered unprocessed data, some of it six weeks old, untouched in the boxes the other volunteers had delivered to her. When Georgia saw it all sitting there, she took John out on the front lawn, wagged her finger in his face, and started chewing him out. "This guy [meaning me] is working 80-100 hours a week, and you wouldn't even listen to his concerns," she shouted.

The following day we taught a new volunteer Karen's function, and the information began to flow again. Karen ultimately finished her book, wrote one of the ecological affidavits for the lawsuit and appeared for its public announcement.

The town planning departments were very pro-development, though less so in Southampton. We continued to attend the meetings of Town Boards, Town Planning Boards and Zoning Boards of Appeal—the public meetings at which citizens were allowed to complain, generally in vain, about a strip shopping center here, a residential subdivision there. We repeated our call for a cumulative impact analysis and a Generic Environmental Impact Statement to determine the minimum area required to preserve the ecosystem.

In our comments at these meetings, we didn't mince words. We openly accused the board members of ignoring environmental law and public needs as basic as drinking water. At first, this angered some board members, and shouting matches broke out. At one meeting I confronted Brookhaven Planning Board Member Anthony Aliperti, who with his family had undisclosed projects before the Planning Board. "You're out of order!" he shouted at me.

"No, the Planning Board is out of order!" I retorted. Aliperti started climbing over the dais to get at me and had to be pulled back by fellow board members holding onto the tails of his suitcoat.

Eventually the Boards learned to listen to our appeals in silence, then go ahead and approve the developers' applications. "Why fight with the Pine Barrens Society?" they figured. "What they have to say won't matter anyway." We attended 72 consecutive meetings of these bodies while the volunteers continued their labors. In so doing we were satisfying the State law requiring that to bring suit, a plaintiff had to demonstrate that he or she had "exhausted administrative remedies," that is, had complained of the illegal actions before suing.

The paranoia grew at town halls, especially in Brookhaven. Autumn came and still the research continued. By this time, they knew something big was up. Amazingly, each town worried only about itself, never realizing that similar activity was going on in the other Pine Barrens towns. We didn't need to send volunteers to the Suffolk County Department of Health Services (another defendant in the suit) because we could get most of the information on those projects from town records. In addition, we had an ally there, an environmentalist with the Department's Office of Ecology. Louise Harrison had been entering the avalanche of development plans on a county map and was worried about their impact on groundwater and the Pine Barrens ecology. She happily supplied maps and other public documents. We were entitled to those documents, but she saved us a lot of hassle. Louise genuinely cared about the environment and wanted badly for us to succeed. She was to provide even greater help later.

Affidavits were prepared by Cryan; Turner; Blumer; David Stern of the State Assembly Water Commission; Renee Easton, a geology professor at Southampton College; Sarah Meyland of Citizens Campaign for the Environment; Dr. Rebecca Schneider of Cornell; and Marilyn England of the Open Space Council. My relationship with Oliver grew more and more strained as I pressed for completion and filing of the petition. "Lew Oliver is an iconoclast who doesn't like to be told how or when to do something," said Cryan looking back. "He acted out often and I frequently had to use my long friendship to keep the client and their attorney from killing each other." At one point when Lew was instructing me as to what I could and couldn't say to the media, I snapped, "We can't win Pine Barrens preservation in court—it's only a means to an end. If we're to win a plan for permanent preservation and the money it's going to take to buy the land, the ultimate battle will be in the court of public opinion. Forgive me, Counsellor. You do the law, but you'll need to leave me to handle the public part."

On September 24, 1989, Brookhaven Town Councilman John LaMura (later to be elected Supervisor and to witness several huge land-use scandals) convened a meeting between the

Society and town planning officials. "We know you're up to some litigation," he declared. "We just want to find out if a compromise solution is possible." We reiterated our insistence on a cumulative impact study and were shocked when he agreed. We briefly discussed the scope of such a study and estimated that it would probably take more than a year. Then came the not-unanticipated letdown. The town would permit no moratorium on construction while the study was being done. That meant that by the time the study was done, most of the projects that were being analyzed in it would have been approved if not constructed. "Forget it," I said.

"Alright, wait," LaMura rejoined, and he asked for a ten-minute recess. It turned into twenty. Later, Buzz Schwenk of the Builders Institute told us that a group of major developers had assembled, and LaMura was seeking their input. The developers acknowledged the threat represented by a sweeping lawsuit but doubted that the Society had the resources to bring it off. This was the single greatest mistake the builders made during the conflict, and they repeated it again and again for years. They constantly underestimated our capacity to wage a large-scale battle. They thought we were a dinky little outfit—which maybe we were—but they didn't realize how persistent we greenies could be and didn't count on the willingness of thousands of Long Islanders to pitch in to save the environment.

LaMura returned. "Well," he said, "at least we tried. I guess we'll probably be seeing you in court." The number of proposed Pine Barrens projects on the Brookhaven agenda for late October was sobering. Developers with many pending projects—including some of the worst—were rushing to win their approvals before now-certain litigation.

Filing the lawsuit was a race against the clock, because the lawsuit could not legally stop any projects that received final approval before it was filed. Anticipating some form of litigation, developers were trying to expedite their projects' approvals, and hoped that those furthest along would receive their final approvals in October. I called Oliver. "Lew, they're getting away," I said of the projects. Given the 30-day statute of limitations on challenging subdivision approvals, I warned that unless the action was filed by November 21, 1989, a bunch of very bad projects would get through. "You can't rush these things," Lew responded.

I pressed everybody for the final push. Cryan handed off drafts and edits of affidavits to Adriana Brako in front of his Manhattan apartment or Joe Colao in front of his office in Queens. An admitted procrastinator, Cryan turned out his best work under pressure. The last week, he pulled an all-nighter, then left it to his wife, Christina, to draw the map depicting all 234 projects under attack in the landmark lawsuit. She spent the whole next night on the floor finishing the map.

Now all of our research was complete and the ball was in Oliver's court. We nagged him regularly, eventually daily. He was surly and not reassuring. Still, we began arranging for the papers to be served and preparing for the public announcement. We knew all hell would break loose when the lawsuit was filed.

We rented the Middle Island Country Club for 11:00 A.M., November 21, 1989, ordering coffee, Danish and juice. A wonderful Port Jefferson couple, Sally Kuzma and Aaron Gottfried, designed and built a customized podium with the Society's name and cutouts for microphone wires. They also created a huge, five-by-eight-foot, wooden picture puzzle map of the Central Pine Barrens with removable pieces the size of the largest areas to be preserved. The project background was an ominous red, while the puzzle parts were dark green. When they were inserted in the map, they represented a fifty-mile-long greenbelt, easy for anyone to visualize. We would use what we called "the Big Board" repeatedly to demonstrate the acquisition alternatives we sought.

We prepared slick press kits, including extensive background information and graphics on Long Island's groundwater system and flora and fauna. There were pages on the economic downside of development and a list of independent experts with contact numbers where reporters could reach them to get background and comments. We arranged for Board members to conduct tours through the Pine Barrens, visiting the most beautiful spots with streams, ponds or other features. We hired our own videographer and even chartered a helicopter to take still and video cameramen aloft for the big picture. Again, I asked Board Members to dress professionally, in suits, ties and dresses, so as not to reinforce stereotypes of environmentalists. And I prepared for my first-ever news conference appearance.

Still Oliver toiled. The document was now more than 1,200 pages, a project-by-project analysis of the 234 proposed projects including those approved by Brookhaven on October 22. Robin arranged with Village Copier in Manhattan to copy the petition and its associated affidavits and notices of service. We asked a notary public and those whose signatures would have to be certified to appear at 10:00 A.M. for the final step before serving the document.

The night before D-Day was horrendous. Oliver needed facts checked. Only Cryan had the answers. But by this point, his wife, Christina, had had more than enough of the Pine Barrens suit. "You're not even on the Board anymore," she complained to him. "Make them stop bothering us." Early on the last night, he stopped answering the phone; eventually, he simply took the phone off the hook. We were on our own.

Robin and her friend, Helen Fogarassy, copied everything but the missing arguments overnight. This would leave only a small but vital component to be retrieved from Oliver and copied in the morning. A terrible windstorm blew in that Thursday evening. Armed with his American Airlines pass for free travel, Mike Deering bounced all over the sky as he headed to Albany to pick up the legal papers. His intention was to bring the lawsuit back to Long Island that evening.

"It's not ready," Oliver told him. And it wasn't, for hours.

Deering phoned me. "What should I do?" he asked.

"Don't leave," I warned. He spent the night on Oliver's couch, rising at 6:30 am and calling a taxi immediately. Deering jumped into the taxi and upon arriving at the airport, he scrambled across the tarmac, up the steps to the plane and flopped into his seat with the nuclear bomb on his lap just in time for the 7:00 am flight.

At that point, back on Long Island our fax machines were broadcasting news releases to media outlets everywhere. Robin and Helen arrived from the city with the photocopied documents at the Middle Island Country Club at the same time as the signatories and the notary. We installed the lectern and the Big Board. My old college roommate, Peter Devens, began distributing passes for the helicopter tour before being told by the pilot that high winds had grounded the aircraft. Finally, at 8:55 am, Deering wheeled in with the last of Lew Oliver's labors. Phew! The document I truly thought I might never see had arrived.

Scores of representatives from environmental and civic groups took their seats behind reporters from the *New York Times*, *Newsday* and several weekly papers, three television crews and as many radio reporters. I was a nervous wreck. Then, just as it was time to start, an inexplicable calm came over me. Maybe it was the import of the announcement or recognition that all of the pieces had actually fallen into place. Bob McGrath handled the introductions, and we were underway.

The speech was concise but dramatic. It explained how development in the Pine Barrens threatened drinking water and habitat, that towns were approving projects one-by-one without considering cumulative impacts, and that the Society was bringing what WPIX-TV, Channel 11 would call "the largest environmental lawsuit ever" to halt the destruction. We explained both the environmental and economic stakes, concluding, "According to law the permit process must stop while the suit goes forward," I said, "So, building in the Pine Barrens stops right now!" The room erupted with applause from the citizenry and incredulity on the part of the media that billions of dollars' worth of real estate development was being halted in its tracks.

We went on to explain the Pine Barrens Preservation Initiative to preserve "a national park-quality greenbelt." Adriana Brako, the student who had spied on the opposition at Pine Valley, popped the picture puzzle parts into place on the Big Board as cameras recorded the action. As she moved back and forth across the board, Turner had flashes of "Wheel of Fortune," and started calling her "Adri-vanna."

It was time for questions and answers. No prepared notes for this part. Roger Stern of News 12 was first. "This is the most extravagant presentation I've ever seen from a community group," Stern observed. "Who's paying for all of this?" I mumbled something about it's all having been donated or paid for by volunteers. I just couldn't believe the question. Our little group had just halted $11.2 billion worth of real estate development to protect Long Island's drinking water—and Stern wanted to know who'd bought the Danish?

The rest of the questions were more thoughtful. Sarah Lyall of the *Times* wanted to know about how the land acquisition program worked in consonance with the lawsuit. Mitchell Freedman of *Newsday* asked: "How many entities were served, today—town boards, planning boards and the like?" It was a tougher question than he realized, because since the papers had just arrived, no one had actually been served yet. I did not want to convey that this was something that had not yet happened. I fished for the right words. "Let's see," I said. "That would be the town boards, town planning boards and zoning boards of appeal of Brookhaven, Riverhead and Southampton and also the Suffolk County Department of Health Services—ten entities in all to be served, today."

When the news conference ended, we answered additional questions from individual reporters and started the Pine Barrens tours. Roger Stern was seen wrapping one last piece of Danish in a napkin and stuffing it in his suit coat pocket for the road. The lawsuit servers fanned out across three towns to deliver the bad news.

The next day, *Newsday*'s Freedman wrote, "In the largest suit of its kind in state history, the Long Island Pine Barrens Society has begun legal proceedings to block all new construction in 100,000 acres of Pine Barrens in central and eastern Suffolk County. The action, which was sharply criticized by political and business interests, stops the towns of Brookhaven, Riverhead and Southampton from issuing new building permits, zoning changes or subdivision approvals within the Pine Barrens." He quoted me as saying, "We've got to stop development before it destroys eastern Long Island. We all drink from the same well. If we destroy it, there's no place else to turn."

Now everyone knew Long Island's biggest battle was joined.

The War Heats Up

"Government, even in its best state, is but a necessary evil; in its worst state, an intolerable one."—Thomas Paine

The reaction to the lawsuit in the development, political and legal world was swift and strong. "Buzz" Schwenk admitted that the Long Island Builders Institute never saw it coming "until the media was calling us for our reaction." Riverhead Town Supervisor Joseph Janoski immediately termed us "environmental terrorists." And every real estate lawyer on Long Island must have thought it was Christmas.

Dozens of developers with projects named in the lawsuit intervened to be parties in the case. When the court convened for the first conference, nearly every prestigious law firm on Long Island was represented, usually in the person of a senior partner. Daryl Conway of Conway and Ceriello sat in the back row of the courtroom tapping on a hand-held calculator while everyone waited for Judge Paul Baisley, who was late, to appear. I turned to his partner Larry Ceriello, who was providing us pro-bono service on Long Island while Lew Oliver toiled in Albany. "What's he trying to figure out?" I asked. "It's 234 projects covering 43,500 acres." "That's not what he's calculating," Larry replied. "He knows how much each of those guys bill per hour and he's calculating how much it's costing the developers to wait for the judge!" His estimate? $23,000 in 1989 money.

Larry termed the Pine Barrens lawsuit, "The Long Island lawyers full employment act and retirement fund." We called it "L.I. Law."

Commencement of the lawsuit allowed us to re-focus on the preservation objectives. Proposed projects were challenged in court as the Pine Barrens towns approved them. As a result of the filing of the suit, nothing was being built in the Pine Barrens of Brookhaven, Riverhead and Southampton. But this was only a means to an end, not our objective. Our goal, of course, was preserving the Pine Barrens permanently. Thus, our task now turned to identifying the land to be preserved and convincing the developers to go along with the plan. This would be a three-part series of events: communicating the need to Long Islanders, selecting the parcels to be protected and establishing a funding mechanism that elected officials would support.

That would require acquisition of at least 100,000 acres of Long Island's Pine Barrens. We had to identify what most needed to be protected. Not a problem: the three founders of the Pine Barrens Society knew this land from the inside out. John Cryan, Bob McGrath and John Turner had walked every foot of Long Island's premier ecosystem and quickly identified the land most important to preserve. Not surprisingly, the parcels in the center of the Island were most undeveloped and even pristine. We knew that to protect a Core Preservation Area of the most sensitive land we would have to offer development potential for less sensitive property on the perimeter of the Pine Barrens. We named these parcels the Compatible Growth Area. Our strategy was to protect the most sensitive land while supplying developers a formula for building their projects on the perimeter. Moreover, this strategy allowed us to protect more Pine Barrens. Rather than to propose 100,000 acres, we targeted 50,000 acres for the Core and another 50,000 acres for the less sensitive areas. There would be preservation and development. For the first time, the developers began to see the conflict as "Let's Make a Deal." Since most of the developers' projects were in the outside area, they could win approval for their own projects by agreeing to the preservation plan. Of course, we didn't tell them this.

So, identifying the land to be preserved was a no-brainer. The Pine Barrens Society leadership, backed by hydrogeologists and other preservationists, knew exactly what most needed protection. It was land previously undisturbed and with water quality benefits as well as habitat protection. Purchasing all this land was estimated to cost as much as $1 billion. It ended up costing $2 billion. Our strategy had to be to continue to obtain public support so that voter-approved dollars went to land and water protection through the Suffolk County Drinking Water Protection Program and not to some pot of money that the politicians wanted to use to balance the bloated budget.

And that wasn't even the biggest problem. Besides needing to acquire the land, there would have to be a regional authority to control and manage it. Who was going to buy the land? Who was going to manage it? Who was going to enforce the laws that created it? To establish a brand-new government entity, the State of New York would have to create a new authority which would oversee and enforce rules and regulations well beyond the influence of the individual towns and with the authority to effectively control a multi-town agency. We're talking about three separate towns, each with three internal bodies (Town Board, Planning Board and Zoning Board), that establish the rules and regulations. The towns wouldn't want this, the developers wouldn't want this, and the state just wouldn't want to be involved (the very people who were in a position to make it happen). A regional authority was considered impossible, and yet it was a necessity.

Alas, the "home rule" mechanism for approving development had been in place for about 350 years. It was brought over from merrie olde England, added to by a fragmented system of suburban developments, put up one at a time with no overall planning and comprised of 13 townships, 2 cities, 97 villages and 124 school districts. In 1990, Long Island had 2.61 million people—more residents than 21 states in the country. This, despite having a land area of only 912 square miles, less than all of the states except Rhode Island. No wonder the Long Island landscape is such a mess!

The result? Land use decision-making on Long Island came from local government—towns and villages. The notion of "home rule," providing for land use decision-making by those closest to the community, sounds sensible. However, political power in towns and villages devolves from the authority to grant development approvals and is the source of most local power and corruption.

We had to demonstrate that local government was largely controlled by development interests through campaign contributions and "payoffs," plain and simple. On Long Island generally, and in the Pine Barrens in particular, sound planning was routinely subordinated to political wheeling and dealing, which regularly pushed or even broke the law. Jennifer Miller, a planner who was ultimately employed by the Pine Barrens Society, summed it up: "Long Island's self-proclaimed planners were more interested in satisfying egos and carving up the pie than in shaping the built landscape to enhance the place."

Miller, a junior aide to Assemblyman Tom DiNapoli, was becoming an active volunteer, spending Tuesday evenings at Lake Panamoka, offering her help. It was obvious that asking her to stuff envelopes would not be the best use of her time, and she quickly rose to handling tactics and strategy. She had remarkable energy and the quickness to grasp what needed to be done and how to go about it made it clear she would be a terrific asset. The 23-year-old Rockville Centre native was enthusiastic about the Pine Barrens campaign and increasingly uninspired by her government job. I asked DiNapoli if he would mind if we "stole" her. He encouraged her "advancement," he told me, and jokingly told her, "I hope you can keep up with him." She could and did.

She agreed to come to the Society for $22,000, exactly what she had been making with the state. Her planning degree from New York University and her legislative skills were crucial as we moved from litigation to legislation. Her salary demands were certainly reasonable for us, but the commute to the East End from Rockville Centre was impractical, given our long workdays, so she wanted a place to live. As an example of the Society's creative, "never say never" approach, we appealed to volunteers and advertised, obtaining a house owned by environmentalists Ann and George Baird on the Peconic Bay in Southampton. Jennifer was thrilled and so were we.

DiNapoli's challenge to "try to keep up" worked wonders. Smart as a whip and fiercely competitive, she knew no hours and never complained. She wore her intelligence and energy as a badge of honor, deferring to no one and nothing. We were alter-egos with a heavy dose of irreverence and humor. She reorganized the office and handled anything where she could spare me the effort, but she consistently checked with me before venturing into anything she thought I might have an opinion about. She demonstrated leadership at all levels, from the volunteers to our environmental colleagues to elected officials. One time, my brother Tom and I were talking about a job that required some finesse and were pondering who could do it. Tom (who spent little time at our office) said, "Get that buttoned-up one."

DiNapoli remembered, "Jennifer was outstanding, and I think her coming out of government helped because when we wanted you to be reined in now and then, she could be helpful in providing another perspective about process and people. Of course, there were times when Jennifer's enthusiasm and intensity rivaled yours—it's hard to believe that anyone could do that —but I think she was an excellent `second' in terms of being out there positive and aggressive in getting the Pine Barrens thing done."

An added bonus was her mother, Rita, whose reaction to news accounts of our work mirrored public perceptions impeccably and consistently. Realizing this, Jennifer took her work home in a most useful way-- by trying public relations strategies out on her mother in advance, making her a one-woman "focus group" that guided our communications decisions. She never steered us wrong.

It should come as no surprise that the people with money and influence with the politicians were going to have their way with Long Island. After all, they owned the land and controlled government decision-making and mostly didn't give a damn about the visual impact, traffic, resulting high taxes and the quality of Long Island's water – the stuff that mattered most to Long Islanders. We knew that the public would agree with this assessment, but first we had to get this message out.

We had to show that "home rule" worked well for developers but not at all well for residents and taxpayers. And, finally, we explained to the public that we weren't advocating a halt to all building, just that Long Islanders should know how much development Long Island could responsibly support without undermining public health and welfare.

Of course, opposition by local officials to a regional plan was to be expected. What set us back was the resistance by state officials – the only people who could create a regional authority. Their explanation? "Land use decisions are made locally," they said, "that's the way it's always been and that's the way it's going to be."

For example, when we talked to politicians—from self-proclaimed planner Lee Koppelman to arrogant State Senator James Lack—about a regional commission with land use decision-making capability, they both balked. They argued that the historically town-defined commitment to local land use decision-making made a regional or ecosystem management approach impossible. Thus, our efforts to effect change were met regularly and dismissively with the "political wisdom" that what we were seeking had never been done before, as though that fact ensured that it couldn't and wouldn't ever be done. They were miles away from the idea that first you figure out what should be done; then you figure out how to do it. The theme, "dream it up and make it happen" was the touchstone of the Pine Barrens Board from the very beginning. Now we had to deliver it.

It was clear that the towns were not going to change their way. The "home rule" approach gave them complete control over what got built and where. Town officials liked their relationships with the developers. Our only hope was to turn to state government for the fix. But the state wasn't even considering it.

Politicians seem like they have zero vision. Most of them don't seek office for some lofty purpose for which elective office is the only route. Not surprisingly, they don't respond to advocacy very well. They understand and appreciate political process and they pride themselves on being realists. For them that means that government can't actually do much of what anyone wants – so they don't even consider doing anything that hasn't been done before.

To say that things can only be done that have been done in the past is to rule out social change before you even start. So, we were frustrated by the disposition of politicians to give us a completely unsatisfactory, totally unresponsive answer to virtually every question asked and every request made. Yet, their view was entrenched to the point where negotiations to settle the Pine Barrens dispute outside of court were prevented in part by the "political wisdom" that the state legislature could not be expected to pass a bill in a single session, because it rarely did. This presumably meant that they could not or would not do so, even if the bill were backed by every man, woman and child in the state (which ours practically was), was written for lawmakers by stakeholders (which ours practically was) and enjoyed a commitment of hundreds of millions of dollars in land acquisition funds (which ours practically did). The not surprising thing about conventional wisdom is that it does not allow for the extraordinary. Politicians told us we didn't have the resources to bring our lawsuit, couldn't win it at any level, wouldn't have the means to carry out the campaign, couldn't get legislation approved or the funds needed appropriated and couldn't get a referendum on the ballot by petition. One of the biggest mistakes politicians and developers continually made was betting against us.

Dealing with politicians is depressing. It's a huge challenge. First problem, incumbents get re-elected. Americans think Congress is doing a uniformly bad job, but voters keep sending their own Congressman or woman back to Washington. One of the early signs of insanity is doing the same thing over and over again and expecting a different result.

In New York State more than 90 percent of incumbent state legislators seeking re-election win. That's our fault. If we keep sending elected officials back, even when we're not satisfied with their performance, we shouldn't be surprised when they don't give us what we want. Government doesn't get better without change. And, indeed, the principal complaint about government is that it can't get out of its own way. Nothing happens, or else it takes forever.

Given their secure positions, politicians quickly come to a simple conclusion, "I'm fixed for life, if I can just avoid doing anything to piss anybody off." At first we didn't realize that. We'd go to a politician and say, "You can protect drinking water, preserve open space and limit new taxes for government services that development produces by supporting this measure," and we'd expect to hear, "Sounds good. Sign me up." Instead, what we heard was, "No thanks, I might piss somebody off."

Now we have neither the towns nor the state amenable to reform. Since only the state legislature could require the towns to protect the Pine Barrens land and water, we needed a strategy to change the state legislature's mind and pass legislation to do so.

In approaching state government, we took the political high ground (if that's not a contradiction in terms). We had a process. Step One: we asked nicely. Step Two: we made it clear that the unresponsive politician was indeed, going to piss someone off—us—and that we were going to be sure everybody else knew about it. The typical reaction to this was something on the order of, "You and what army?"

A basic tenet of our overall strategy was not to promise or threaten anything we couldn't actually deliver. That meant we really had to have an army. It became essential to count on having to assemble the army and prepare the arsenal before we asked for anything as basic as, "Let's find out the environmental and economic consequences before we pave over Long Island."

We knew that success would require beating the politicians up a couple of times—before they realized that we could and would back up our warnings. But they never did. As candidate Jim W. Gettys said to Charles Foster Kane in *Citizen Kane*, "they're going to need more than one lesson and they're going to get more than one lesson."

We also found that few politicians could differentiate between a special interest and the public interest. To most of them, anyone who was at their door was a lobbyist, and they couldn't make the distinction between a real estate developer with only his own pecuniary interest and an environmental advocate whose agenda benefited everyone. But they had no trouble seeing the difference in power between the two groups. The special interests could attend fundraising events for the politicians and endorse them for election. The non-profit environmental and civic groups are precluded by means, morality and law from doing so. It also belies the notion that elected officials view themselves as public servants. In meeting after meeting, the politicians gave us the impression that they were doing a giant-sized favor just by seeing us. The special interest lobbyists had bought their access and were regularly treated as pals.

Politicians have no idea what the world looks like to real people. To begin with, they think everybody wants to be like them. When it occasionally gets through to them that people hate them, they think it's because they're jealous. For example, Michael LoGrande described my early advocacy efforts in public forums as a "short cut to the ballot box," suggesting that political ambition was driving my agenda. Dealing with the politicians was the most unpleasant part of my job: I would never have even considered a career in politics.

They also have no clue as to how the public regards their press conferences and photo opportunities. Routinely, public officials announced a land acquisition or other environmental action with a news conference or media event dominated by other politicians, usually with the same party affiliation. On one occasion Suffolk County Executive Robert Gaffney told a cabinet member that he would "punish" the Pine Barrens Society for our public criticism of his land acquisition record by not including us in his press events. "Amper won't get to be up there with us," the official quoted Gaffney as saying.

The trouble for politicians is that people expect politicians to say good things about each other, especially members of their own party. People see it as horse-trading and pay no attention. When non-partisan advocates and citizen activists commend an elected official, that counts for lots more—especially, as in the Society's case, where we enjoyed a reputation for criticizing those who obstructed our environmental objectives. Here again, the politicians were projecting their own inclinations to self-promotion. The Society actually preferred not to appear at such events. When a politician stands next to me at a podium, he looks like an environmentalist, from which he clearly benefits. At the same time, I look like a politician, from which I clearly don't. In fact, there were other elected officials who saw their job as reform and not merely as a path to re-election. They included the eventual sponsors of the Pine Barrens Protection Act, Assemblymen Tom DiNapoli, Steve Englebright and Fred Thiele and Senators Ken LaValle and Caesar Trunzo. And George Pataki, who succeeded Cuomo as governor, fully supported the preservation process. As it turned out, these public officials were very encouraging, as we shall see.

The way we referred to politicians depended on how we felt about them. We called opponents "politicians"; supporters were "elected officials" or "leaders." We always referred to them by their proper titles, no matter how well we knew them. The business lobbyists invariably called them by their first names, even out of their presence. They wanted people to know they were in with politicians. That was the last thing we wanted.

The bottom line is good politicians were few and far between.

Every good story needs a bad guy. And that was the developers. The ""War of the Woods"" was a battle between the interests of all Long Islanders (clean water) versus the interests of developers making money by building stuff – regardless of its impact on the environment and the economy of Long Island. Let's face it, Long Island was overdeveloped way before the effort to save the Pine Barrens. And, of course, all we were doing was asking for a study to determine the impact of Pine Barrens destruction before the builders constructed 234 real estate projects, regardless of the adverse impacts.

The environmentalists warned me about the "enemy" early on. They were variously described as "greedy," "money-grubbing," "sleazy," "soulless," and "just plain bad," if you like adjectives; "land rapists," "con artists," and "slime," if you prefer nouns.

I suspected that they were merely wired differently. Upon arriving at the crest of a hill affording a spectacular natural vista, I thought, an environmentalist gasps, "Let's preserve it for everyone," while a developer encountering the same vista says to his partner, "Let's develop it and make a killing." Developers, I thought, were not so much evil as misguided, lacking a sophisticated perspective and value system concerning matters of ecology and preservation. Whatever the truth, I operated throughout the campaign as though I were right, while I found it increasingly difficult to refute the characterizations of my mentors in the environmental community.

Understanding how the developers thought and worked, it was logical to map a strategy for campaigning against them. Our communications campaign needed to characterize the developers in a way with which the public would identify. It was clear to the public the developers were trying to advance their own agenda, not the public's interest. I knew we had to debunk the developers' claims and get the people's interest instead of the developers'. Most of all, we needed to show that the public interest had to come before the developers' selfish goals and the way to ensure that was to determine how much more development Long Island could tolerate and still protect something as basic as our drinking water. Thus, it was just sensible to find out first how much land and water protection is necessary before we "green-light" massive overdevelopment on top of our most sensitive land and water.

One thing is clear: Long Islanders know that Long Island is overdeveloped. They see it in the impenetrable traffic which has gone from bad to worse. They see it in the badly designed downtowns and they recognize it in the intolerable taxation we face---twice the national average. Our message: what's good for the developers is what's bad for us. All we had to do was say it. I could just imagine the nodding heads in front of the television as we explained our position.

I knew what to expect. We knew that the developers would paint us as zealots. We knew they would call us anti-growth and job killers. I planned our answers. We reversed the developers' "zealot" argument with a sensible recommendation: that you should study before you build. We knew the public agreed that the Island was already overdeveloped, and it made good sense to find out whether the development of 234 new projects would undermine the already declining water quality of Long Island's Sole Source Aquifer. All of our water comes from beneath our feet.

Our trickiest communication challenge was the developers' touting of jobs. Yes, building produces jobs – for a limited period -- and Long Island builders have a record of limiting employment or bringing it in from off-Island. Our position: construction jobs for a few are good, but they're temporary. And the resulting construction leaves all of us with debris contaminated water, from Great Neck to Montauk.

They claimed that limiting development would hurt the economy. Calvin Rafuse of the Long Island Builders Institute (LIBI) said, "This adversarial legal tactic has wasted thousands of taxpayers' dollars and has been virtually the straw that broke the back of the regional economy." Not so, it's the opposite. In fact, overdevelopment hurts the economy. It brings higher taxes for new government services including transportation infrastructure, new schools and other government expenses. Long Island's economy is a mess, and much of it because of overdevelopment. Builders tell you development reduces taxes. When did that ever happen? Our response was just the opposite. We needed a slogan that was easy to remember and impossible to forget. We explained simply that "deer don't go to school." We didn't think it would be hard to demonstrate that Long Island's high taxes are directly attributable to overdevelopment. If building lowered taxes, why are Long Islanders being taxed out of existence? Another nod of heads in front of television screens.

The developers made their campaign personal. In fact, public relations professionals hired by the developers later acknowledged that part of their strategy was to discredit the messenger, since our environmental arguments were so hard to debunk. Robin had a hard time with the personal attacks, but they genuinely didn't bother me a bit. I understood the developers' strategy and knew it would never work. The people who were doing the name calling didn't know me at all, and the characterizations and accusations didn't ring true or seem right to the overwhelming majority of Long Islanders. This helped to make the builders seem even more villainous.

"Mr. Amper wants to scare everyone to death that the water will be polluted and make it impossible for anyone to live on Long Island," said LIBI Executive Director "Buzz" Schwenk, "and it's a big lie." Name calling was a consistent tactic used by developers to try to discredit our effort. Of course, history shows that contaminated water has become the Island's largest environmental challenge, with remedy estimated in 2020 as $8 billion. Still, the land beneath the Pine Barrens remains our purest drinking water source.

In fact, signs held by supporters of the "mini city" planned for the Pine Barrens by mega developer Wilbur Breslin said simply, "Stop the Amper Recession." I don't believe that Long Islanders bought the notion that we were responsible for the recession. It was just another method of name-calling that didn't ring true and didn't discourage us.

The level of harassment had been about what we had expected at the start of the initiative. Some had feared far worse. Security consultants had issued dire warnings about what the Society might face. We didn't know if what the developers were doing was an intentional strategy or the product of their actually hating us. We didn't worry much about what the developers, contractors or associated institutions might say or do, but we took reasonable precautions.

At the outset, for example, Board Members and I transferred ownership of our real property, our houses, cars (we didn't have a lot of stocks and bonds) to our spouses' names. We made sure that personal litigation was not going to wipe out any of us. Next, I have never been a spokesperson for any of my clients; I design communications; someone else executes it. In this case, we were warned that high visibility was better for my health. They were more likely to kill me if I was not in the public eye. "Some of these guys will kill for a lousy unpaid debt," our security consultant explained. "You're talking about stopping more than $8 billion in development. Money isn't funny to these guys."

My thinking was that making a martyr of me would have assured enough public support to wage the war the developers thought we couldn't afford to wage. Robin was instructed that if anything happened to me, a "Memorial Fund" was to be announced immediately. We joked that my funeral would be the most successful fundraising special event in Society history.
Early in the campaign, the Long Island Association's James Larocca asked me ominously whether I worried about Robin's starting the car in the morning. A security guy actually suggested a remote car starter, but we rejected the notion as paranoid. There were a couple of telephone death threats, but the police who heard the tapes agreed they weren't serious. In the only serious discussion we ever had about personal safety, Robin asked late one night after someone tried to drive my car off the road, whether I was prepared to die for the Pine Barrens. I hadn't thought about it. After a minute, I answered, "No, I'm not. But I'd only be killed for talking about them and I'd be willing to die for free speech, if necessary."

Spying and efforts to discredit were more real. Financial and background checks were done, private investigators took pictures from a rowboat "trying to document an alleged cocaine habit," the cameraman told an acquaintance. Others shadowed us in cars, far more obtrusively than in the movies. One night as Jennifer drove home alone, she stopped and confronted a guy she'd seen following her car. "Follow Amper if you want to," she shouted into the private eye's car as he hastily rolled up his window, "I just work here." She conspicuously wrote down his license plate number and he was quickly off the assignment. Somebody replaced him in a couple of days.

Our garbage can was regularly emptied into the back of a van. We burned strategic documents and household papers. Except to monitor our increasing debt, there wasn't too much of use to them anyway. However, this may be part of why they kept underestimating our staying power.

We were warned against drinking more than two drinks at a restaurant, then driving. "They'll have your DWI on television the same night," a cautious supporter warned. We never hired anyone who applied for jobs with us during the war years—only those we already knew and never anyone under 21. When the Board met, we played music to make remote listening more difficult, even though we never had evidence we were being listened to. We did use the phone, even for tactical purposes, without thinking much about it, because, we were told, phone tapping is usually avoided. It seems some people "in the industry" take liberties with the law, so they try to avoid doing things that might invite involvement by the federal government.

The developers were convinced from the beginning that the Society lacked the resources to win the war. They talked constantly about imminent bankruptcy and warned against negotiation, which they felt would "empower" us with credibility. However, then vice-president of the New York State Builders Association, Bob Wieboldt, saw early on the benefit of "creative engagement." When other Long Island builders argued that the Pine Barrens suit would require the filing of petition after petition for years, as development projects were approved by the towns, Wieboldt replied, "They may be only environmentalists, but they do have word processors."

Wieboldt told a developers' group in 1999, "Go ahead and march out in red coats, make your members feel good and tough, beat your drum and fly your flag if you want, but it might be better to start wearing green yourselves and stand behind the trees where you can start picking off the environmentalists, too. You won't look as heroic—you're not marching in step and all that —but at least when you walk away from the battlefield half your men will still be alive." Alas, most of the developers never appreciated Wieboldt's sage advice.

Wieboldt was big in stature and long on brains. More than any of the other development advocates, he saw the seriousness of the Pine Barrens Society and its prospects for success. He played a major role in ending the "War of the Woods." Not only did he understand the developers, he understood the environmentalists, too. While the two of us fought fiercely for our causes, Wieboldt's wit and wisdom allowed for civilized and productive dialogue.

Our campaign was moving. The lawsuit was effectively halting the development of the 234 projects proposed collectively by the three Pine Barrens towns. Donations were beginning to come in and our media presence was winning public support as we emphasized the need for a study to establish what land had to be protected to assure clean water and natural beauty. Now it was time to directly save the Pine Barrens by purchasing Pine Barrens land in the order of ecological priority.

We had meeting after meeting with planners at Suffolk County and in the three towns to establish the priority of acquisitions. Clearly, the undeveloped land in the center of the Pine Barrens would be our first goal. This land would become the Core Preservation Area, if and when a Pine Barrens Preservation Act could be achieved. We also mapped the next most important land on the perimeter of the Barrens. Then we campaigned with the towns and county to increase the rate of land purchases. We celebrated key acquisitions making certain that government officials got all the credit. And we nagged public officials who were dragging their feet. Public attention and support grew.

Suffolk County's Drinking Water Protection Program had been approved on Election Day in 1987 during Michael LoGrande's short time as county executive. Halpin put it back on the ballot in 1988 and it was during his administration that county planners began saving environmentally sensitive land by purchasing key parcels using the quarter-cent the voters had approved at referendum. It took a little while to get the land purchases underway, but by 2020, over 100,000 acres had been preserved. Water protection was the key objective but land of critical environmental value was another key goal. By 2020, voters had put up more than $2 billion for Pine Barrens protection.

The Pine Barrens Society was always focused on the next priority acquisition. In the spring of 1990, the Society had its eye on the 1,400-acre "Hampton Hills" proposal. The project was one of the largest developments pending in the Pine Barrens and it lay in the center of the Pine Barrens we sought to preserve. We really, really wanted it.

A developer named Barry Beil had acquired the property and proposed building a 307-home luxury subdivision. Construction of it would have cut the Pine Barrens in half and discouraged the assemblage of an eventual 50,000-acre nature preserve. Beil and his supporters argued that the environment would be protected by "clustering." In short, clustering meant cramming all of the homes they wanted to build on much of the land environmentalists wanted to save.

Developers argued that the clustered development would allow preservation of the rest of the land for "free," saving the $14.7 million cost. Of course, this was simply their way of getting to build as much as they wanted. And it assured that every parcel of land in the Pine Barrens would be spoiled by fragmented development.

Environmentalists supported the acquisition as key, observing that high density development was antithetical to preservation of an ecosystem. In fact, for many people the Hampton Hills acquisition defined who was an environmentalist and who wasn't. Englebright, Thiele and most importantly Halpin favored full preservation. Koppelman, Schwenk and Southampton Town

Planning Board Chairman Roy Wines and Planning Director Tom Thorsen favored clustered development.

Alas, Andrew Walker, director of The Nature Conservancy (TNC) called Hampton Hills a good cluster plan. This came as no surprise to us. At one point in the early battle, Walker publicly praised the developers' lobby for supporting efforts to win passage of the Drinking Water Protection Program. I was furious. I had pulled him aside and warned him that while we didn't expect TNC to lead the preservation effort, we would not tolerate his supporting the developers' assertions that they were part of Pine Barrens preservation. Ultimately, government officials and a majority of their constituents agreed that preservation is preservation and clustering is development.

It was clear to us that if clustering was accepted as an alternative to land preservation there would be a lot more building and a lot more loss of open space. Here again, public support of our effort was key. We knew that most Long Islanders eschewed high density development and valued open space. They hated what they termed suburban sprawl and the high taxes that dense development produced. So, town politicians were not going to be eager to approve development their constituents abhorred.

Throughout the "War of the Woods," the developers kept repeating publicly that they supported and contributed campaign funds to the Drinking Water Protection Program, which they did. They then opposed every acquisition ever made under that program.

Bob Wieboldt, who became Executive Director of the Long Island Builders Institute after the legislation and plan were completed, admits, "LIBI was paranoid that government was going to buy up every parcel, leaving none for development. The Society's appearances on TV and in the press at acquisition ceremony after acquisition ceremony increased that perception. Time and time again I had to assure them that the state and county didn't have the money to buy up everything," he said.

Beil received fair market value for the property, twice what he had paid for it years before. The Society's and Group for the South Fork's litigation certainly took its toll, as did the demise of Pine Valley way back in December, 1990, but Beil persuaded at least some environmental leaders that he'd also had a change of heart.

"We talked a lot about it at home," Beil told *Newsday*. "I questioned what I had been told—that the project would not harm the environment. You start to say to yourself, `They [his environmental consultants] could be wrong. Which side would I rather be wrong on?'" His daughter entreated him to preserve the land. It turns out that the preservation of Hampton Hills was not the exclusive accomplishment of the Pine Barrens Society. It was probably Beil's daughter's opinion that made the difference.

At first a critic of County Legislator Steven Englebright's comparison of the Hampton Hills project to "anchoring 307 houseboats on the Croton Reservoir," Beil later accepted the analogy. He concluded, "How many steaks can you eat, how many suits can you wear, how many houses can you live in?" Whether a true convert or persuaded that the politics had turned to the environmentalists or that his daughter was right, we didn't care why Beil changed his mind about Hampton Hills -- merely that he did.

Suffolk County Executive Patrick Halpin staged the Hampton Hills acquisition announcement at the golf club which the parcel surrounded. The occasion brought together the Society's three founders for the first time in years. It seemed so fitting. The size and beauty of this Pine Barrens parcel left us with a feeling. We had won Hampton Hills, we were on a roll. When Englebright arrived, I charged across the patio and threw my arms around the man who had so championed this particular piece of Pine Barrens, so startling that Halpin's security man instinctively reached for his gun.

When the ceremony ended, the Society's Board Members ordered drinks from the developer's bar. Beil's partner, James Zizzi (later to become president of the Long Island Builders Institute), retained ownership of the golf club. Then we sat on the patio, rolling out maps of the adjacent Pine Barrens, discussing the next logical acquisitions. If this was the "War of the Woods," our army had captured the high ground and was already mapping strategy for capturing the next key territory.

"The developers didn't win the Hampton Hills fight because their underlying argument was wrong," Thiele explained. "The idea of adding another 307 houses in the very core of the Pine Barrens was ridiculous. To me the acquisition was one of the best deals we ever made. We were able to protect the largest and most strategically-located parcel at a price of between $9,000 and $10,000 an acre, far less than we were paying for land in the more developed west end of the County," he said.

Almost all of the building projects were completely stalled. One that was not came from the man environmentalists viewed as the biggest and baddest developer of them all, Wilbur Breslin. He was short, conservatively dressed and well-connected. His past projects included controversial battles over permits and broken promises. The volume of his past projects and the size of the next one made him the most powerful developer on Long Island.

The sheer magnitude of his proposed project dwarfed every other building project in the region. We termed this "mini city" "Willy World," a variation on the National Lampoon film "Vacation," with Chevy Chase, that portrayed the world's biggest amusement park, "Wally World." Unlike most of the projects threatening the Pine Barrens, Wilbur Breslin's proposed project for Yaphank was not a subdivision but a commercial development, exempt from the automatic stay that our lawsuit prevented. On October 16, Breslin received the first of the many approvals he would need to undertake construction of the "mini city" in the Pine Barrens. The 2,100-acre mega-project located at the intersection of William Floyd Parkway and the Long Island Expressway called for the Island's largest shopping center, 12,000 units of residential housing (more than in Ozone Park, Queens, we were fond of saying), and more office and commercial space than the Chrysler Building. Brookhaven Town granted preliminary approval without hearing from the public at the final meeting.

Breslin's association with *Newsday* publisher Robert Johnson assured him of *Newsday's* editorial support, and his promise of construction jobs won him support from the labor unions. But there wasn't much the labor unions could do with most development on hold. The Island's most powerful developer, Breslin had the ear of the Long Island Association, Long Island's biggest business group, although President James Larocca minimized Breslin's influence on the LIA.

At first, Breslin dismissed the Pine Barrens Society and me as "too small to count," in the words of LIBI's "Buzz" Schwenk. "`Amper lives on a postage-stamp lot in a middle-class community, and the Society has no budget,' the developers kept telling themselves. `All we have to do is hold out,'" Schwenk remembered.

But Breslin's first problem was not with the Society, but with the pesky Open Space Council (OSC), an underfunded, not-for-profit group which had it in for Breslin's project like no other. OSC, headed by ornithologist Marilyn England and environmentalist Dan Morris, was concerned about the effects of the project on the Carmans River headwaters and adjacent preserved Pine Barrens, dogged Breslin every step of the way. They immediately challenged the Breslin approvals on project-specific grounds – different from the basis of the Pine Barrens Society lawsuit.

OSC argued in court that even if the court wouldn't order a cumulative impact analysis of all 234 projects in the Pine Barrens, that it must insist that Breslin at least consider all the parts of his mini city plan before Brookhaven Town could approve the mall. To do otherwise, they argued, would constitute illegal segmentation of the project.

Breslin was unbowed and pressed ahead as though the litigation did not exist. In fact, he brazenly promised, through his attorney, Herbert Balin, that he would begin construction in late 1990 or early 1991. He said he had lined up four anchor stores, essential to a mall of this size, though he refused to identify them. Later, when pressed, Balin claimed that Breslin had obtained agreement by a Nassau County department store owner, Alan Fortunoff, to be a major tenant, but Fortunoff quickly made it clear he would never locate there.

Also dogging Breslin was environmental champion, Van Howell, whose clever tactics and masterful illustrations characterized Breslin as a megalomaniac, gobbling up Long Island. Howell called department stores warning of the negative public reaction that leasing in the Breslin Mall would mean and staged demonstration after demonstration, drawing big crowds and waving banners with such slogans as "The Road to Hell is Paved by Breslin."

Equally smart, strategic and creative, Howell made killing "Willy World" his personal crusade. If we needed a cartoon, illustration or demonstration, there was Van. He had a terrific sense of humor, substituting satire for anger. Van Howell was an offbeat, self-styled environmental advocate. He worked on several of our campaigns as a thorough researcher and great grassroots organizer. He was also a talented artist and his brilliant caricatures infuriated the bad guys in campaigns such as Pine Valley and Wilbur Breslin's proposed megadevelopment. He and the Society shared a similar perspective. He called our work "the image of guerrilla environmentalism."

One day, a huge billboard at the site of the proposed mall, which the day before had read, "Breslin: Building for Tomorrow" had been flawlessly altered to read, "Breslin: Building for Big Bucks." The entire sign was removed before sunset and was never seen again. The Society didn't take on guerrilla tactics like these but didn't care that others used them.

Breslin's mantra, "They're killing us," repeated again and again, showed his frustration. He was very haughty but thin-skinned. He was very concerned about his public perception. His mini city was "planned" and "balanced," he argued, offering 2,000 jobs and featuring "amenities." At one public hearing, a representative allowed as to how the parking lots would recharge 60 million additional gallons of water to the aquifer because it wouldn't be absorbed by trees and other plants! Preposterous!

The developers' public relations professionals were "Buzz" Schwenk of the Long Island Builders Institute; Gary Lewi of the Manhattan-based Howard Rubinstein Agency, representing the Association for a Better Long Island; and Howard Blankman, who ran the Island's largest public relations firm, representing Breslin. Between them and the developers, we couldn't lose. Later, Schwenk confided, they never collaborated and never coordinated their offense or defense. Some of the top communication professionals in the region never seemed to grasp that they simply lacked a credible argument as to why we shouldn't find out first how much development our groundwater could survive before letting them pave over the Pine Barrens.

We recognized at our initial strategy session that the developers would raise the job issue. We estimated that it might take two years before they fully developed that tack, but we could blunt it only so far. The minimum wage jobs at "Willy World" would require four wage earners to afford the cheapest house in the development project, we would explain. The construction jobs would be over in a year or two as Breslin brought in outsiders to rush completion of the mall, rather than maintaining long-term local employment, we would argue. Finally, we would point out that all construction could resume immediately if only the fat-cat builders would permit drinking water protection for their families and everyone else on Long Island.

The only formidable showing by the developers came at the presentation of Breslin's hefty, 26-pound Draft Generic Environmental Impact Statement at Brookhaven Town Hall on August 4, 1992. Breslin's people were assigned to create a large public meeting in front of the Brookhaven Town Board. Town Board meetings were usually calm, boring procedural meetings at which developers provided information on their projects, knowing that the Board would very likely approve the development.

This one would be different. Breslin knew that we would be there, as well as the Open Space Council, to speak against the Environmental Impact Statement. He decided to bring a contingent of his own. And what a contingent! Nearly 700 union laborers attended the public hearing in an organizational operation involving union leaders and Brookhaven Town Board member John Powell, who would later be convicted for taking bribes from a private carter for access to the Brookhaven Town landfill and conspiring to traffic in stolen trucks.

The builders' union marched to the hearing behind a bagpipe band and packed the auditorium beyond fire department limits. They held signs of protest, but few seemed to know why they were there. They had been told that the environmentalists were blocking jobs. The union participants didn't know how or why. They were just told to show up on time if they wanted to work. The organizers prohibited admission to the hearing by environmental and civic leaders and the general public. Concerned citizens were angry that the labor unions and Breslin were trying to exclude them from expressing their concerns about "Willy World." Breslin's P.R. team produced a hand truck containing the volumes of the Draft Generic Environmental Impact Statement.

That morning, we received a call from a man representing that he was a "Sergeant" at the "Sixth Precinct" who wanted to know how many people we planned to bring to the meeting so they could provide "appropriate security." "We're not taking sides on the issue," he assured me. "We just want to maintain public safety." "Not many," I told the non-cop.

We suspected that this was merely a way to determine the magnitude of turnout Breslin forces anticipated. We also thought it likely that the attendees would not understand the environmental issue or why they were there. We decided to produce a short brochure for distribution to the union members expected at the hearing. It explained the history of Breslin's other trouble-plagued development projects, reminded them that management had not been a good friend of unions in the past, and pointed out that the mall was not ready to go. We added that while we wanted them to go back to work, the only obstacle was Breslin's refusal to consider the drinking water and habitat issues. To avoid actual combat between the construction workers and the leaflet distributors, we recruited Pine Barrens Society Program Manager Jennifer Miller, her teenage sister Mary and several of Mary's girlfriends. No "real man" was going to smack a little girl, right? They distributed our literature to the labor union representatives.

I arrived at a media circus at 6:30. Joe Colao and Vinny Scandole shook their heads as the car reached the parking lot. "Hey, Amper," Colao warned, "I don't like the looks of this." There were as many construction workers outside as in the auditorium and they were waving professionally-printed signs that read, "I'm Broke and I'm Mad. Save My Family, Vote Yes," and others, "60,000 union families are watching: We All Want to Work." This was a good message which could have won them a lot of support. But the message got swept away in the ugliness that followed.

Scandole was in front and Colao behind me as we waded through the angry throng. The girls were brought in later through a side entrance we asked to be opened. A burly construction type met me at the door. He shadowed and intimidated me for three hours, never moving a foot from my body, wherever I went, glowering, making profane comments and occasionally jostling. Joe and Vinny stayed with me. When one of the laborers made a crude remark in front of the girls as they distributed the leaflets, Jennifer gently scolded, "There's no cause for that, sir."

The leafleting idea was brilliant. It turned out that most of the construction workers didn't really know why they were there. They knew who the enemy was but didn't know anything about the issue. They had merely been told that if they wanted to work, "be there."

Patti Ann Browne covered the spectacle for News 12. We knew each other from past encounters on other stories. Either to maintain her professionalism or out of fear of what association with me might produce for her, she never acknowledged me and frequently avoided even looking my way. She did a completely fair piece.

Newsday was something else. The paper sent seven reporters and photographers. In story-after-story, they covered the angry members of the International Brotherhood of Electrical Workers, Local 25 or other union members, and Breslin's Draft Environmental Impact Statement, giving short shrift to the environmentalists' position. A tradesman in an underwear shirt posed with his wife and three kids and a "Stop the Amper Recession" sign, while a black pine casket was featured with the words, "The Death of the Long Island Economy." There was a column entitled "Of Aquifers and Hungry Kids," and a sidebar about the atmosphere in the mob scene. While they made no reference to the Society's public comments, they asked me how I felt about the "goon" who had been assigned to heckle and menace me. I described him as "sort of a guardian angel."

The lead story was co-written by Jim Puzzanghera, a straight-shooting journalist, and newcomer Gary Witherspoon, who might as well have been working for Blankman. As he interviewed me, he kept saying, "Mr. Amper, you can't argue that the Breslin project isn't good for the economy." Blankman beamed as I tried to explain the economic argument against development for the umpteenth time. He had orchestrated a great show and was enjoying the scene. He should have. It was the only effective thing they ever did.

Town officials and police repeatedly urged me to leave. "Not until the Society's testimony is heard," I said. Visibly shaken, but hanging tough, Bob McGrath sat by me at the speaker's table as I was jeered by the raucous crowd upon introduction. "Once we've answered the question as to how many acres must be preserved to protect drinking water and how many acres can be developed, Long Island's drinking water will be safe and these people can go back to work," I declared. To the frustration of Blankman's P.R. handlers, the crowd of construction workers cheered.

When I finished my remarks, a real police officer approached me. It seemed that the impatient union members outside were being calmed in the tradition of the airlines. There was plenty to drink, and the beer wasn't cooling tempers. "We simply cannot any longer assure your safety," he said bluntly. "It's time, Amper," Colao urged. We evacuated the "women and children first," then I was escorted by the police, Scandole, Colao and Brookhaven Town Councilman John Powell (who repeatedly protested that he had had nothing to do with the demonstration, even though nobody had even charged him with doing so) all the way to a car which had been backed literally into a corridor in the building. A volunteer went to the main door to announce that I was coming that way, drawing the near riot away from the actual departure point.

"I'm a street guy from the Bronx," Colao said to me, "and I've been in a lot of tense and threatening situations, but I've never seen anyone braver in my life." I was truly startled. I knew that the meeting was intended to be intimidating but doubted that personal harm would come to me at a public meeting broadcast on television. "Joe's right," Scandole said, "That was one scary scene." Now, out of the parking lot and onto a country road, Joe pulled over to allow the two of them to take off their sport coats. It was only then that I realized they were both wearing shoulder holsters with loaded guns.

News 12's coverage was straight down the middle. The reporting captured the thugged-up event as well as the reasonableness of our testimony that we were just trying to determine whether overdevelopment was threatening water quality. *Newsday's* was highly biased toward the developers. This event was probably the only time in the preservation campaign where the bad guys put points on the scoreboard, especially on the need for jobs. Fortunately, there was never a repetition of the pro-development show.

To no one's surprise, Brookhaven Town approved "Willy World." So, that gave us one more challenge to be overcome. Still, the Breslin project had a subordinate residential component in it, which our lawsuit could delay, depending on how the courts ruled. As a powerful developer, he knew that this battle was not yet over.

If we didn't like the developers very much, they hated us. They termed us "extremists," "eco-terrorists," advocates of "no growth" and lots worse. Donald Partrick, a president of the Long Island Builders Institute in 1990, said, "Their purpose is to stop all progress on Long Island, regardless of the damaging effect on the economy. There are some people who believe that it would be better to have grass grow on the Long Island Expressway." This was real animosity on the part of the developers – not just a strategy.

We used television effectively and affectively, even when the news was bad. A year after the filing of the historic lawsuit, I got a 5:30 A.M. call from the assignment editor of News 12 Long Island, asking me if I could be ready for a 7:00 A.M. "live interact" with News Anchors Lea Tyrell and Carol Silva.

"What's a `live interact' and what's the subject?" I asked. "A `live interact' is where you're interviewed in a remote location by the anchors in the studio, and the subject is the court ruling against the Society by New York State Supreme Court Justice Paul Baisley." That's how I found out we had lost the first round of the Pine Barrens lawsuit.

I wiped the sleep from my eyes, instantly accepted the heretofore theoretical but anticipated defeat, got up, showered and dressed for my first "live interact." It was wild. First, they staged me in front of a partially frozen pond in the Pine Barrens, not a half mile from my home. Then they gave me an earpiece through which I heard rock music. What had they told me a "live interact" involved?

The field producer, a young woman who looked like she was on her first assignment, told me she had been instructed not to tell me what I would be asked. Absolutely fair, given our strategy of trying to avoid saying anything with which we thought fewer than 75% of Long Islanders didn't already agree, I hadn't a clue what to expect, but anticipated the worst. I was not wrong.

The music was suddenly interrupted, and I heard a burst of static, then "Rainbow Communications" (the parent company of News 12 and a subsidiary of Cablevision) and a commercial for a local car dealership. The satellite transponder had shifted from a rock radio station to News 12. The meaning of "live interact" became clear as my left ear was filled with the crisp diction of News 12 anchor Lea Tyrell, an ardent environmentalist but stern professional, reporting on the judge's decision, concluding with, "End of battle, end of war: is that how you see it?" Talk about a loaded question.

I responded with, "Oh no, not by a long shot." I said, "The judge has agreed that the Pine Barrens is an environmentally-sensitive area, that development in it would threaten drinking water and he's gone a step further and said that government has not put on the books any plan to protect the Pine Barrens, so his hands are tied." I explained that the case would be decided by appeals courts and concluded, "I don't think Long Islanders need to worry that their drinking water has been adversely affected by this limited ruling today, and I think the developers are wrong by a long shot if they think they have any go-ahead to build in the Pine Barrens now."
The developers had won the first battle, the not-unexpected dismissal of our case in the lower court. Justice Paul Baisley had ruled that a cumulative impacts analysis could not be mandated because there was no clear "policy or plan of government" to guide the preservation and development of the Pine Barrens. The confusing ruling seemed to say that if there had been a preservation plan, we could have obtained a court-ordered study about preservation needs, but without a preservation plan, no study could be ordered.

"Preposterous," concluded Professor Philip Weinberg, Chairman of the Environmental Law Department at St. John's University. "That's like a bank refusing you a loan unless you can prove you don't need the money," he said.

The ruling forced one of only three media mistakes the Society ever made. Because we had expected a lower court loss and didn't want to exaggerate its importance, we issued no press release on the ruling. *Newsday* got the story from the developers, but Sarah Lyall of the *New York Times*, who had covered the litigation's launch a year earlier, learned about it from her competition. She was mad as hell. I tried to explain that we simply didn't view the decision as "all that important," but knew she was right. I received an important reminder: that you must consider the story from the reporters' and editors' points of view, not merely your own, if you are to be a respected news source and not merely a public relations person. We never made that same mistake again.

Not a Plan; Not a Clue

"Study how a society uses its land and you can come to pretty reliable conclusions as to what its future will be …. [The] destinies of most of man's empires and civilizations were determined largely by the way land was used." —E.F. Schumacher

The Pine Barrens Preservation Initiative included the environmentalists, the developers and the politicians. But there was a fourth player—the so-called planners. The Pine Barrens "planners" were mostly agents for developers. What they planned was high density development in the midst of Long Island's premier ecosystem. The developers would tell the planners what they wanted to build and where, and the highly paid planners would enthusiastically oblige.

The bottom line is that, with rare exception, Long Island's so-called planners lacked the vision to use planning tools to effect some great, noble and lasting character of landscape for the benefit of society. They merely wanted to be among those "important" people who were "calling the shots." In many cases Long Island planners were simply developers who knew how to build stuff.

"Planning is Good." That's the name we gave to a slide presentation that the Regional Plan Association (RPA) often showed. It contrasted unchecked development, randomly situated, versus well-designed communities, compactly built with little shops and pedestrian-friendly roads, bike paths and walking trails assembled around a village green. RPA was what all planners should be.

The LIA's Larocca said, "The principal threat to Long Island as a place to live, work and raise your kids has been its pattern of development, which marched forever eastward without applying any of the lessons learned from earlier chapters." Jennifer Miller, the Society's Program Manager, put it even more bluntly: "The landscape is our legacy. Our planners let us down." Who could argue with the premise of planning? It makes sense to decide what you want the built landscape to look like and work like, instead of merely responding to each developer's whim to create a strip shopping center here, a residential subdivision there, with malls and industrial centers littering the landscape.

Good planning such as the design of Washington D.C. and A.T. Stewart's Garden City, Long Island are widely recognized as models of thoughtful design. Alas, the building rush that followed World War II produced plenty of places to live, but with little consideration to aesthetics. The thin, fish-shaped island, extending for 125 miles east of Manhattan, was deliberately carved up by planners who were, in too many cases, doing the bidding of builders with big bucks. They were less like designers than development application processors. Instead of determining what Long Island should look like—where people would live and work and play —Long Island's planners usually responded to the applications of individual landowners with rubber-stamp approvals.

Much of what we now call suburban sprawl was the product of wealthy real estate speculators working in cozy cooperation with local government. The most prolific among self-proclaimed "planners" was probably Robert Moses. His biography, *The Power Broker: Robert Moses and the Fall of New York,* by Robert A. Caro, documented a seemingly endless series of dreadful development projects that compromised natural treasures, despoiled the landscape and ruined established neighborhoods on Long Island and around the state.

Robert Moses indelibly marked the landscape by his creation of distant state parks and the highways that made them accessible to New York City. As suburbs grew, more highways made new areas accessible for shopping centers, office parks and more homes. But that suburban sprawl then brought more highways, which in turn brought more sprawl—a vicious cycle that undercut the region environmentally, economically and in terms of quality-of-life. Between the end of World War II and the early 1960s, Nassau County was effectively paved over. In the summer of 1963, Harry Guggenheim, the publisher of *Newsday*, assigned a new reporter, Robert Caro, to do a series on planning in Suffolk County. Caro interviewed Lee Koppelman, who seemed like the only man in Suffolk who was thinking about planning. Koppelman, the former landscape architect from Queens, was Planning Commissioner under Suffolk's first County Executive, H. Lee Dennison, and remained the county's chief planner for almost 30 years. Caro's series, "Suffolk: The Sick Giant," helped persuade Guggenheim to bring Nassau and Suffolk leaders together to create the Nassau-Suffolk Regional Planning Board, with Nassau politician and former Republican National Chairman Leonard Hall as Chairman and Koppelman as Executive Director. The Regional Planning Board was never going to work because it had no authority.

Once Koppelman actually did something useful. In 1978 he authored the "208 Study," so named for a section of the Federal Water Pollution Control Act, which evaluated land use and groundwater protection. That same year, the federal government designated Long Island a "Sole Source Aquifer," and the study led to the state's creation of nine state-designated Special Groundwater Protection Areas under the Sole Source Aquifer Protection Act. Sadly, the state legislation called for strictly voluntary actions, but at least it led to the introduction of water protection concerns on the part of the Suffolk County Department of Health Services. The designation increased awareness that a large population which drew its water from beneath its feet would need to take extraordinary precautions to protect its groundwater, and thus its drinking and surface waters. The 208 Study presciently presented future groundwater threats, and government began to take seriously Long Island's aquifer protection.

The study reflected Koppelman's career view that upzoning and clustering were adequate to protect Long Island's underground drinking water reserves and to preserve open space. In reality, upzoning ensures development on every parcel—the very definition of suburban sprawl—and clustering ensures lots of it.

What's worse, this approach to land use guarantees the loss of the opportunity to aggregate the vast areas of contiguous open space necessary for the very survival of the Pine Barrens ecosystem. Every time a project is clustered, open space ends up a patchwork of whatever isn't built upon. From Froelich Farm in Huntington to Hampton Hills in the Central Pine Barrens to Hither Hills in Montauk, Koppelman opposed acquisition for preservation and lobbied strongly for clustered housing development. Fortunately, he lost every time. Nevertheless, at Hither Hills on the South Fork, a 777-acre county park bears Koppelman's name. Those who thought this was in recognition of Koppelman's commitment to open space should know that the developer, Nicholas Biase, made the naming a condition of his sale of the land to the county after Koppelman fought East Hampton Town officials and the environmental community to the end, in support of the builder's application for a clustered subdivision.

In 1993, the Regional Planning Board accepted a $486,000 Koppelman study, paid for by the Federal Aviation Administration, recommending a cargo jetport in the Pine Barrens at Calverton and approval of the SGPA water protection plan, which depended on town enforcement of massive five-acre rezoning. In a May 9, 1993 article in the *New York Times*, reporter John Rather wrote: "...Even as State Environmental Commissioner Thomas Jorling certified the water plan as complete, developers and environmentalists joined in depicting it as insufficient to settle how development should proceed in the 100,000 remaining acres of Pine Barrens. What is still urgently needed, they said, is a binding plan administered by a state agency that would delineate areas for building and areas where it would be barred. In a split between Mr. Koppelman and the critics, Mr. Koppelman has insisted that no state agency was needed. He also predicted that there would be no chance that the State Legislature would approve such an agency." All the way to the end, Koppelman was a hindrance, as we will see.

Rather concluded, "The opponents assert that Mr. Koppelman has become an impediment to a binding development plan. People close to the dispute said last week that it appeared that Suffolk County Executive Robert J. Gaffney faced a choice between Mr. Koppelman and an unlikely group of builders, environmentalists and town officials favoring a binding plan. Mr. Koppelman has not participated in the talks among the developers, environmentalists and public officials, participants said."

"Koppelman thought that he was being pre-empted," Schwenk, of the Long Island Builders group, recalled. "Besides, he couldn't have pulled it off anyway and he knew it," he added. Everyone agreed that Koppelman was so invested in his SGPA Plan that he never considered the need and the opportunity to preserve Long Island's largest remaining expanse of open space through a regional plan with the force of law.

Ray Cowan, Regional D.E.C. Director explained, "Lee was trying to continue his role as broker for all things great. He was trying to use Article 55 (the Special Groundwater Protection Area Plan) to solve the Pine Barrens problem, but the environmental community was not behind him. Article 55 passed in '88 and was finalized in '92, although we weren't particularly enamored of it. It had significant shortcomings, so we commented on it, as did the environmental community. [D.E.C. Commissioner Thomas] Jorling had a meeting with environmentalists that really set off Koppelman. He had to do an addendum because of that meeting, and it really rankled him something terrible. He's probably never gotten over it. But the long and short of Article 55 is that it doesn't really carry the force of law." Cowan continued, "I don't want to take anything away from Lee Koppelman's role over the past 35 years, but as far as the Pine Barrens Protection Act and Plan are concerned, I think I can say he played no role at all."

Bob Wieboldt of the state builders' lobby observed, "Much to his regret, Koppelman was sort of irrelevant, definitely a fringe player. To this day, his position is, `I had the solution with five-acre zoning and that would have saved it all anyway,' and his position hasn't changed to this day. That was the biggest mistake we ever made. Committing us to a low-density solution for the Island was stupid. Every time you do that, you just chew up the land."

Former Suffolk County Planning Director Steven Jones raised an even larger problem with the SGPA plan for developers. He said, "The SGPA Plan was a Master Plan that could have brought back the Pine Barrens Society lawsuit to force cumulative impacts consideration, and developers definitely didn't want that." He proved remarkably prescient when the drinking water battle spread to Long Island's East End in 1999. Jones concluded, "The thing that distinguishes the Pine Barrens Plan from the SGPA recommendations is that it is a regional plan with teeth." Asked about Koppelman's role in the development of the Pine Barrens Plan, Steve Jones said simply, "He played a valuable role by staying out of it." More about Steven Jones later.

In his excellent book on the history of *Newsday*, Robert F. Keeler says "Koppelman was a creation of *Newsday*, and indeed the paper repeatedly described him as the dean of Long Island planners." He was one of its most-cited sources, both in news accounts and in editorials. Even when he wasn't quoted, he shaped *Newsday*'s editorial position on planning and land use issues because of the symbiotic relationship between them.

Former Long Island Congressman Robert Mrazek, a Democrat, described Koppelman to *Newsday*'s Frank Lynn as far back as 1982: "He is extremely sensitive and ingratiating to the press." Former Suffolk County Legislator Anthony Noto, a Republican, said, "*Newsday*'s endorsement helps him." As late as the turn of the century, a *Newsday* profile of Long Islanders who most influenced the 1900s said, "His greatest victory may have come in persuading elected officials to preserve acre-upon-acre in eastern Suffolk. Together with environmentalists he was a driving force behind the conservation of 65,000 acres of Pine Barrens to protect Long Island's drinking water." The rest of us must have been out of town that day.

Koppelman created the Pine Barrens Review Commission, the window-dressing advisory group meant to suggest government commitment to preservation, but a body without teeth. It rarely opposed Pine Barrens development projects, and when it did it was generally overruled by the more powerful Suffolk County Planning Commission, as in the case of the critical Hampton Hills subdivision, or by the towns themselves, especially by Brookhaven, with a majority-plus-one vote. The Commission was comprised of some good, well-intentioned people, but they accomplished little.

Koppelman never criticized this. Instead, he accepted a $175,000 a year job as "planning czar" for Brookhaven (on top of his Center for Regional Policy Studies post) while it was reviewing Wilbur Breslin's mini city in the Pine Barrens. He later charged the Pine Barrens Society with "selling out" Pine Barrens preservation to Breslin and widely shared this revisionist fantasy, as if anyone could forget who was calling the planning shots in Brookhaven at the time. In terms of both his understanding of and his role in Pine Barrens preservation, he was completely out of it.

In 1999, Bruce Lambert, a reporter for the *New York Times*, quoted Koppelman: "I learned my first lesson from Moses," Dr. Koppelman said. "My relationship with Moses was sometimes stormy. The word 'planner' was anathema to him. We would raise questions like, for example, why the Long Island Expressway didn't have a mass transit rail running down the median. He was totally opposed. So, I was another of those pointy-headed, long-haired pains."

Lambert went on, "Although Dr. Koppelman describes himself as politically independent and above party machinations, he has often run circles around the pols. Desmond M. Ryan, director of the Association for a Better Long Island, a developers' group, said: 'He is a political entity unto himself.'

"The secret? Dr. Koppelman said: 'The politicians could never figure out what the source of strength was. My secret was somewhat like Robert Moses. He had Gov. Al Smith, and for the first 12 years, I had [former Suffolk County Executive] Lee Dennison. I was untouchable.' At least until Mr. Dennison retired."

By the turn of the century, and with the success of the Pine Barrens Protection Act well established, Koppelman shifted his public pronouncements, increasingly encouraging land preservation as though he had done so all along. Call it revisionist history, legacy buffing or an evolving sense of what Long Island needed all along, he ended his long career an outspoken supporter of saving what was left.

Another planner who was very much involved in the struggle between preservation and development was Michael LoGrande. At the end of his career, he served as Chairman of the Suffolk County Water Authority, which supplied water to more than 350,000 households by 1999. LoGrande had served as a town planner and later Supervisor of Islip, as Acting Suffolk County Executive and later as Executive Director of the Association for a Better Long Island— the commercial developers' lobbying organization. His protestations to the contrary, LoGrande was less a planner than a political figure, public administrator, and head of a developers' group. He simply used his background as a planner for credibility's sake. In fact, he was a developer in disguise. With all of these "planners," we had to keep reminding ourselves that they were indistinguishable from the developers for whom they worked.

LoGrande "was a man conflicted," as the Open Space Council's Marilyn England put it. "I always thought of him as a big supporter of open space and drinking water protection," she explained, "but I had a sense that somewhere under it was the desire to keep the building community happy."

Suffolk Planner Steve Jones saw it differently. "Mike LoGrande had the credibility of having been an elected official, a supervisor, and he had a planning background. As County Executive he had proposed the Drinking Water Protection Program, and it didn't hurt that he had the money and staff at the Water Authority to get the ball rolling." Jones didn't mention LoGrande's stint at ABLI, the builders lobby, where he was an outspoken critic of the Pine Barrens Preservation Initiative and me.

LoGrande had a traditional, conservative philosophy. Of land in need of protection, he said, "Buy it, don't regulate it." And he often reminded attendees of meetings he chaired of a lesson learned in his past. "Don't forget the Brooklyn Rule," he would say, lecturing with his index finger waving. Applied to Pine Barrens preservation, LoGrande meant that if you wanted to preserve land, you had to buy it from the owner, not restrict its use through rules and regulations. Applied more colloquially, he explained the Brooklyn Rule as "put up, or shut up."
LoGrande was a mercurial man who could chat amiably one moment and fly completely off the handle, the next. He admitted to once having thrown a chair at Koppelman, though the instinct is understandable. As Islip Supervisor, he supported state preservation of the Oak Brush Plains, but also supported clearing virgin Pine Barrens there to move a railroad station. He introduced the quarter-cent sales tax yet pressed the developers' agenda at ABLI. As Jennifer Miller put it, "Talk about standing firmly on both sides of preservation."

He initiated what was termed his "LoGrande Lunches," involving stakeholder efforts to obtain a preservation agreement. He worked hard to win the support of Pine Barrens town supervisors, explaining that their contribution to a historic accomplishment meant more than the loss of home rule in a limited area. He persuaded Suffolk County Executive Robert Gaffney to spend a full day in the New Jersey Pinelands, which helped win Gaffney over to the side of preservation. He was even-handed in his chairmanship of the Advisory Committee after the Pine Barrens Act was approved. He immediately grasped the concept and potential of the Consensus Group of builders and environmentalists who met at the Long Island Association and dramatically influenced the shape of the Comprehensive Land Use Plan once the legislation was approved.

Ironically, LoGrande admitted he was not a champion of participatory democracy. He said, "I don't believe in democracy. I believe in benevolent dictatorships of superior intelligence, people of great integrity. That's the government that really works. Louis IX was probably the greatest leader ever known, at least in modern times. That's because he had unlimited power and extraordinary integrity."

One of LoGrande's first acts after passage of the Pine Barrens law in 1993 was to consolidate all operations of the Pine Barrens preservation effort at the Suffolk County Water Authority. The Society and the Long Island Builders Institute agreed to select Raymond Corwin, a Society Board Member at the time and an employee of the Suffolk County Water Authority, to serve as the newly created Pine Barrens Commission's Executive Director. Corwin was an avid environmentalist but was perceived as an impartial administrator who would consider the interests of environmentalists and builders. Like LoGrande's selection as Chairman of the Advisory Committee created by the Pine Barrens Act and mine as Vice-Chair, the selection process had been expected to be controversial, but stakeholder agreement to select people who were expected to be fair avoided divisiveness at a critical juncture. Unexpectedly, in 2010, a heart attack struck down Corwin, a terrible loss.

Next, LoGrande recruited the Regional Plan Association to do "community outreach" for the Comprehensive Management Plan of the Pine Barrens Act. "There was resistance to having the Long Island Regional Planning Board involved in any way, shape or form," Steve Jones explained. "That was something that the builders, the environmentalists, the towns, county and state all agreed on, right off the bat." He was right. By now, Koppelman had alienated just about everybody. The new Pine Barrens Act gave him a seat on the 26-member Advisory Committee, and that was all.

The Regional Plan Association and its Executive Director, Robert Yaro, had advised the Society during the pursuit of legislation. Yaro had worked with Cape Cod-based planner Armando Carbonell and with New Jersey Pinelands Executive Director Terrence Moore. Yaro observed, "Every acre of Long Island is zoned for development, and when you zone for development, not surprisingly, you get it. If you want preservation, you need to plan and zone for it." While displaying a slide of beautiful, unspoiled wetlands, Yaro said, "And this is Flushing Meadow before Bob Moses improved it."

Yaro was a savvy regional planner whose organization advanced sweeping changes to the way the Tri-State metropolitan area is developed and reformed. Released in 1996, the RPA's third regional plan, "A Region at Risk," advanced recommended directions for economic development, environmental preservation, transportation and a host of other planning issues. An hour-long introduction to the plan aired on New York City's Public Broadcasting System station, Channel 13. Narrated by WNBC-TV's newsman Chuck Scarborough, himself a Long Islander, it featured the Pine Barrens Preservation Initiative as a model of good planning.

Yaro's dry, informal and conversational style made him understandable and likeable. But the RPA was long on generalities and short on specifics. The RPA hired a sincerely motivated and hard-working landscape architect employed by the Suffolk County Water Authority. Donna Plunkett was to inform and involve the community. RPA then banked the remainder of a $90,000 contract. Buzz Schwenk claimed that the RPA "did nothing." The Society thought they did worse. Her presentation to local civic groups contained little if any explanation of how the Pine Barrens plan would affect the community. It raised more questions than it answered and inflamed unfounded fears about everything from future land values to taxes. The Society, adept as it was at public education, was never even considered for the task. Instead, we had to run around behind the "road show" clarifying issues, then follow-up with articles and letters to the editors of local newspapers to assuage community concerns. When her contract with RPA ended, Plunkett was employed by the Commission, where she did outstanding work evaluating development applications and visiting sites, among other duties. She was a real standout then.

The RPA recognized and encouraged the protection of the Pine Barrens plan and was a champion of its accomplishment. Its "service" to the Pine Barrens Commission was a big disappointment.

Steven Jones played a significant role in the Pine Barrens saga – sometimes for better and sometimes for worse. Jones had served as Islip Town Planner when LoGrande was Supervisor and helped with the re-use plan for the former Central Islip Psychiatric Center, once home to the New York Institute of Technology's eastern campus. He arrived at the Suffolk County Planning Department in September 1993, right after the Pine Barrens Act was signed into law and just as the two-year process of putting together a comprehensive management plan had begun. In between his government jobs, he had been involved in real estate development for a decade, something that was "kind of scary to some of the environmentalists," in Jones' own words. You bet.

He admits to having been very pro-development on the Suffolk County Planning Commission. He supported clustering instead of acquiring environmentalists' most coveted Pine Barrens parcel, Hampton Hills, and he maintained that drinking water protection was not the motive of the Pine Barrens Society in its push for preservation but that water protection was just a mechanism to protect the Pine Barrens ecosystem. Of course, it was both.

When the national magazine of the American Planning Association covered the Pine Barrens Preservation Initiative in January, 1993, less than six months before the Pine Barrens Act made history, Jones wrote in response, "...Not only is the aquifer beneath the Pine Barrens unnecessary for current [water] supplies, but is arguably unnecessary for future supply as well [since] pumping from this aquifer and distributing water long distances is economically not even on a par with desalinization." Water Authority Chairman LoGrande would not agree.

Jones added, "It is absolutely remarkable how the Pine Barrens Society quickly moved on the open space preservation issue, which gained little public acceptance, into an `us versus them' issue of rapacious builders poisoning the water supply for their own financial gain without a care for the residents of Suffolk County. It played to the fears of people, was positively demagogic, and frighteningly effective." Today, Suffolk County is facing contaminated water supplies county-wide, except in the Pine Barrens.

Our response reminded planners of the federal and state protective designations, that 84% of voters had supported LoGrande's Drinking Water Protection Program, and that the state's highest court had concluded the need for centralized, long-range regional planning for the Pine Barrens. I declared, "Planner-for-hire Jones would have us believe otherwise. Ignoring Long Island's historic commitment to groundwater protection, he suggests that preserving its purest supply is unnecessary and transporting it impractical—both contradictory to neighboring New York City's policy and practice. He opposed cumulative impact consideration, apparently in favor of myopic project-by-project approval, as though if no one project will harm drinking water, surely 250 of them won't either. When consultants to developers ignore legitimate public concern to advance their clients' projects, they are no better serving the developers than their neighbors and they're not advancing sound planning at all."

Years later, Jones mellowed and became more supportive of preservation efforts, well before declining water quality became an island-wide problem. In fact, the whole matter of the relative benefits of preserving the Pine Barrens was ridiculous. Koppelman, Jones and others argued that drinking water could be protected even if the Pine Barrens weren't. But Pine Barrens preservation also preserved habitat, prevented taxes for new government services, increased property values, improved quality-of-life, attracted tourists and preserved Long Island's natural history. When Long Island preserved the Pine Barrens, it reaped all of these benefits.

Relations between environmentalists and Jones improved after he returned to government. He swiftly jumped into the task of preparing the first land use maps, authoritatively showing existing land use and the preservation objectives. He borrowed interim standards and guidelines for development from the Pine Barrens Review Commission, only now they weren't merely voluntary and couldn't be overridden by town government.

Perhaps Jones' greatest contribution to Pine Barrens and drinking water protection was his preparation of a report on the quarter-cent land preservation program. Between its raids of funds from the Drinking Water Protection Program, the Suffolk County Legislature, led by anti-environment County Legislator Alan Binder, sought an audit to demonstrate that the program wasn't working. We feared a whitewash.

Instead, Jones professionally and methodically traced the program from its inception, favorably evaluated its environmental accomplishments and reported how its economic benefits reached everyone in the county, no matter how far from the Pine Barrens they might live. When Pine Barrens-like protection was extended to the South Fork, Jones played a leading role in planning efforts. Referring to all of Suffolk's land preservation programs, he concluded, "These programs, in the aggregate, have contributed mightily to the high quality of life in Suffolk County. Most often quoted by business executives, residents and visitors is their view of a remarkable mix of suburban and rural qualities, scenic beauty, open space and clean water within such a short distance of the New York urban center, which all combine to make Suffolk County the special place that it is." This wasn't just talk. When the preservation effort shifted to the East End in the late 1990s, Jones rolled up his sleeves and went to work.

After helping to develop purchase criteria for the county and ranking candidate parcels by priority, he let his politics interfere again. He agreed with Gaffney administration officials and denied the Suffolk County Planning Commission this critical information in connection with their consideration of zone change and other applications by developers. Before legal challenges and intervention by the County Legislature, the county lost its top-ranked parcel for preservation to a golf course development as a result of this "go along to get along" decision. Here again, politics was allowed to subordinate sound planning and important preservation objectives.

Like so many other planners, Jones was co-opted by the development-at-any-cost crowd, but his commitment to sound planning won out at the end and he spent the rest of his career as an environmentalist.

The involved town planners were a mixed bag. Marty Shea, under the leadership of Supervisor Fred Thiele in Southampton, did a first-rate job on upzonings, code changes and the town's western Generic Environmental Impact Statement, which the Society, a frequent critic of government, called "visionary." His predecessor, Tom Thorsen, frequently behaved like an agent for developers, especially over Hampton Hills. Carole Swick, Planning Commissioner of Brookhaven during the preservation effort, was smart and cared about the Pine Barrens, but she was an easy tool of the political powers-that-were, ensuring business-as-usual in Brookhaven Town. During one of the periodic wildfires that broke out in the Pine Barrens, Brookhaven Planning Board Chairman Charles Sullivan allowed as to how these fires could be avoided if the Pine Barrens were developed. I compared it to the U.S. Army major in Vietnam who said it was necessary to destroy the village in order to save it. And Riverhead Planner Richard Hanley consorted with Supervisor Jim Stark and the Town Board to threaten rejection of the Pine Barrens Plan right up to the last minute.

Perhaps Kevin McDonald best described our experience with planning prior to the Pine Barrens Preservation Initiative. "The Pine Barrens statute lifted planning away from those who were merely processing and toward looking at the big picture," he said.

Town and County Planning Departments and Planning Boards were part of the government bureaucracy, which was pro-development. They may have called themselves planners, but they didn't plan. They just gave the developers what they wanted and made not insignificant money in the process. Some of them could maybe plan, but jobs for planners mostly put them in a position where they had to be nice to developers. So, development usually won out at the expense of good planning. That is, until the Pine Barrens preservation campaign prevailed. It was not just the legislation or the lawsuit, but two decades of persevering pressure for preservation.

"In the end," Jennifer Miller said, "the Pine Barrens were preserved not by the sycophantic planners, but rather by those who were indifferent to the powerful, except as a means to obtaining their enlightened vision of Long Island. They were people who not only did not curry favor with the politicians, developers and planners, but who stood up to them and occasionally ran over them to achieve their dream. They created a national park-quality greenbelt which responded to our need for drinking water, even as it nourished our souls."

She said, "The Pine Barrens Preservation Initiative has given the next generation something even more valuable than pure, fresh drinking water or a sense of history, even a sense of place. It provided the best gift we can give to our children: a sense of hope that if something is worth doing and you work hard at it, you can achieve your dreams."

Ray Corwin put it simply. "If the Pine Barrens Society hadn't taken on its work and done what it did, there wouldn't be a Pine Barrens Preserve." Sara Davison of The Nature Conservancy, put it another way, telling an interviewer, "I would say that but for Dick Amper, the Pine Barrens Preservation Act and Plan would not have happened. He was the lead protagonist and key strategist, and at times he was very difficult. He was on a mission to get this done, and nothing was going to stop him."

The Pine Barrens *is* Long Island's agora, its heart and its soul. It's the space that represents our commitment to inspiration, environment, economic and personal health and our dedication to the democratic principles that allowed us to preserve it. Tomorrow will be different for what Long Island did in the Pine Barrens. Its citizens protected its precious natural history and heritage and ensured a critical supply of pure drinking water for its future.

The Rip-Off

"Our government is not the master, but the creature of the people. The duty of the state toward the citizens is the duty of the servant to its master. The people have created it; the people, by common consent, permit its continual existence."—Franklin D. Roosevelt

We had to acquire the land and we thought we had the money.

It was obvious to us that we couldn't preserve the Pine Barrens without a lot of money. It was also clear that the politicians were trying to steal those dollars to balance the budget. Land use decision-making on Long Island came from local government—towns and villages. Government officials at the local level argued that who better than they were in a position to decide what should be built and where. We had to show that "home rule" worked well for developers but not at all well for residents and taxpayers. And finally, we reminded our neighbors that we weren't advocating a halt to all building, just that Long Islanders should know how much development Long Island could responsibly support without undermining the public health and welfare.

Our next job was to persuade public officials that land and water protection would be politically popular. Clearly it would take political movement, unprecedented on Long Island, to pressure county and state government to direct necessary funding to preservation. We needed to show the politicians that the public was squarely behind water and land protection and that public officials would benefit from advancing this ambitious agenda. Selling the program seemed like an insurmountable goal but once the politicians saw how popular the preservation programs were, they quickly embraced land and water protection.

The pro-environment leaders who first envisioned assembling funding for Pine Barrens and water protection knew that $56 million was a drop in the bucket when it came to acquiring large blocks of Pine Barrens. They guessed $560 million would be needed and the Society began identifying the specific parcels to be protected and the sequence of their purchase. In the end, preserving the Pine Barrens would cost $2 billion!

On Election Day 1987, voters were asked to decide the fate of a referendum such as none before. Voters had the opportunity to approve a referendum for the Suffolk County Drinking Water Protection Program, the funding mechanism by which a majority of Pine Barrens land would be protected. This was a major development! You can't preserve land without paying the property owner full market value for the property. So, placing a ¼ cent sales tax on a referendum ballot would provide millions of dollars for land preservation in the Pine Barrens – if, and only if, the public approved. They did – big time! Suffolk County voters voted six times beginning in 1987 to voluntarily tax themselves to the tune of $2 billion through 2020. The approvals were conditioned on the premise that the money generated be used to protect land and water and not for any other purpose.

The initial funding was supported by 84% of voters and opened a new day on land preservation in general and on Pine Barrens protection, in particular.

Where there's big money, there's bound to be monkey business. Sure enough, the County politicians turned their sights on the Drinking Water Protection Program to fill holes in the County's bloated budget.

Suffolk County political leaders wanted to remove millions of dollars from the drinking water program for alleged "tax stabilization." But they were worried because of the overwhelming public support for drinking water protection. So, they asked freshman legislator Tom Finlay to propose a November referendum which would have removed $120 million. We freaked! This was a potential catastrophe. We knew that for the Pine Barrens to be protected, raiding the needed funds had to be prevented. We overwhelmed Finlay with demonstrations in front of his Brentwood office, rallies at the legislative chamber and an avalanche of post cards and critical press. The proposal quickly died in committee. Finlay was not re-elected to the legislature, but his name lives on in the vernacular of Long Island environmentalists. To Finlay someone became shorthand for the strategy of deluging a politician with career-ending criticism.

In October 1991, Democrat County Executive Patrick Halpin asked the Suffolk Legislature to raid the preservation fund of $24.3 million to overcome a shortfall in the 1992 budget. Police pension costs were reported as the cause. Yet again, we freaked! It was clear that continued preservation of land and water was doomed if county executives or the county legislature, for that matter, could bag the money the public had put up for land and water protection. That had to stop.

Halpin and the Legislature argued that a little–known provision in the 1988 law permitted the redirection of a portion of the revenue generated for "tax stabilization." Most environmentalists familiar with the law intended these dollars to be used to compensate local government in cases where the loss of taxes resulting from the acquisition of land created short-term fiscal shock. A common claim of the developers was that Long Islanders could not afford to take Pine Barrens land off the tax rolls because of lost revenue. Of course, they never bothered to point out that when land was developed, the costs of providing government services to the resulting population far exceeded the tax revenues collected. In any case, the Drinking Water Protection Program did provide for tax relief.

It was obvious that the legislators supported the rip-off and were glad that Halpin had initiated the raid. I guess it shouldn't have been a surprise. Anyway, we immediately went to the Legislature to protest, and criticized the raid in the media. If the politicians weren't responsive to environmentalists, maybe they would be more responsive to the public criticism we were about to heap on them. You can only imagine our frustration that members of the 18-member Suffolk County Legislature had no problem with the Halpin raid. Once again, we were thrust into the role of attacking politicians for their support of the rip-off of public funds intended for water quality protection. Appearing on television and in print, we called the slimy politicians "a pack of lying thieves." We angrily asserted, "You cannot balance the budget unless there is a relationship between how much you're spending and how much you're taking in. And ripping off $24 million from this program will neither balance the budget nor do right by the people you are supposed to serve."

This was a strategic decision--essential to get public response. It left me open to being called a zealot, and the developers played this card constantly, for years. What we found from polling was that the public didn't buy it (or else that the public wanted a zealot) because the polling showed that 70% of polled voters were completely on our side.

Then, working with the Long Island Neighborhood Network, we brought a lawsuit challenging the rip-off. We were cautiously optimistic that state judges would not bless a legislative panel's acceptance of an out-and-out raid of public funds. Alas, we were denied "standing"—that is, the right to bring a legal action. The Court concluded that neither group would be impacted in a manner or degree different from the public at large. In 1991 the Court of Appeals, New York's highest court, expanded on "standing" in the landmark *Society of Plastics Industry v. County of Suffolk*. It said that a trade organization (like the plastics industry) could not claim "standing" in an environmental suit because they were not an environmental group. Finally, in 2009, in *The Matter of Save the Pine Bush Inc. v. Common Council of the City of Albany*, the high court finally established a standard for "standing" that included environmental groups aggrieved by decisions of government, but that was too late to help in this case.

Despite our unhappiness with the court decision, we were gratified that most of the press, including *Newsday* columnist Bob Wiemer, condemned the raid. Here again, we went around government, including the courts, and won broad public support which resulted in critical letters to the editor and complaints to elected officials themselves. But we still hadn't stopped the raid on the funds.

One of the most difficult challenges in waging the "War of the Woods" was that one day you were throwing ticker tape at a supportive politician only to throw darts the next day. Halpin had become a leader in land and water protection (admittedly on the basis of our pressure) so the Society decided to honor him at our annual fundraising gala, only to have him sell us out when county budget demands went badly. Halpin's point man and person responsible for acquisitions was a sincere lawyer named Kevin Law. Knowing that Halpin was to be honored by the Society on the weekend before the general election in which Halpin was seeking a second term, Law struggled to contain the damage.

After some prodding by the Society early in his administration, Halpin and Law had moved out smartly, buying an average of 2,500 acres-a-year in 1989, '90, and '91—an accomplishment never to be even approached again. Halpin was an outspoken supporter of Pine Barrens preservation who had stood up against pro-development critics in support of the acquisition of Hampton Hills, the largest single tract ever acquired under the Drinking Water Protection Program. He richly deserved the Society's award for "Outstanding Contribution to Long Island's Environment."

Still, Halpin's role in looting the fund was anathema to everything we sought. The Board of Directors assembled hastily to consider withdrawing the award. Law pleaded Halpin's case to the Board. He argued that Halpin had had no choice, that there would still be enough money to complete the preservation program and, after all, he had purchased more land than his predecessor, and, ultimately, his successors. He reiterated the Legislature's insistence that the Drinking Water Protection Program permitted use of funds for "tax stabilization."

In the end, In the absence of being able to demonstrate that Halpin's and the Legislature's action was fatal to Pine Barrens preservation and not eager to create an election eve scandal that might influence the result, the Board begrudgingly agreed to present the award. Fearful that he was in unfriendly territory, Halpin stayed at the Society's Fourteenth Anniversary Dinner Dance only briefly. We invited his opponent, Robert Gaffney, to speak as well. Three days later, Gaffney defeated Halpin. Our organization was consistently non-partisan.

It was clear that Gaffney had learned a lesson from Halpin – the county could take money from the land and water protection fund and get away with it. It was at his hand that the second raid on the Pine Barrens fund occurred. Even more nefarious than Halpin, Gaffney accepted the Society's top award in 1995 for having guided formulation of the Pine Barrens Plan as the state Pine Barrens Commission's Chairman, then bagged $24 million from the Drinking Water Program the day after the election.

"Fool me once, shame on you. Fool me twice, shame on me." It was clear that unless the Drinking Water Protection Program were changed, the fund would be raided again and again. It was equally clear that soon the program would lack the funds to pay for land in the Pine Barrens. The Society excoriated Gaffney and the legislature. For his part, Gaffney contended that it was not he but the legislature that had done the dirty deed. But he did not veto the bill that purloined the money, claiming that the legislature had the votes to override. He was kidding no one.

Our attack on the politicians was swift and devastating. A big rally produced scores of demonstrators with placards reading, "Clean Water, Not Dirty Politics." We used every verb available to describe the redirection of dollars from stole, pilfered, filched and robbed to plundered, looted, burglarized and ripped-off. We demanded that the money be restored.

The scandal generated many stories, editorials and letters to the editor. All were intensely favorable to our position. A January 30, 1996 column by *Newsday*'s Paul Vitello quoted me in response to a question about how we had recently honored Gaffney and were now excoriating him. "I say we should treat them like the rats they are. We give them cheese pellets when they do the right thing and electric shocks when they do the wrong thing." Vitello decided to use the quote to start his column. The politicians were pissed.

In his column he argued, "In religion, in the criminal statutes and in certain matters of the heart, Right and Wrong are enemies who never meet except in mortal combat. In politics, however, it is hardly ever like that. Right and wrong in politics are more like a married couple who after many years together start to look alike."

He continued, "Richard Amper, the environmentalist who more than any other single person, has kept developers away from the Suffolk watershed known as the Pine Barrens, is probably more of a religious type than a political one. He says he knows right from wrong. He says people should keep their promises. He gets mad when politicians use sweeping generalities to take credit for things and use lawyerly technicalities to avoid blame. You know how they do that. You sort of accept it as the way politicians are. Not Richard Amper." I was genuinely outraged at the raids and knew that I was "articulating the public rage," as expressed in the film "Network." I was definitely "mad as hell and not going to take it anymore."

The legislators were livid. Having survived the last raid, they apparently thought the reaction, this time, would be muted. But there was no way the Society could permit future raids and still secure the money needed to complete Pine Barrens purchases. We needed to plug the loophole in the original legislation to prohibit the use of the funds for any other purpose than preservation. The County's predilection for bagging referendum money was to haunt us for years.

Perhaps the most flagrant abuse of the land preservation money came at the hands of Suffolk County Executive Steve Levy – a short, mustached and arrogant know-it all. In 2006, a live television program about land preservation turned into a confrontation which spilled off the air when Levy took umbrage at charges by me that he was too cozy with developers and wasn't buying open space and farmland fast enough. The occasion was a special edition of News 12's "At Issue" discussion forum, broadcast live on August 10. The Society and more than 100 other environmental, civic and business groups including Levy signed onto a plan advanced by The Nature Conservancy to save 35,000 acres of open space and farmland before the final build-out of Long Island, projected by planners for 2015. I told the TV audience that meant that to preserve 35,000 acres in 3.5 years, the rate of combined state, county and town land preservation would have to increase to 10,000 acres per year. Levy bragged that under his administration, Suffolk preserved more than 1,000 acres per year, nearly twice that of his predecessor, Robert Gaffney (but not nearly as much as Halpin). I pointed out "clearly that was still not enough. Environmentalists called for extending state, county and town funding programs to at least 2030 so that government could "buy now and pay later" on the strength of future revenues before land prices go any higher or the land is lost forever to development.

The conversation became heated and exploded near the program's end. In response to a viewer's phoned-in question, I said elected officials, including Levy, had to get off the fence and side with the public instead of the special interests before Long Island's economy and environment were both undermined. I pointed out that Levy had accepted more than $35,000 in campaign contributions from developers in the last three months alone. Levy visibly bristled and a shouting match began between us. The moment the program ended Levy jabbed his finger at me and said, "You're dead. Our relationship is over. Don't even bother calling my office ever again." Then he stormed off the set and out of the studio. The confrontation made news for weeks with News 12 re-broadcasting the show and clips of the heated verbal exchange and *Newsday*, relating the conflict in its Sunday political column. I concluded, "This isn't personal. If Suffolk continues to buy 1,000 acres a year for the next 3.5 years, we will end up preserving 3,500 acres when everyone agrees we need 35,000 acres."

In 2011, the county legislature approved a budget resolution raiding nearly $30 million from the water fund to the general fund. The bill was signed by Levy. The county took the money and used it to balance the budget again.

After the county's attempt to divert money from the Drinking Water Program to plug holes in the county's General Fund, for fiscal years 2011, '12 and '13, we filed a lawsuit over its use of the fund for purposes not approved by the public. We sued for the specific purpose of requiring the return of those illegally diverted funds. The county sought to dismiss the lawsuit. The Society continued this litigation for over a decade, ultimately winning decision after decision.

To this day, Levy insists that a mandatory referendum is not required, even when the intent of the original referendum is changed. Worse still, he denies that Long Island's water quality is threatened by groundwater contamination. As recently as August 12, 2019, he claimed, "the latest baloney is that our drinking water is so polluted it will soon be undrinkable." The reality is that top scientists agree that our watersheds are badly polluted, and the cost of remediation is estimated at close to $8 billion.

Paul Sabatino, a former counsel to the Suffolk Legislature and later a Deputy County Executive, eventually said that the county transferred the money illegally because voters had specifically approved it for the sewer fund. "If politicians ignore that and just say 'no, we're going to do whatever the heck we want,' there have to be consequences." After Sabatino left government, he became a forceful advocate for the Society's position that laws that were established by referendum could only be changed by a subsequent referendum. He, and Pine Barrens Society attorneys Jennifer Juengst and Regina Seltzer, won lawsuit after lawsuit, preventing future raids. The three were honored by the Pine Barrens Society in 2015.

Levy was a mess throughout the rest of his term. After an investigation by the Suffolk County Attorney, Levy agreed on March 24, 2011 that he would give up $4 million from his campaign fund and would not seek re-election. It was never revealed what he had done or why he had agreed not to run again. Ironically, Thomas Spota, the County District Attorney, was later convicted himself of concealing police brutality and was forced from office.

Supreme Court Justice Joseph Farnetti ruled against us in 2012. We appealed, eventually winning the case in November 2014. On August 27th the New York State Court of Appeals, the state's highest court, declined to hear Suffolk's appeal.

To prevent future raids, we added a provision to the newest preservation referendum that no part of the Drinking Water Protection Program could be altered in any way without a new mandatory referendum. Still, succeeding Suffolk County Legislators continued to re-direct funds to plug holes in their bloated budgets, forcing the Society to go to court to halt the practice. Finally, in 2014, the Appellate Division of State Supreme Court rendered an inarguable decision that the Drinking Water Protection Program, having been created by referendum, could not be altered without an affirmative vote at a subsequent public referendum. Alas, in a series of appeals by succeeding administrations—specifically under the administrations of Steve Levy and Steve Bellone—the litigation was dragged out for eight more years. In the end, the Appeals Court agreed that any law created by referendum could only be altered by a subsequent public referendum. The court ordered the county to repay the funds raided by Levy--$29.4 million. A frustrating element of the "War of the Woods" was how long and hard you had to press to obtain common sense good government.

Meanwhile acquisitions were continuing. The Pine Barrens Society was busy trying to keep land preservation going by identifying key parcels, prioritizing Pine Barrens parcels specifically and filing lawsuits against projects that should never have been approved.

Photo Gallery

A key to the success of pine barrens preservation was the role of the public. The Long Island Pine Barrens Society educated Long Islanders on the desirability of preservation of Long Island's premier ecosystem. Citizen support, as evidenced by crowds at numerous rallies and at the election booth, pressured politicians and developers to support the wildly popular preservation effort. Republicans and Democrats, lobbyists and developers came together to save the pine barrens. More than 75% of eastern Long Islanders actively supported our campaign and celebrated the victory with us. What a triumph!

TREASURE IN PARADISE: The Pine Barrens forest, forever secured. Credit: Georgia Schwender.

TOP. **THE BEGINNING:** The Long Island Pine Barrens Society kicks off its preservation effort on November 21, 1989. Credit: Long Island Pine Barrens Society.

𝕿𝖍𝖊 𝕹𝖊𝖜 𝖄𝖔𝖗𝖐 𝕿𝖎𝖒𝖊𝖘

Metropolitan News

NEW YORK, NEW JERSEY, CONNECTICUT / WEDNESDAY, NOVEMBER 22, 1989

Suffolk Is Sued to Block Plans For Subdivisions in Pine Barrens

By SARAH LYALL
Special to The New York Times

MIDDLE ISLAND, L.I., Nov. 21 — An environmental group sued Suffolk County and three of its towns today in an effort to block hundreds of subdivisions planned for Long Island's Pine Barrens.

Much of the Island's drinking water comes from an aquifer beneath the Pine Barrens, a 100,000-acre swath of land in central Long Island that is one of its largest remaining open areas and is home to rare species of plants and animals. The environmental group, the Long Island Pine Barrens Society, contended that the governments had failed to consider the cumulative environmental impact of the subdivisions proposed there.

About half the land is publicly owned; of the remaining acres, 42,000 are being considered for development now, according to the Pine Barrens Society.

"We're directing the governments to determine what the total effect on the drinking water and rare and endangered species will be if development continues," the society's executive director, Richard Amper, said at a news conference here.

The suit by the society, filed in State Supreme Court in Riverhead, seeks to halt further administrative action by the county or the towns of Brookhaven, Southampton and Riverhead on 230 subdivisions that have been approved within the last 30 days or that have permits pending.

Under state law, said Lewis B. Oliver Jr., the lawyer for the Pine Barrens Society, further action on the projects named in the suit is halted until the court reviews the case and decides whether a cumulative environmental study is warranted.

Lawyers for the governmental bodies named in the suit — the town boards, planning boards and zoning appeals boards of the three towns, and the county's Health Services Department — said it was too early to assess the immediate effect on the subdivisions.

Thomas Boyle, Suffolk's County Attorney,

Continued on Page B5

FIT TO PRINT: New York Times announces environmentalists' lawsuit, blocking development in Pine Barrens. Credit: New York Times.

PINE BARRENS PRESERVATION: Society founders John Turner, Robert McGrath and John Cryan with New York Governor George Pataki supporting Pine Barrens preservation. Credit: Ted Curry Photography.

HAPPY COUPLE: Pine Barrens Society Executive Director Richard Amper and wife, Robin, celebrate preservation purchases in the Core Preservation area. Credit: Ted Curry Photography.

LONG ISLAND LEADERS: Assemblyman Tom DiNapoli, Society leader Richard Amper, developer Wilbur Breslin, business leader James LaRocca, State Senator Ken LaValle and New York Governor Mario Cuomo at bill signing. Credit: Newsday.

WINNERS ONE AND ALL: New York Governor Mario Cuomo signs the Pine Barrens Preservation Act, flanked by Long Island leaders. Credit: Newsday.

THE AUTHOR: Pine Barrens Society Executive Director announces the preservation of the Pine Barrens. Credit: Newsday.

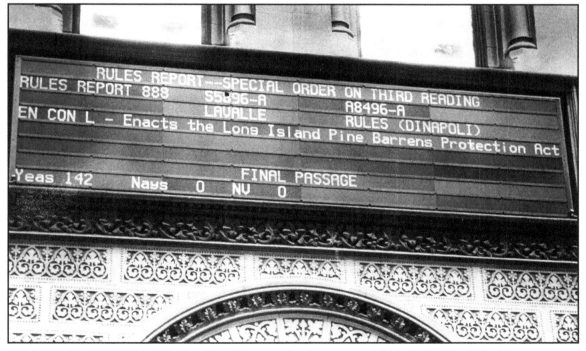

UNANIMOUS VICTORY: The Pine Barrens Act is approved 142-0. Credit: Sally Kuzma.

SPONSORS: Assemblyman Tom DiNapoli and State Senator Ken LaValle flank Pine Barrens Society Executive Director Richard Amper. Credit: Ted Curry Photography.

PUTTING IT TOGETHER: Suffolk County Executive Patrick Halpin puts together the pieces of the Pine Barrens. Credit: Newsday.

PINE BARRENS CROWD: Environmentalists and media cheer supporters at a preservation rally on Long Island. Credit: Long Island Pine Barrens Society.

STRANGE PARTNERS: Developer Edwin "Buzz" Schwenk forges a rare partnership with Pine Barrens Society Executive Director Richard Amper. Credit: Ted Curry Photography.

GETTING STARTED: : Community representatives campaign to prevent development at Long Island's Lake Panamoka. This started preservation efforts. Credit: Long Island Pine Barrens Society.

CASINOS IN NY?
State Leaders Agree on Amendment
To Allow Gambling Upstate / Page A3

UNABOMBER
New Threat to Blow Up a Plane at L.A.
Disrupts Travel, Halts Mail / Page A3

Newsday
THE LONG ISLAND NEWSPAPER

THURSDAY, JUNE 29, 1995 • SUFFOLK   50¢

THE PINE BARRENS
Saved

Peconic River, just east
of the LIE overpass

Pataki, LI Officials
Sign Historic Pact
Creating a Sprawling
Forest Preserve

Pages A6-A7

PINE BARRENS PRESERVED: Long Island newspaper covers the preservation of Long Island's premier ecosystem in June 1993. Credit: Newsday.

NEWEST HIGHWAY SIGNAGE: The Pine Barrens Society announces the introduction of the Pine Barrens to Long Island highways. Credit: Long Island Pine Barrens Society.

Citizens Battle

Government of the people, by the people, for the people,
shall not perish from the Earth – Abraham Lincoln

It was clear that the only chance to remedy these rip-offs was to create a new referendum that explicitly prohibited future raids. Dubious about the prospects, we nonetheless went to a sympathetic Suffolk County Legislator, Nora Bredes of Setauket. An active opponent of the Shoreham nuclear reactor, she could be counted on to try to help. A member of the Democratic minority, she had occasionally formed coalitions with some Republicans to create progressive legislation. Besides, she had voted against the Gaffney raid, and the Republicans weren't real chummy with us just at the moment.

To our amazement, she persuaded two Democratic colleagues and three Republicans to sponsor a bill that would put on the 1996 ballot a referendum which effectively said, "We've stolen more than the public can tolerate, so we agree to steal no more." Even The Nature Conservancy applauded. Sara Davison, TNC's Executive Director, promised us her support of the legislative action and the referendum.

"When something looks too good to be true, it's usually because it is." The old chestnut proved painfully true. At the next meeting of the Republican Caucus, Party Leader John Powell ordered Republicans off the bill. "We're going to need that money again," he reportedly told the Legislators.

Davison called to tell me that if the Republicans were off the bill, so was TNC. We were flabbergasted. "We can't be partisans," she told me. "Wait a minute!" I snapped. "That's exactly what you are if you support protecting the environment when Republicans do and oppose it when they don't." The fragile relationship between the Society and TNC was about to shatter. "Please," she urged, "let's not talk about this in public, and we'll see what can be done."

The Pine Barrens Society knew exactly what had to be done. The Suffolk County Charter provided for a referendum by public petition. No referendum by public petition had ever been put on a county-wide ballot in New York State. The Neighborhood Network's attempt to put a public petition on the ballot in 1993 had failed, and no other had even been tried.

My old college roommate Peter Devens should have suspected he was being sandbagged when I invited him to lunch in Riverhead. Laid off from virtually running American Airlines' operation at LaGuardia in one of the '90's "downsizing" corporate moves, he had some time on his hands. Unapologetically but appreciatively, I meant to use it.

He was on to me. "So, what are the scum of the earth politicians up to now?" he asked. I explained our predicament and he asked, "So, what do we have to do?"

"I haven't the slightest idea," I replied. "It's never been done before. We'll just have to figure it out as we go along"

"Count me in." Pete was one of those guys who could do whatever you needed to have done. An extension on your house, fixing something that no one else could fix or building just about anything.

The petition process and drive were more complex and demanding than every previous undertaking. The law required precise legal procedures and language. Petition carriers and signatories had to be registered voters, we needed notaries, and any errors invalidated whole pages of signatures. We faced daunting filing timetables with the Suffolk County Clerk, the Legislature and the Board of Elections. The obstacles seemed insurmountable. But seeking passage of a loophole-closing referendum seemed unavoidable. Without a prohibition on future raids, the funds needed for Pine Barrens preservation simply disappear. We had to do it.

We were both well organized and naive. We agreed to activate Pine Barrens preservation partners in the signature-gathering process, using the legal and canvassing skills of the Neighborhood Network, which complemented our community organization capacity. We knew that our efforts had made the public staunch allies, angry at government. The challenge was to mobilize our resources to capitalize on public antipathy. We had to get people mad-- really mad. And that was actually easy.

As with the initial Society outreach, we started by approaching our friends. Pete met with or contacted the Sierra Club, Long Island Greenbelt Trail Conference, Neighborhood Network, Open Space Council, and New York League of Conservation Voters. Bill Steibel, Laurie Farber and Bobbi Josepher of Sierra were helpful, as was Joshua Klainberg of NYLCV. We asked environmental groups to reach out to their members for financial support and appealed to foundations to support our general-purpose activities so that we could use member contributions for active advocacy. The Rockefeller Brothers Fund and RBF Board Member Abby O'Neill understood instantly and helped.

In February, 1996 it didn't take Pete two weeks to realize that environmental volunteers weren't going to begin to do the job. He came to me soberly one cold night with the bleak news. "This ain't going to make it," he said.

We determined that we would have to hire a legion of paid petition-gatherers, "mercenaries in a holy war," Devens called them. Recruitment started the next day. "Part Time: Earn $10 per hour evenings and weekends" we advertised. Devens worked the phone doggedly. He succeeded in recruiting the workers who would need to get the necessary number of signatures. Three days later, he had one less voice and 123 petitioner prospects.

"Still, not enough help," he complained. We recruited Laurie Cordes, a motivational, even charismatic young former canvas coordinator for Neighborhood Network who had a valuable and very much needed skill: she knew how to train and motivate people to extract from the public the commitment to force the political system to work.

Among the training admonitions was not to try to convert the "irreconcilably lost" and not to exhibit any coercion or hostility. Good advice, but some people know when [or how] to improvise. For example, while delivering supplies to the noble troops of the Concerned Citizens of Montauk, I watched two silver-haired veterans of many East End environmental campaigns being approached by a self-assured man in his mid-thirties. He said, "I don't know anything about this issue and can't be bothered."

"It's for drinking water and it's good, young man. Sign it!" one of the petitioners snapped.

"Yes, ma'am," the yuppie answered, and we had one fewer signature to collect. Thank you, mom.

Another time one tired and admittedly irritable intern, Joan Carlson, on loan to the Society from the U.S. Fish and Wildlife Service in Vermont, encountered an even more self-satisfied Manhattan executive on a cell phone as he entered the Amagansett Post Office the very same day. Talking animatedly as he entered to collect his mail, he waved off the petitioner with a "too important" swing of his hand.

Having obviously solved all of the world's problems with the completion of his call, he emerged from the Post Office with his mail in hand and a barely tolerant willingness to, at least, address the young volunteer. "What are you selling, and what does it cost?" he asked impatiently."

Overcome by too many hours and too many assholes, Joan replied, "Democracy. And it's free!" The man signed.

Of course, democracy is not free and it's not easy, as the petitioners and all of us learned, if they did not already understand it. With as much pragmatism as idealism, they plugged away at the banal but essential task of meeting the constitutional process called "Initiative and Referendum."

Night after night, Pete and Laurie interviewed petition-gatherer candidates, selected the capable and trained them. Then in the morning Pete would get up and "deploy" them to their "beachheads." I don't know where the military nomenclature came from--Pete had no military service background--yet he soon became known as "The General." Perhaps it was his rote, detached, unemotional and effective approach to the assignment; perhaps it was *Newsday*'s continual characterization of our crusade as the "War of the Woods."

By April, Pete and Laurie had deployed 83 "troops," and signature collection was in high gear. Under New York State and Suffolk County law, we were obliged to collect a number of signatures equal to five percent of the voters in the last gubernatorial election, in each and every one of the ten Suffolk County towns. Failure by a single signature in a single town would be mortal to the referendum drive.

Throughout, the countdown clock ticked. Under Election Law, there are a series of hard deadlines that must be met to place a referendum on Suffolk County's ballot. Once the required number of signatures are gathered, your petition bounces back and forth between the County Clerk and the Board of Elections to be validated and placed on the ballot. If you stretch out the timeline to its maximum, your signatures would need to be submitted to the County Clerk 160 days before the election. Assuming the maximum delay allowable under law by everyone involved in the process, we calculated that by deliberate delay alone, we could be kept off the ballot if we did not have the signatures collected and filed by May 29, 1996.

Doing the math, we saw that we were not going to make it. Mindful of the Society's gospel, "Don't threaten or promise to do it if you can't bring it off," we were desperate as we looked the deadline in the eye. By this time, meetings at Pete's location or mine were out of the question; not enough time. We agreed to meet at the Radisson in Islandia, equidistant between Pete's house and my office. To avoid being overheard, we sat on a grassy bank near the north service road of the Long Island Expressway. It was a moment of truth.

"Once we go beyond May 29, we can be knocked off the ballot by coordinated use of maximum delays at each point," I explained. "I'm sorry," Pete replied. I explained the situation to Pete. "What should we do?," I asked.

Pete pondered long before answering, "It looks like we're only going to miss your deadline by a week, or even less. At that point they *could* run out the clock on us. If they realized their play right away, AND reacted at once, AND the different departments all got their acts together. But then these are bureaucrats we're talking about." "My sentiments exactly," I replied. We stood up, wiped the newly-cut grass shavings off our butts and went back to the campaign.

By now, the "disqualification rate" had become a force to contend with. Even though our volunteers were trained to obtain only the signatures of registered voters, it turned out that voter registration is not something citizens are really honest about. We discovered that consistently between 18 and 26 percent of petition signatories were not registered voters. Since petitions solicited by non-registered voters are also disqualified, we made certain by Board of Elections checks that all petition gatherers were registered voters. We applied the same standard to petition signers.

First, we purchased the current electronic file of registered voters, then transferred it to computer discs. We then rented ten personal computers and installed them in my house. Then we recruited as many volunteers to nightly check the petitions against the registered-voter files, effectively "challenging" our own petitions. In this way, we could be assured that we would not fall short of the requisite number of signatures in any town by virtue of a signatory's not being a registered voter. Our confidence level increased, and we could re-deploy petitioners daily to the towns where we needed the greatest number of additional signatures. Additionally, this reduced the number of "safety signatures" we needed to collect.

On Earth Day, April 20, a bunch of us headed to Suffolk's Heckscher State Park. Thousands from all over poured in, families at a time, to celebrate Earth Day. Pete had them backed up three and four deep in five columns signing the petitions. He checked in with his 17 other petitioners county-wide by cell phone. Suffolk County Executive Robert Gaffney took an Earth Day publicity hike of the Pine Barrens with the Long Island Greenbelt Trail Conference. The group seemed more enamored of the official attention than aware of how this otherwise credible group was being used by those who had ripped off the Pine Barrens fund. The group claimed they used the hike to promote acquisition of additional Pine Barrens. To be fair, the Greenbelt Trail Conference had sought a hike with Suffolk Executive Gaffney for two years and lobbied other county and state leaders for more money for preservation. And this group generally stayed out of politics. Still, the Earth Day hike made Gaffney look "green" while we were battling him over the re-direction of funds for preservation.

The Suffolk County Fair was held the following week. Pete worked so hard and stayed on his feet so long that his scholastic football injuries took him off his feet by the fourth day, despite the near-constant application of ice packs to his knees by his increasingly annoyed wife, Chris. By the middle of May, we still had 33 weary petitioners working at 27 different locations. Our campaign was now spinning in greased grooves.

On May 29, the *New York Times* had caught the military fervor of the latest battle in the War of the Woods: "To hear Peter M. Devens tell it, a petition drive to stop Suffolk County officials from taking money intended to protect the Pine Barrens water supply and using it to balance budgets has been a lot like a military campaign," John Rather wrote in a story. "We landed on the beaches of the East End and consolidated the twin forks," Devens was quoted. "Then we mounted a two-pronged attack along the north and south shores. We took Heckscher Park on Earth Day. Now we are in a mopping up operation. It's a war out there, and unfortunately the elected officials are the enemy."

It was all the computer checkers could do at night to check what the petitioners had been doing during the day. In the last days of the drive, we fielded an around-the-clock team to make sure our signatures were good. Robin and I slept from about 1 A.M. until 6 A.M., while the checkers worked in the spare bedroom. The computer operations continued all the while.

Suffolk's largest town, Brookhaven, "fell" early. Huntington and Babylon were the last bastions of resistance. On May 28 Peter joined us at my home. Amid the clutter of PCs on every table, and every other flat space, we collectively concluded that the struggle was over, the battle won. It was as if everyone simultaneously recognized the significance of our accomplishment. "We did it!" rang out in unison.

We hastily prepared for a news conference the next day. We descended on the offices of the Suffolk County Legislature and Clerk, our hand truck full of bound signatures, and little American flags waving from the podium to announce the democratic achievement of which we assured the audience, Thomas Jefferson would have been proud. Then we wheeled the stack of town-by-town signature books into the Clerk's office.

Greg Cergol of News 12 told the story through the eyes of one of the few true volunteers, a Manorville citizen advocate and mother of two, Sarah Nuccio: "For the past few months, housewife Sarah Nuccio of Manorville has been giving her daughters a lesson in democracy. They travel Suffolk County together collecting signatures on this petition. The petition calls for an Election Day referendum that, if approved, would prevent Suffolk lawmakers from taking money from a fund intended to protect the Pine Barrens water supply. Today they presented over 36,000 signatures to County officials. An army of volunteers collected those signatures in just seven weeks, and if the signatures pass muster at the Board of Elections, the effort will mark the first time in New York history that a citizen-led referendum has made it on a county-wide ballot."

The Suffolk County Legislature didn't know quite what to make of the submission. County Legislative Clerk Henry Barton provided the obligatory certification of submission. Days later the political caucus gathered again to determine the appropriate response. Some argued that the Legislature ought to challenge the petition as the developers had challenged the Neighborhood Network's ill-fated petition of 1993. "No way," one Legislator argued. It was one thing for developers to challenge environmentalists; another thing entirely for elected officials. For all their hubris, even politicians were bright enough to realize they couldn't try to sabotage the petitions of their own constituents. "Besides," another legislator allowed, "It is extremely unlikely that the Pine Barrens Society would make a crucial mistake like submitting a defective petition." For the first time, we had overcome the historical underestimation of the Society. Seven years after we had pledged to ourselves never to threaten or promise something we could not deliver, our enemies had given us our due.

Anxious that delaying tactics could still prevent certification of our referendum for the ballot, we pressured each reviewing group to move the process along, without any public tip-off that the establishment, collectively, could derail the plebiscite. Since we were only seven days away from getting the referendum on the ballot on time, it didn't take long to get out of the window of vulnerability. By the time the Board of Elections certified the number of signatures, we were out of the woods. No challengers emerged, and we were never worried about a challenge to the petitions themselves, having pre-challenged every signature.

Once we had the signatures necessary to put the issue to the voters, the Pine Barrens Society owned the agenda. It was probably the first and maybe the only time we were in a position to dictate the terms of Pine Barrens preservation. The legislators realized that they had no choice. If they fought for their own bill, they'd only look bad, make voters mad, and lose anyway when election day came.

When it works, democracy is swell.

Our referendum petition worked quickly. The Republican legislators joined with their Democrat counterparts and swiftly approved a new piece of legislation, eliminating the "tax stabilization" loophole and ensuring some $32 million for the acquisition program. That suited us fine. Their bill would take effect immediately upon passage. Publicly-placed referenda are usually delayed one-year to allow county government to adjust to the fiscal implications of any citizen action.

The County Executive's people tried to use this advantage to get us to support the legislators' agenda instead of our own. "Why campaign for competing referenda?" they asked. "We'll assure you the needed funds and then we can all unite behind County government's referendum." "After all," they argued, "Our referendum would kick in sooner and protect the Pine Barrens sooner as well."

In theory, we agreed. But we wanted assurances that $8 million a year would be spent to complete acquisition of the remaining Core Area parcels by 2002. Members of the Consensus Group, including SCWA Chairman Michael LoGrande, agreed in early July to seek a commitment from County Executive Gaffney to this effect. It was only in this way that everyone could agree to support the County Legislature's version of the loophole-closing referendum. We agreed to meet with Gaffney on July 8, 1996 to complete the agreement. It seemed a done deal.

We gathered at the County's temporary lodging in a Hauppauge office complex during the County Center's asbestos clean-up operation to pen the final agreement. Incredibly, it didn't work. Importantly, Gaffney did not attend. Despite his inclusion in all previous plans and agreements, LoGrande chose the role of apologist for the administration, to curry favor, but to no useful purpose. He told those assembled that County Executive Gaffney had no obligation to accommodate the Society even though the overture for an agreement had come from the County itself. Alas, Gaffney's handlers, grateful for LoGrande's support, didn't see the pitfall. LoGrande, who had served briefly as Acting County Executive to fill a vacancy, had lost his election bid to Patrick Halpin and never gotten over it. His sycophantic behavior toward Gaffney was the product of his awe of the office he could not himself hold onto.

Ignoring the understanding reached only days before, LoGrande argued both that no agreement need be made, as Gaffney could be counted upon to do the right thing, and that there was no certainty that $8 million a year was necessary—the very basis of the agreement to support the County referendum instead of our own. The meeting adjourned amid acrimony. LoGrande continued his defense of Gaffney and soon ordered everyone out of his office.

We had no real cause for concern. Even if it would take longer, we still had a referendum that would enjoy almost certain passage. The referendum with the largest number of votes would prevail. Moreover, the next day, the Advisory Committee of the Pine Barrens Commission was scheduled to meet at the Water Authority to consider which referendum to support. James T.B. Tripp, of the Environmental Defense Fund and a Board Member of the Water Authority, had been selected to introduce the resolution requiring the $8 million annual commitment as a condition of support for the County's and LoGrande's preferred referendum.

The meeting ended at 5:00 P.M. We had only until 8:00 the next morning to respond to the challenge represented by the turn of events. Quickly the phone calls went out to volunteers. We recruited a sign-making committee and urged News 12 to send a camera, if not a reporter, to the Water Authority the next morning. We promised them a confrontation of dramatic proportions and the capability to "pick up" the story later in the day.

It was a grassroots organizer's dream come true. Early Tuesday morning, we arrived at the Water Authority headquarters in Great River to be greeted by dozens of enthusiastic demonstrators. Inside, I sat in the meeting room alone except for a News 12 cameraman who had already recorded cover pictures, or "B-roll," of the demonstrators and was hastily getting ready for the "confrontation pictures" for which he had come. It didn't take long.

Next came the saboteur of the previous day's meeting, LoGrande. He was hot as a hornet. Before the meeting even started, he marched into the room fuming. "How dare you embarrass me in front of the County Executive!" he sputtered. "I've got a good notion to call this whole meeting off! This is my facility, and I won't have it used to embarrass my friend!"

"Now, just a political second," I retorted, charging from the back to the front of the room, only inches from LoGrande's nose. "You created this crisis with your ass-kissing performance yesterday in contravention of everything everybody had agreed to last week." Wagging my finger in his face and obviously lecturing, I added, "You do anything you think you can get away with, but at the end of the day, you and County Executive Gaffney are going to buy on to our requirements for endorsement of your referendum or you're going to watch voters approve ours on the ballot." LoGrande shook his jowls and scowled.

I walked back to the end of the room, satisfied that I had given News 12 the promised confrontation. To my astonishment, the cameraman approached me apologetically, saying, "Shit, I didn't have the camera microphone hooked up." Knowing the thin-skinned LoGrande as I did, I concluded that this posed no lasting problem. It took absolutely no effort to send LoGrande up the wall all over again. Assured that the cameraman was now ready, I charged back to the front of the room, pointing my finger threateningly, "And another, thing," I continued. "How dare you threaten a process that could end this confrontation that you created only yesterday?"

"Don't you dare tell me what to do!" LoGrande responded, and News 12 had the sound and pictures for a story that started, "There was a meeting today on the environmentally-sensitive Pine Barrens. It's a highly sensitive subject for many Long Islanders. The latest on the Pine Barrens saw a heated shouting match between two of the key players in the dispute. "

LoGrande didn't talk to me for weeks.

The Advisory Committee, on the motion of Jim Tripp, adopted a consensus resolution promising to support only a referendum assuring $8 million worth of Pine Barrens acquisitions per year. The electorate made it law on November 5, 1996. It was one of our finest hours.

The Suffolk County Drinking Water Protection Program was one of the most successful in U. S. history. Despite paying two-and-a-half times the national average in taxes, Suffolk voters extended the quarter-cent sales tax program, over and over, generating more money for land and water protection—more than $2 billion—than 45 of the 50 states in the union.

To protect themselves from future raids, voters added the requirement that no part of the Drinking Water Protection Program could be altered in any way without a new mandatory referendum. Still, succeeding Suffolk County Legislators continued to re-direct funds to plug holes in their bloated budgets, forcing the Society to go to court to halt the practice. Finally, in 2014, the Appellate Division of State Supreme Court rendered an inarguable decision that the Drinking Water Protection Program, having been created by referendum, could not be altered without an affirmative vote at a subsequent public referendum.

Cuomo's Jetport: An Idea That Wouldn't Fly

"You may fool all the people some of the time, and some of the people all of the time, but you cannot fool all the people all the time."—Abraham Lincoln

The Pine Barrens Preservation Initiative was a well-designed strategy, which was, for the most part, seamlessly executed. That's why we were so shocked when we were sandbagged by one of the country's smartest and scariest people, New York Governor Mario M. Cuomo. And it was bad.

An avowed environmentalist, Governor Cuomo was among the brightest, most articulate politicians ever to grace our governmental stage. A Rhodes scholar, a radio commentator, even a professional athlete, he was truly a man for all seasons. An oft-mentioned candidate for President, New York's 52nd Governor first needed to be re-elected to an unprecedented fourth term in 1994. Long Island's economy, as well as the state's and the nation's, was in trouble, so Cuomo was touring the state to propose a series of "New New York" economic initiatives. There were specific programs for each region in the state: "New York City in the New New York" or "Long Island in the New New York."

We received an innocent-enough sounding call on November 1, 1991 from Mark Grossman, the amiable Department of State representative and Long Island operative for Governor Cuomo. His official title was Regional Director on Long Island but what he prided himself on and was appreciated for was his good showcasing of Governor Cuomo on Long Island. Mark called to ask for several Pine Barrens photos for a presentation Governor Cuomo had scheduled for the next week. "Scenic shots," Grossman said, "something reflective of the Governor's appreciation for the land." We obliged, producing several compelling Pine Barrens images on 35 mm slides. We were professionals. We were obliging. We were sandbagged.

In return for our cooperation, we were offered "reserved seats, right up front" for the Governor's November 14 dog and pony show, sponsored by the Long Island Association at the Huntington Hilton. Cuomo was a strong, articulate speaker. He told an audience of nearly 1,000 that as a Long Islander he well understood the needs of Long Island in the challenging 1990s. The program featured a five-minute, multi-image slide show that had to have cost five thousand dollars. The program depicted Mario Cuomo as leading New York into the new millennium as a progressive thinker and economic doer, and its centerpiece was an over-the-top proposal to create New York's fifth major airport on U.S. Navy property being leased by the Grumman Aerospace Corporation at Calverton to assemble and test military warplanes, in the heart of the Pine Barrens! The program was available on video for campaign presentations across the Island.

We were aghast. This was not part of any of our plans and fighting it would demand extraordinary and probably unattainable resources. We did not need New York's Governor to decide that a key part of his re-election campaign strategy was to win agreement in favor of an airport in the Pine Barrens.

Michael Deering and I sat speechless as Cuomo concluded. "We were blind-sided," Deering said, "I wouldn't want to be Mark Grossman when you catch up to him." "To hell with Grossman," I replied, and headed off Cuomo's slow moving entourage of staffers and media.

When the Governor saw me waiting for him, he strode confidently toward me. Mario Cuomo was never known to avoid a verbal confrontation. Not content with a mere sound bite, he was the master of on-the-fly media gun fights. This involved his stopping to engage in sound-bite debate with an opponent, then arrogantly striding on as if to suggest the unworthiness of whoever had the gall to disagree with him. This time, I was it.

"Now Dick," he said, "because you're an environmentalist, you're expected to take the large view —the high ground," Cuomo began. The broadcast media pressed closer.

"A jetport in the Pine Barrens?" I countered. "You don't expect us to sit for that!"
"To start off," he pointed out, "there's no such word in the English language as `jetport,'" Cuomo pedantically replied.

"There is today," I said, "And tomorrow it's a Pine Barrens Jetport and the day after that it's the Mario M. Cuomo Pine Barrens International Jetport," I fumed.

"I'm really disappointed in you, Dick," Cuomo concluded, moving away.

"The feeling is mutual, Governor," I responded. "At least I have a reason."

After the media had trailed Cuomo to his car, they returned to me. One reporter reminded me that Cuomo had, after all, explained in his presentation that he was a Long Islander and knew what Long Island needed. I pointed out that, in fact, the Governor lived in the New York City borough of Queens—not a place most Long Islanders consider Long Island—and that in fact, he lived almost equidistant from Kennedy and LaGuardia Airports, not areas Long Islanders envied. Most Long Islanders, I observed, didn't share the Governor's affection for commercial jetports.

"So, what does this tell Long Islanders about Cuomo as he heads into his reelection campaign?" a newspaper reporter asked. In my final and most grievous indignation, I answered, "You can take Cuomo out of Queens, but you can't take the Queens out of Cuomo."

My relationship with Mario Cuomo was over. He was so vindictive; he would hurt himself to spite you. He sought to undermine our work in every way imaginable through the remainder of the preservation initiative, even to the end of his political career. The term "jetport" however, stuck. It appeared regularly on T.V. graphics and newspaper accounts of the controversy.

We were in big trouble. This was not in the grand design. And the Governor had launched a major political campaign with enormous fanfare without our having any response planned at all. We sent word to my brother Tom, to Alan Singer and the rest of the Society's Board. We were going to need minds and manpower, pronto. With a slick video on the street promoting the Jetport, our first instinct was to produce our own video as quickly as we could. We agreed to reach out to local elected officials who we expected to oppose a jetport on Long Island's East End. We then organized the largest direct mail effort in the organization's history—a letter to every resident within 15 miles of the proposed facility.

The support of other East End environmental and civic groups was an immediate priority, and Sherry Johnson, the former Society Board member who was now Program Coordinator for the North Fork Environmental Council, rose to the challenge. She immediately began researching other airport conversions, noise issues, fuel, deicing and maintenance chemicals and other threats to groundwater and more. Kevin McDonald, vice-president and principal advocate for Group for the South Fork, promised funding support and Hamptons opposition. And a group of previously unheard-from civic people from nearby Wading River created a new group, Citizens Against East End Jetports, headed by civic activist, Mark Lembo. They used the plural to oppose the possibility of developing nearby Gabreski Airport in Westhampton Beach should the Calverton drive fail.

As quickly as we reacted, we fell further behind. Lee Koppelman of the Long Island Regional Planning Board announced that he had received a $400,000 grant from the Federal Aviation Administration to study the feasibility of the jetport. We freaked. The F.A.A. was aggressively pursuing airport conversions, and the Regional Planning Board and Koppelman personally had been touting its benefits for years. It was sure to be a whitewash, but it would give the jetport momentum.

Like so many self-proclaimed planners, Koppelman talked a good game. He made matters worse because instead of using his position as a bully pulpit, he sucked up to developers and the politicians that helped them. Over the years, he advocated for open space preservation, transportation-friendly development and groundwater protection. He lectured and wrote about the wisdom and need for long-term regional planning. All the while, towns and villages were approving development, business-as-usual. And, when Koppelman was reminded that the Island was being systematically destroyed on his watch, he replied, "If they'd listened to me, this would never have happened."

That was the principal problem with Koppelman's approach to planning. He ignored the realities of land-use decision-making, preparing studies and issuing reports and plans that produced little in the way of reform because they were strictly voluntary and lacked any teeth. He was strictly old school. He did not see the Pine Barrens as an important region, but rather merely as lots to be carved up.

Back when the Society began preparing its litigation, I sought out Koppelman to obtain a bit of his celebrated vision and sage advice. Indeed, he had served every Suffolk County Executive since the office was created and headed the highly visible Long Island Regional Planning Board. With an opportunity to shape the future of 100,000 acres of Pine Barrens, he would certainly have a valuable perspective.

Instead, I found Koppelman to be a pompous, pontificating relic of the poor planning that had made Long Island such a mess. He had a whiny, pretentious voice, honed by decades of affectation. It was as if his slow delivery and pedantic diction were saying, "Despite my tremendous intellect, it will be difficult for me to convey even my simplest observations to a person with your limitations."

We knew Long Island leaders would oppose the project if they knew about it. Tom set out at once to write the script for a video which became known as "An East End Jetport, the Shoreham of the '90s." The long title reflected our recognition that the only way to prevent this was through vocal, local opposition on the magnitude of surrounding efforts to open the last nuclear power plant in the United States at Shoreham, Long Island. Public opinion had overcome all odds and closed the plant before a single kilowatt of power had been sold.

East End Supervisors, led by Fred W. Thiele of Southampton and the usually pro-development Riverhead Supervisor, Joseph Janoski, quickly came out against the jetport plan. They were joined by Shelter Island Supervisor Huson "Hoot" Sherman, a Democrat and a pilot. We had bi-partisan opposition.

Tom was writing a great script. We booked a crew, scheduled the locations and tried to raise money from anti-jetport groups all at the same time. East End resident George Plimpton, the actor, writer and all-around personality, agreed to narrate the piece, pro bono.

Cuomo, Koppelman and the FAA were cast as the bad guys, pressing for a project that would "devastate the economy, decimate the environment and destroy eastern Long Island's quality of life." Experts in each area were matched with local residents to show how bad "this nightmare jetport would be." Plimpton's sonorous voice drove home each point, and the opposition of local elected officials made the 15-minute video even more compelling.

We shot the piece in a single day. With a limited budget, we taped at seventeen separate locations, starting at 5:30 A.M. with beautiful shoreline and farmland scenes on the East End. We contrasted this with scenes filmed at LaGuardia Airport, thanks to Peter Devens, who obtained New York Port Authority permission to shoot taxiing commercial aircraft from the top of a moving truck in what felt like the coldest weather I'd ever experienced. The taping ended at last light in the backyard of a resident near Kennedy International Airport.

Entreating Long Islanders to "make your political officials uncomfortable with your discomfort," Ira Gordon, a Cedarhurst resident who lived on a Kennedy Airport approach pattern, shouted over the roar of an approaching Boeing 737 visible above his house. An audio glitch made the first "take" unusable. I threw up my hands in frustration.

"Don't worry, we can do it every 90 seconds until midnight," Gordon explained. And, right on cue, another airliner appeared on the exact same approach, and Gordon tried again. "You must get yourselves organized," he admonished, "because once this is established you will not be able to move it. You will not be able to change things. We've been trying to change this for 40 years." By now, he was yelling at the top of his lungs to avoid being drowned out by the aircraft overhead. "Long Islanders must put their foot down. You must get your act together. This noise is very intrusive, and it will make your lives absolutely miserable." We took seven "takes" for safety. Each was better than the last.

On February 17, 1992, we held a rally at Suffolk County Community College's Riverhead Campus which drew 200 jetport opponents. Kevin McDonald and Mark Lembo enumerated threats represented by a Jetport at Calverton. We also premiered the video on a huge screen for an enthusiastic audience. We followed it with a demonstration of the noise levels to be expected from the introduction of commercial jets at Calverton. Sherry Johnson played sounds from a railroad crossing bell (at 70 decibels); an excerpt from a Billy Joel concert (100 decibels); and finally, noise from a Boeing 727 taking off (125 decibels.) The high-powered amplification/ speaker system deafened the crowd and produced dramatic pictures of an auditorium full of people, holding their ears.

The event was very well covered by the regional media, including WCBS-TV, *Newsday* and the *New York Times*. A bright intern, Lisa Bruschetti, distributed copies of the tape. We told her to give broadcast professionals the video on broadcast-quality videotape, while print and local reporters were to receive VHS -- a home video format.

In the one story recounted in this book for which I cannot obtain a second source, it is alleged that *Newsday* publisher Robert Johnson waited for the jetport story to be filed by veteran reporter Tom Morris, then requested a copy of the jetport video. The intern confirms this much: that viewing *Newsday* as major media, she supplied professional format video to Morris. Morris confirmed that he had done his reporting on the basis of the video as aired at the rally and never referred to the tape supplied him. The person who claimed to have been with Johnson in his office that night remembers that Johnson, unable to play the tape on the home video system in his office, grabbed it and threw it across the room, shouting that *Newsday* was supposed to be *the* communications source on Long Island and couldn't even play a video put together by a bunch of tree huggers. He left exasperated.

This was only a beginning for the jetport opposition, but an auspicious one. Shy and unassuming, Sherry Johnson made the jetport battle the professional fight of her life and made decisive contributions. For his part, Mark Lembo added the benefits of an allied group focused solely on the jetport. Funny thing about Mark, he loved doing public appearances. Time and again, he told me how much fun he was having on television debates and in community forums.

That's something I could never wrap my head around. How could you like it? I never once enjoyed being on T.V. When a program was over, I could enjoy it only if I thought I had nailed the messages we wanted to convey, regardless of the questions asked. Doing so required concentration under fire, and we never enjoyed it until afterward and only if we made the points we set out to make. In addition, there were few good reasons for a new airport on the East End, so we easily won debate after debate. Moreover, the public didn't like the idea, so persuasion wasn't very hard.

The first meeting of Lee Koppelman's Long Island Regional Planning Board "feasibility study" was coming up. Held January 21, 1992 at the County's H. Lee Dennison Building in Hauppauge, it was packed with print, radio and television reporters, few of whom had ever attended a meeting of the regional board. We had sent them our ambitious press kits charging that the "fix was in from the start" and to make sure they came, we told them that community organizations would boycott or walk out of the first meeting, charging Koppelman and the FAA with bias and collusion.

Sherry Johnson, trembling with nervousness amid all the attention, Jeff Fullmer of Citizens Campaign for the Environment and I attacked the honesty of the "feasibility study." I demanded an evaluation by an impartial group. Then, by arrangement, Johnson and I walked out.

Newsday, principally Bob Johnson, attacked the protest in a lead editorial, "Why Should LI Heed Environmental Walkouts?" Again, calling us "zealots," *Newsday* acted as though the walkout was an uncontrolled, emotional outburst, despite the fact that the paper, like the rest of the media, had received the press kit announcing the protest tactic days before. It was still another example of *Newsday*'s believing their own public relations creation, namely that Pine Barrens defenders were emotionally out-of-control extremists—messengers who should be ignored. It was an error that the development-at-any-cost crowd continued throughout the campaign, long after it became obvious that it wasn't working. It not only didn't bother us, we were glad they were sticking to an ineffective strategy.

We created a steady stream of events to keep the issue in front of the public. We organized a march involving sign-toting mothers and children at the Grumman-leased airfield targeted for Cuomo's jetport. There was a protest burning of the first draft of the Koppelman study suggesting that the Calverton conversion was feasible, despite the failure of similar efforts. And then there was the confrontation with Koppelman by activist Richard DiDonato of another new organization, the Citizens Planning Board.

DiDonato, a handsome actor who lived in nearby Mount Sinai, had agreed to sit on the study's citizens' advisory committee to "monitor" developments. At a key meeting chaired by Koppelman, he was prepared to challenge the validity of the process of the feasibility study. Print and television media were certain to be in attendance.

We rehearsed DiDonato's confrontational protests, at which he ticked off grievance after grievance intended to provoke the holier-than-thou Koppelman. It worked. In a classic television performance, DiDonato so riled Koppelman that he charged off the dais, screaming uncontrollably, waving his arms in the air and threatening to knock DiDonato's block off. Tom Junor, a big man who served on the county's planning commission, physically intervened to prevent fisticuffs. Looking back on the jetport fight, Kevin McDonald of Group for the South Fork, which co-sponsored the video, said, "It was amazing how Koppelman and the Regional Planning Board played the role we assigned them every time, not knowing that it was a pre-designed skit."

We couldn't afford to do much paid advertising during the Pine Barrens Preservation Initiative, but the jetport campaign was a notable exception. We decided to run a full-page ad in *Newsday* and the *New York Times* one Sunday, intended to expose where the politicians stood on the jetport issue. There were those who were opposed to the jetport, including Assemblyman Englebright and East End Supervisors Thiele, Sherman and Janoski. There were the bet-hedgers who said they would withhold their position until the Koppelman Feasibility Study was complete, including Congressman George Hockbreuckner, State Senator Kenneth LaValle and Brookhaven Supervisor John La Mura. Finally, there were two politicians supporting the jetport: Governor Cuomo and Suffolk County Executive Robert Gaffney. These three categories of position were characterized respectively as "The Good," "The Bad," and "The Ugly" in an ad headlined, "Will the Last Politician Off the Jetport Please Turn Out the Lights (On Your Career)." Cuomo's Long Island aide, Mark Grossman, pleaded for us not to run the ad, right up to the newspapers' deadlines. Finally, he begged, "There's got to be some way to get my guy into bad and out of ugly!" The ad ran.

Proponents of the jetport plan hired former Suffolk County Deputy County Executive Tom McAteer to advance their cause. He was hired to debate me in a series of discussions about the proposed jetport. McAteer was known to be politically savvy and influential.

Ostensibly, McAteer worked for the East End Executives, whose activity consisted of attending monthly dinner meetings at Suffolk County Community College featuring business speakers. This group was formed by the publisher of the *Long Island Business News*, Paul Townsend, a conservative knuckle scraper who never saw a development plan he didn't love. He supported more highways—the cause of Long Island's suburban sprawl—and like-minded, "more of the same" projects, while he opposed anything that smacked of environmental protection as "anti-growth." He argued, incredibly, that there was no need to protect Long Island's groundwater or Pine Barrens and often quoted Lee Koppelman to support his view. Yet he appeared at hundreds of early morning breakfasts and late night dinners, demonstrating his strong, if frequently off-base, commitment to the Long Island he loved.

He greatly admired "Buzz" Schwenk, giving him gallons of ink. Later, Schwenk explained that the breakfasts, lunches and dinners Townsend organized were originally designed to encourage advertising and subscriptions for his *Long Island Business News* but grew to be real forums for pro-business insiders.

Schwenk also admitted that McAteer's salary could not possibly have been borne by the East End Executives who paid for their own dinners and little else, and was probably paid by a larger, pro-development and anti-Pine Barrens group in western Long Island.

Neither McAteer nor I personalized the series of jetport debates. Instead, we frequently adjourned for post-debate Pepsis or other drinks, depending on the time of day. This helped us avoid acrimony and kept us focused on the issues rather than the personalities.

The jetport proposal died more quickly than we expected, I think for two reasons. First, it was a bad idea. I think Governor Cuomo and County Executive Gaffney quickly realized that a commercial jetport was not going to be popular in a rural area. But more important, our campaign against it was very effective. Within a period of eight weeks, we had produced a compelling video, run a campaign ad in *Newsday* and the *New York Times*, conducted a citizen's march and anti-jetport demonstration and an assault on Koppelman's jetport plan. As important as it was to kill the horrific jetport proposal, we couldn't allow it to delay or interfere with the campaign to save the Pine Barrens. So, we threw everything we had at the jetport plan to get it out of the way. And we did.

There Is No Reality: It's All How It Looks on T.V.

"The basis of our governments being the opinion of the people, the very first object should be to keep that right; and were it left to me to decide whether we should have a government without newspapers or newspapers without a government, I should not hesitate a moment to prefer the latter."—Thomas Jefferson

As we have seen, victory after victory can be ascribed to our mastery of the media. Using print, radio, television and direct mail, our case for preservation of the Pine Barrens won out over the selfish objectives of the developers. Yes, we were better, more effective communicators than the builders' lobby, but we also had the advantage of a message that resonated with Long Islanders while the developers were promoting overdevelopment. We were sensibly arguing to find out how Long Islanders would be harmfully impacted by Pine Barrens development while the builders were selling 234 construction projects that nobody needed or wanted.

While it's true that *Newsday* was Long Island's only daily newspaper at the time and it had a circulation of 711,000, the Island was just a small part of the biggest megalopolis in the country —making competing for media attention either very difficult or very expensive.

Editorials variously characterized us as "parochial," "dogmatic," "nothing whatsoever-in-my-backyard," "Long Island economy be damned," and "extremists." Some were very personal. In an editorial written after settlement talks broke down and shortly before oral arguments before the State's highest court, *Newsday* editorialized, "Amper had his chance and he blew it. His goal is to duplicate a New Jersey Pine Barrens administrative mechanism on Long Island. That would require legislation ceding extraordinary power to a special Pine Barrens council. The agency would be given power to override local zoning. Even if Amper and the developers had agreed to that, translating such an agreement into legislation would have been difficult." Of course, that's precisely what we asked for during the negotiations; no more, no less. It's identical to the pre-Johnson era *Newsday* editorial position. It's exactly what we ended up with.

We met with the editorial board but soon abandoned the tactic of reasonable explanation. These meetings gave us a chance to explain to the editorial writers of the paper what we were doing and why. My brother, Tom, quickly advised against further efforts to "move their thinking a degree or two," choosing instead to "let them make their knee jerk attacks, then demand the opportunity to answer in an Op-Ed piece or Letter to the Editor. Take the free kick on goal," Tom advised, "Let's see who the people believe."

As I've said before, in the news pages, we usually enjoyed fair coverage. At first, news about the Pine Barrens was relegated to the local "town" pages. But after the lawsuit, the story earned county-wide coverage and soon Long Island regional attention in all editions. *Newsday* was important to our public education efforts, and we knew how important it was to opinion-shapers and policymakers. There might be little we could do about Bob Johnson or the editorialists, but damned if we couldn't get the story of Long Island's struggle to save itself environmentally and economically, covered in "Long Island's newspaper."

From 1989 to 1993 there were more than 200 newspaper articles per year on the Pine Barrens story along with an average of 100 T.V. stories and as many radio reports. At first, the story of a small, heroic "David" group of ragtag warriors fighting to save our children's drinking water, struggling against "Goliath" real estate developers, was going to get enough press to make us larger than the sum of our parts. Conversely, the disposition of reporters to "balance" the story ultimately results in giving equal weight to both sides, however more worthy one is than the other.

So, by the middle of the campaign, *Newsday* was treating developers' arguments and positions as though they had the same merit as ours. We took the question of balance to Managing Editor Tony Marro. "*Newsday*'s stories have degenerated into nothing more than `He says, she says,'" I argued. "You're content to write that Breslin says development is needed to sustain our economy and Amper says the same development that is threatening our environment is devastating our economy."

"Residential development costs more in new government services than it collects in taxes," I pointed out. "*Newsday* didn't earn all those Pulitzers hanging in the lobby by quoting Breslin and Amper," I reminded him. "Talk to an economist and report the truth for a change," I suggested. With Long Islanders paying twice the national average in taxes and per student school costs soaring above $12,000 in 1990 money, the economic arguments in favor of more development began to deteriorate, because most Long Islanders could read their tax bills. It was not because they read *Newsday*. I told Marro, "matters of opinion should be balanced but not matters of fact."

James Ledbetter occasionally exposed *Newsday*'s misbehavior in his "Media Blitz" column in the *Village Voice*. He picked up on Karl Grossman's complaints about Bob Johnson's secret meeting on development in the Pine Barrens and later charged the editor with censoring a cartoon which depicted the painting of a "Buy American" billboard with the painters having fallen asleep on the scaffolding before finishing the message. In its place, Ledbetter claims, Johnson inserted another anti-environmental editorial.

Those who understood what we were up against were impressed. The LIA's Jim Larocca, on whose board publisher Johnson sat, said, "I thought it was masterful—the management of the public information against the challenge of a hostile publisher. It was extraordinary. I can't think of too many big policy fights in recent times where an advocate was as consistently successful in getting their story told on their terms."

On the T.V. side, the top journalist was News 12's Patti Ann Browne. She lived in Bayside, Queens with her twin sister, an insurance executive with Lloyd's of London. Browne was named

News 12's Environmental Editor, a high-sounding title that meant even more work, to cover a true news "beat" while doing everything else required of the high visibility, low-paying job at News 12.

Patti Ann Browne was a gem. She took her job seriously, but never herself. She was down-to-earth and unassuming. She was honest, candid and fair. We had lunch occasionally (Pat Dolan always insisted that news sources never pay; you could share, or News 12 picked up the tab—no shallow *quid pro quo*.) She dug for stories, worked hard to be fair, and shared herself, her family, friends, job, enthusiasm and frustrations. We cultivated relationships with other reporters but considered Patti Ann Browne a friend, though we never had very much time together. When we did, we got along famously; then we went back to work. She was assigned to cover the momentous hearing on Wilbur Breslin's "Brookhaven Town Center"—the largest development proposal ever advanced on Long Island. Her report was straight down the middle. She was also assigned to cover the legal challenge in the courts and ultimately the signing of the Pine Barrens Preservation Plan by Governor George Pataki, attributing to unnamed sources (not us) the characterization of our effort as "Long Island's greatest achievement."

But seriously, no one covered the Pine Barrens Preservation Initiative more or better than Patti Ann Browne. It wasn't until years later, after she had moved to Fox News, that the Pine Barrens Society honored her at its 2011 Environmental Awards Gala with its award for "Outstanding Contribution to Long Island's Environment." In her acceptance speech, she said "I've been a journalist for more than 25 years. I've covered many issues at the local, national and international level. But to this day, I'm proudest of my coverage of the Pine Barrens Society's efforts to preserve Long Island's greatest resource. As a Long Islander raising my family on Long Island, it is a source of great pride to me."

News 12 aired debate after debate on the Pine Barrens issue. From "Long Island Talks Business," hosted by the LIA's James Larocca, to "At Issue," a weekend confrontation between those representing conflicting interests, we were granted a forum essential to the success of our campaign. In some 24 major televised debates, the Society was able to advance its arguments that we ought to know the economic and environmental effects of our public policy before paving over Long Island with 234 projects we didn't need and couldn't afford.

The developers did poorly. With all their resources and some pretty savvy representatives, they simply hadn't an argument. They trotted out spokesman after spokesman, starting with Vincent Polimeni, then President of the Association for a Better Long Island. I'm always suspicious when an organization chooses a name that doesn't say what it's all about. We were the Long Island Pine Barrens Society. They were the Association for a Better Long Island? We quickly translated ABLI to mean the Association to Blacktop Long Island. This was closer to the truth.

Vince didn't fare too well. I was still awkward and uncomfortable on set, but at least I had a believable argument. It was tough for the developers to sell the idea that we should let them do whatever they wanted, whenever they wanted regardless of the economic and environmental impacts.

The Society's president, Mike Deering, and Gary Lewi, representing development interests, watched from the control room. "I was impressed at the non-confrontational tone of the exchange," Deering remembers. "The Society's arguments were calmly and reasonably conveyed and Polimeni couldn't make his case." Larocca spun questions and interpreted answers so as to help Vince, but he was not blatantly biased.

Charles Mancini, president of the New York State Builders Association, was next, followed by Edwin "Buzz" Schwenk, and the succeeding ABLI heads, former Suffolk County Executives Michael LoGrande and John V.N. Klein. ABLI certainly had some prominent, experienced spokesmen, but, none of them could make a case on News 12 or on Public Television's "Contact Long Island" or the succeeding "21 Edition." We were simply asking for a study to find out where and how much development could occur atop Long Island's purest water supply. Arguing against us on this matter was an absolute impossible position.

Most of the programs were taped, and the Society's Board asked me to call immediately after the recording to advise the board members of how we did. Truly, I never knew. Eventually, I postulated that one cannot simultaneously transmit and receive—that one either executes his or her "game plan" pro-actively as planned and rehearsed or reacts to the program, as the builders regularly did. The only way to evaluate a performance was to view and review programs after they aired to identify effective tactics and strengthen skills. My brother helped enormously, making suggestion after suggestion on how to improve. To a man, the developers' representatives in the long series of televised debates seemed largely unprepared, with the exception of John Klein. He appeared, at least, to have a strategy, even if he didn't have a strong argument. The developers trotted out almost a dozen spokesmen, never once besting the environmentalists.

News 12 asked tough questions but took no sides. On one occasion, Suffolk County Executive Robert Gaffney responded to our umpteenth challenge to his moribund acquisition program with slanderous charges that I was "a phony and a fraud," who was making false charges to encourage fundraising to pay my salary. Frankly, Gaffney wasn't buying any land and News 12 aired his unsupportable charge. To my amazement, Pat Dolan called the comment protected free speech and denied the Society an opportunity to respond.

Politicians conveniently forget that our founding fathers (and contemporary courts) give citizens almost limitless entitlement to criticize government—that's a principal purpose of free speech. But private citizens, even those as public as I, enjoy greater protection against defamation, as were the statements made by Gaffney about me.

Newspapers and radio and television stations are responsible for what others say, because they are the ones spreading it. Against the expressed will of the Society's Board, and especially President Alan Singer's and my own wife's rare interjection, I refused to sue for libel. The son of a journalist and one who had advanced his cause by the use of a free, unfettered press, I declined to press a case of clear-cut malice so as not to "chill" free speech, even on the part of a desperate and irresponsible politician. I felt that a libel lawsuit would harm free expression and open, honest coverage of the news greater than any harm done to me or my reputation by the Gaffney slur.

I figured there was a better way to fight back: hit Gaffney where it obviously hurt—his dismal record on preservation. Ultimately, I persuaded a bright, enterprising young *Newsday* reporter, Jordan Rau, to lobby his editor for an in-depth piece that dramatically demonstrated how Pine Barrens purchases had declined 80 percent after Gaffney's election. I researched and fed the reporter page after page of irrefutable evidence that a preservation program that had purchased an average of nearly 2,300 acres a year under the previous administration was now acquiring an average of fewer than 500 acres. Apart from delaying the preservation process, the lagging acquisition program posed the specter of a successful "takings" case, where a private property owner convinces a court that his land use is being unlawfully restricted without just compensation. That could have resulted in the Pine Barrens Act's being declared unconstitutional under the Fifth Amendment, which protects land from government seizure. In fact, such a case had already been brought, and the prime defense was the existence of state and county land acquisition programs.

Newsday had a rock solid and important story and went for it. They planned a 2,000-word feature that would run on the front page of the Sunday paper—the primo placement. As the deadline for filing the story approached, I was on the phone refuting county denials right up to the last minute. Responsibly, the reporter would call the county, the county would respond, and the reporter would call me back to get my take on the story. By this time the story was about much more than hammering Gaffney—it was the declaration that would turn the tide and set the course. I was persuaded that this was a story critical to the completion of the Pine Barrens Preservation Initiative. Realizing that gave me another thought. What would the headline be? What would I want it to be? Editors write headlines, not reporters, but a reporter's working title, if it's good, sometimes makes the headline. I called Jordan one more time. I got his voice mail, a device invented, I think, by phone carriers to require five phone calls to produce one actual conversation. I said, "For what it's worth, the working title for this piece ought to end up a banner headline, 'Promised Land!'" It landed just that way on my driveway and that of the County Executive on Sunday morning. Acquisitions doubled that year and tripled the year after. Then again, the next year was an election year.

We wrote numerous editorial replies and commentaries and appeared on Public Broadcasting's "Inside Albany," challenging Long Island's governing bodies to advance our environmental objectives. The Society's Board agreed that I would be its single spokesman, and that held true, except for a handful of sound bites, for ten years and more than 2,000 news accounts. The last thing you need in a focused campaign is a dozen spokespeople, all touting a different message.

Often, we thought a particular story was unfair and complained to the reporter about it. Like challenging an umpire's call in baseball, no one expects a reversed call. But it keeps fair reporters honest, and every once in a while, a succeeding story corrects the error or spins it your way.

Occasionally, a reporter will be as annoyed at an event as you and report it that way. Such was News 12 reporter Don Crawford's characterization of one of Wilbur Breslin's "Willy World" public hearings. He reported, "The Brookhaven Town Planning Board meeting was something less than a lesson in democracy. The Board allowed no one from the audience to speak and even badgered some audience members who rose to their feet to shout comments from the floor. That constitutional question went unanswered like all the questions the audience had at the Brookhaven Town Board. The Board opened the meeting with an announcement. No public comment would be taken. No one would be allowed to speak except Breslin's attorney." A video sound bite featured environmentalist Jane Edsall standing and shouting `What about democracy?'" It was the first time most people had a chance to see and hear the way Brookhaven conducted many of its meetings on proposed development projects, especially for well-connected builders.

Despite all the differences between us and *Newsday*'s editors during Robert Johnson's tenure, and even with a real journalist, Pat Dolan—despite all the shortcomings of the media, their bias toward a good show, the "he says, she says" journalism and the capacity of big business to overwhelm public interest—it is undeniable that the Long Island Pine Barrens would never have been saved had it not been for "the fourth estate." The news media, however sensational, however predictable, for the most part tells Americans what's going on, fairly and accurately. Across the board, print, radio and television covered the Pine Barrens Preservation Initiative fairly and accurately. Without that coverage the Pine Barrens would never have been saved.

In the absence of an advertising budget the size of our adversaries, without a grant larger than all of those we ever received, the Long Island Pine Barrens Society would plainly and simply have been unable to get its message out sufficiently to win the public support necessary to stop paving over Long Island and preserve our water and our land. Journalism's highest purpose is to educate citizens so that they can shape government policy in our democracy. This issue resonates today; whatever their faults, their mistakes, despite all differences of opinion, if there weren't strong and independent news outlets able to tell people what's going on, our governments could do or not do almost anything they pleased. In the end Long Island reporters did a first-rate job covering the "War of the Woods."

In and Out of Court

"The human race is challenged more than ever before to demonstrate our mastery, not over nature but of ourselves."—Rachel Carlson

Usually loquacious, with quick rejoinders during debates, I remember being stopped cold by a fourth grader's question at an elementary school presentation. "What does the Executive Director of the Pine Barrens Society do?" a precocious young girl wanted to know. I really hadn't thought about it. "I guess I just type and talk," I answered. She seemed appropriately unimpressed. Actually, I did both, a lot.

Winning is the inevitable result of refusing to lose. It requires a constancy of striving that is evident in nearly all great accomplishments. The Long Island Pine Barrens Society demonstrated an indefatigable drive to succeed, which despite periodic setbacks, allowed the group to advance its goal and to capitalize on every opportunity.

We scheduled an eighty-hour work week. Monday through Friday we booked appointments with public officials, attended hearings, gave lectures and appeared at environmental and civic group meetings from one end of Long Island to the other, from 7:00 A.M. until 10:00 P.M. with an hour for lunch and dinner. Saturdays were spent writing letters, testimony, releases, white papers, speeches, newsletters and direct mail. That was also the best day to meet with volunteers and to update our environmental colleagues concerning ongoing developments. Sunday was supposed to be a sabbatical, but it rarely turned out that way. Invariably, the quieting of the phones invited more serious writing, such as Op-Ed pieces and major policy addresses.

We worked from my house, which avoided the drain on scarce resources paying rent would have required and provided for the shortest possible commute each morning and night. It also reflected the grassroots nature of the campaign. We may have looked big and powerful to the bad guys, but the good guys understood the human dimension of the crusade as they attended homey meetings, sitting informally in my living room or around the dining room table.

The work was overwhelming and incessant. In addition to the education and advocacy work, there was the constant pressure to raise funds. We built our membership through direct mail appeals targeting residents of individual towns and villages where there was opposition to specific local projects. Civic associations, garden clubs and environmental groups made organizational contributions, as well.

One of the best early surprises greeted me as I checked my answering machine after returning from another worthless meeting at Brookhaven Town Hall. "I'm looking for the Richard Amper who is heading the Pine Barrens preservation project," the caller said. "This is Bill Moyers." I returned the call to the Public Broadcasting System number he had left. He said he had been following our activities in *Newsday* (where years earlier he had been publisher). "My successor is obviously not very sympathetic, and it sounds like you could use some help," Moyers explained. He was on the Board of Directors of the John and Florence Schuman Foundation and quickly arranged for the Society's first grant: $25,000, more money than we had ever before seen.

Later, Michael Northrop, a bright, enthusiastic, program officer for the Rockefeller Brothers Fund, asked to visit. He had been following the story in the *New York Times* and thought our use of communications might be a model for some of their other grantees. He orchestrated several large grants that helped keep the Society in the game in which the developers thought we couldn't compete. The Society quickly turned the $3,500 it had accumulated before I started to $50,000 in 1989, $75,000 in 1990, and $100,000 in 1991.

It still wasn't enough. Legal and printing costs were exorbitant. I missed paycheck after paycheck, at one point going unsalaried for more than a year. Robin and I consumed our savings, ran up our credit cards, and only Robin's salary kept the bank from taking our house. Bob McGrath urged me to hire an assistant, but we couldn't figure out how we would pay one. Fundraising (which he tracked more closely than any other board member did) had gained, and the court victory hadn't hurt. Increasingly, wealthy East Enders, some recruited by author and radio personality Sherrye Henry, were making large donations. Up to this point donations were averaging $23.

On the war front, we appealed the lower court decision to the Appellate Division, retaining possibly the finest environmental attorney in New York State, Michael Gerard, then of Berle, Kass and Case (later of Arnold and Porter.) He was bright, knowledgeable and very much interested in what was not just the largest but the most important environmental case of the decade. With a slight build and big steel-rimmed glasses, he authored the environmental case law and policy journal for the profession and had an impressive list of environmental victories under his belt.

His adversary was a former appellate court judge himself, Leon Lazer. Retained by Wilbur Breslin, he knew most of the judges in the Second Department and was highly respected. The thrust of the bad guys' case was that the environmental study wasn't necessary, and that the *de facto* moratorium caused by the case, and especially a reversal of the lower court ruling, would prove catastrophic for Long Island's economy.

Environmental Advocates and other non-profit organizations began signing on to our land and water campaign. The Sierra Club Legal Defense Fund, Citizens Campaign for the Environment, New York State Assembly Water Commission, North Fork Environmental Council and Group for the South Fork all filed briefs in the appeal.

In July 1991, we came up with the idea of trying to recruit New York State Attorney General Robert Abrams into joining the lawsuit as a friend of the court. The Attorney General's involvement would support the legal validity of our litigation. Alas, persuading him to join our campaign wasn't easy. I nagged Abrams' chief of staff with several suggestions as to why the A. G. should join our crusade. I pointed out that he was the state's defender of the law. Another day, I reminded Abrams' top aide that the A.G. was popular on Long Island and water quality was an important issue.

Abrams declined several written requests, but I pressed for a personal meeting. I called several more times and spoke to the assistant who seemed personally sympathetic but offered no encouragement about Abrams. I simply wouldn't give up. One morning, about 9:30, the assistant called and said, "Be here by 3:00 pm. You've got five minutes." It took me nearly three hours to reach Abrams' downtown Manhattan office from my eastern Long Island home, that day. As I cursed the traffic, I kept wondering why I was "wasting" all this time and effort to have a man tell me to my face what he had already conveyed through aides twice before. The meeting was nothing to him--five minutes. I was the one who had to schlep the length of Long Island and back.

By the time I arrived, I was anything but not ready. He greeted me amiably, I thanked him for seeing me and quickly ticked off the three reasons he should sign on. First, the case was a good one both in terms of our arguments concerning environmental law and the chance to win the appeal. Second, he was running for U.S. Senate and his support for a key swing constituency, Long Island, might be decisive. (He eventually lost a close race.) Third, there could be no more important role for an attorney general to play than as advocate for the public's health, given the drinking water issue. " He paid close attention, nodding often.

"Fine argument," Abrams said when I finished. "Did you ever consider practicing law?" To my astonishment, he agreed to do it, just like that. I wondered later whether he was already leaning toward doing it; why else would he have given me the meeting? Maybe he wanted to meet me to see if I was buttoned up enough to do a news conference right. Or perhaps he had seen that I knew how to get press and he wanted to be a good guy I'd remember when the cameras started rolling. His involvement was announced days later at news conference we organized on the Supreme Court House steps in Mineola, attended by hundreds of supporters bused from the East End and a horde of reporters.

The Appellate Court in Brooklyn heard oral arguments on September 23. News 12's Pat Dolan covered the story personally. He knew the court usually banned cameras, but he planned to interview the litigants and do a stand-up from the courthouse steps. To everyone's surprise, Chief Judge William Thompson invited him to tape the proceedings. "The public should be able to see and hear a case of this much importance to them," he said.

After brief presentations by Gerard and Lazer, Appellate Justices Thompson and Thomas Sullivan asked each side tough questions. Why, they asked Gerard, was a new study needed, given the volume of other studies in the past? They challenged Lazer, asking wouldn't contamination of the Island's drinking water pose a huge economic as well as environmental problem? And the judges lambasted Brookhaven Attorney Denise Molia for arguing that

Brookhaven had no legal obligation to conduct such a review at all. We left, persuaded that the judges had heard and understood our case, but we were uncertain of the likely decision.

The October 6, 1991 cover of *Newsday* blared the latest in a series of land use scandals in Brookhaven Town, the largest on Long Island. "Public Acts, Private Deals" was the title of a major investigative report that went on for pages to document how top officials of Brookhaven, including Supervisor Henrietta Acampora, had used their public offices in ways that benefited them and their friends. It described a system in which favored developers got anything they wanted, while those not connected struggled. *Newsday* pointed to consulting fees paid to a town planning board member who voted in favor of a subdivision, then received part of a commission on the sale of the property. Another planning board member voted for a zone change requested by a fellow planning board member who owed him $75,000 from an earlier joint business venture. The story cited example upon example. While we had nothing to do with this news, it played into our hands.

In fact, environmental and civic leaders routinely referred to the town as "Crookhaven," and had for years. Name-calling in political battles is a common tactic. We used it very effectively. The term "Crookhaven" drove developers and politicians crazy throughout the "War of the Woods"— not because it wasn't true, but because it was. Buzz Schwenk, who knew both Suffolk politicos and real estate development, flatly admitted that everyone knew the cost of a zone change in terms of cash or purchasing tables at the party fundraiser.

The land use scandals in Brookhaven were legion. In July 1990, the Brookhaven Town Board voted to purchase a tiny bay front lot in Shirley for $660,000 at the behest of Supervisor Henrietta Acampora. County officials insisted that the price paid was many times higher than the property was worth and that it wasn't needed for parkland. It turned out that the landowner was a friend of Acampora's who frequently included her in free junkets to Atlantic City. I knew Acampora, of course, from the fight to Save the Lake, when she told me how many dimes she might have from all the times people had promised to expose her to *Newsday*. It seems she knew an even better source of income. Other scandals involved town engineering consultant John Johnson, Brookhaven Town Attorney Phillip Sanderman (who later represented the home builders' lobby in Pine Barrens negotiations) and many Town Board Members or Planning Board Members. Many were indicted and some convicted.

By far the biggest of the land use scandals involved Port Jefferson automobile dealer John McNamara, a business titan and Brookhaven's largest real estate developer in the 1980's. McNamara made millions of dollars by rezoning properties and "flipping" them to other developers to build on newly approved sites. McNamara's business model was perhaps best typified by a transaction in Setauket, where he purchased an idle piece of farmland for $1.1 million, had the property rezoned by the Brookhaven Town Board and one year later sold the property for close to $13 million. In April of 1991, the General Motors Acceptance Corporation found that McNamara had created a "Ponzi Scheme" that used their financing to obtain loans to support McNamara's empire. He told federal prosecutors he had systematically bribed various elected officials to obtain approvals to develop his various properties. In short, when the prosecutors went after him, he offered up the elected officials. Brookhaven Town Planning Board member Anthony Aliperti was convicted. A fourth defendant, Peter Sapienza, a former Brookhaven Planning Board member, pleaded guilty to extortion and tax evasion. Brookhaven Town and Suffolk County Republican leader John Powell was convicted of racketeering and extortion in 1999 for running a motor vehicle "chop shop." He was accused of using his influence to help "friends" get special privileges at Brookhaven's controversial landfill. McNamara, who pleaded guilty and testified against the government officials, was sentenced to five years in prison. He was also ordered to repay General Motors more than $412 million in outstanding loans within three years of his release. The scandals were not directly linked to the Pine Barrens fight but demonstrated the cozy relationship between the politicians and the developers. We never missed an opportunity to use the scandals to discredit the developers and politicians.

Neither *Newsday* nor the prosecutors ever found more than the tip of the iceberg. This emboldened the wrongdoers. Nevertheless, it used to infuriate Acampora's successor, John LaMura, when we publicly responded to charges of systematic corruption with, "That's business as usual in Crookhaven."

1992 brought immediate good news. The same judge who had ruled against us in the lower court ruled that Brookhaven had erred by approving Wilbur Breslin's shopping center plan without considering the rest of his "Willy World" complex of homes and office space. Ruling in a case brought by the Open Space Council, Justice Paul Baisley said such an approval of part of a larger plan by the same developer on adjacent property constituted illegal "segmentation."

The next day, *Newsday*'s front page shouted, "Mega-Mall Stalled—The "War of the Woods." It was a major victory for environmentalists, and OSC's Marilyn England was jubilant. The ruling meant that town approval of the project was overturned and sent Breslin back to the business of conducting a more comprehensive environmental review. This demonstrated, I said, "what environmentalists and civic groups have been saying for years: in approving projects for their builder friends, Brookhaven is not merely acting irresponsibly; they're breaking the law."

Throughout the legal process, another drama was playing itself out in a separate arena. Veteran planner Lee Koppelman's Long Island Regional Planning Board was preparing the Special Groundwater Protection Area Plan for the Island's nine state-designated aquifer protection areas. Citizen groups attending meetings on the plan criticized it as strictly voluntary and lacking teeth.

Citizens Campaign for the Environment, an early supporter of the Pine Barrens Initiative and one of three organizations that canvassed door-to-door for public support, was leading the effort to strengthen groundwater protection in the plan. They had created an umbrella organization of concerned groups called the Coalition for the Protection of Long Island's Groundwater.

A lawyer and groundwater expert, Sarah Meyland, headed CCE with assistance from a sharp married couple, Jeffrey Fullmer and Adrienne Esposito. We supported their efforts and they supported ours; they led the SGPA battle while we fought on the litigation front.

The Appellate Division ruling was overdue. Chief Judge William C. Thompson had taken personal charge of the case from the outset. One member of the five-judge appeals court panel had recused himself, leaving only four judges to hear oral arguments. A ruling was slow in coming. Were they deadlocked? This might account for the ruling's delay.

The wait ended March 10. Our Long Island lawyer, Larry Ceriello, called to say that an aide to his wife, a practicing attorney in Manhattan, had stumbled across the decision while researching another appellate matter. The news, he reported sullenly, was not good. We asked that she obtain a copy of the opinion and fax it to us. We notified Gerard, who wanted to see the decision for himself before assessing our position.

I read the ruling as it came off the machine. The first few pages recounted the facts and laid out the issues. The diction was dry, and the challenge of the case explained. But, as I read on, our position gained favor. It sounded like our arguments were being accepted. Because it was a fax, I couldn't simply skip to the back and read the decision. As the pages slowly crept from the now old-fashioned machine, I became increasingly persuaded that the opinion I was reading could only end up with a decision to overturn the lower court and order the cumulative review we sought.

My suspicions proved correct. Judge Thompson had empaneled a fifth judge who supported our arguments. By a three-to-two margin, the Appellate Court had reversed Justice Baisley's decision, concluding that not one of the 234 projects pending in the Pine Barrens could go ahead until the combined effects of all of them had been considered. To this day, we don't know who misread the opinion.

The majority opinion, written by Thompson, concluded, "...Cumulative Impact Review as a means of ensuring that projects are approved in conformity with a legislative program is as logically compelling here—if not more so—than it was in the Save the Pine Bush case. In Save the Pine Bush, the projects were independent, functionally unrelated actions proposed by different sponsors, whose cumulative impacts could nevertheless have resulted in deleterious environmental impact within a well-defined, ecologically-sensitive area. In the present case, the various projects—although functionally unrelated—are similarly linked by virtue of their potential to adversely affect an irreplaceable natural resource within a discrete geographic area." Our position in a single paragraph!

Robin and I called Board Members, *amici*, and every environmental and civic leader we could reach. We rented space at the Radisson Hotel in Islandia for 11:00 A.M. the next day and prepared a release and background press kit. The co-founders were delighted. "Better than [preserving] Hampton Hills," Turner exulted. "Alright!" McGrath exclaimed. "Congratulations, Dick," Cryan responded, savoring the import.

We loaded the podium into the back seat of the car for the next morning, finally crawling into bed about 4:30 A.M. It was going to be a great day. By 7:00, we were up faxing releases and giving radio interviews by phone. Tom and I talked about the importance of strategizing on how to use the ruling to create momentum in the direction of a preservation plan. The builders had dropped the ball in not publicizing their win in the first court ruling, as Buzz Schwenk later acknowledged. "We really fell down on the job by not publicizing the first court ruling, because it would have made us look like we were right about the issue," he said. Not us – we had no intention of repeating their mistake.

Despite the short notice and a weekday business schedule, the room was packed with supporters. Norman and Liliane Thurau, who had done so much of the research, were joined by Sarah Meyland of Citizens Campaign, David Stern of the New York State Water Commission and Laurie Farber from Sierra. Appellate co-counsel Phillip Weinberg of St. John's University Law School was on the dais with attorney Larry Ceriello and Society Board Members Joe Colao and Vinny Scandole, the intrepid duo from Pine Valley days. Janet Smith and Gladys Belmonte represented our enthusiastic volunteers. There were hugs and kisses for half an hour while the media assembled. The *Times*, *Newsday*, and News 12 were there, and WNBC's Roger Stern, who had witnessed the inauguration of the legal effort while at News 12, was back to report the victory for his new employer. "Yes! Yes!" I exclaimed as the news conference began, my hands over my head like a victorious sports figure. Gerard explained the implications and importance of the ruling, and co-founder and then President Bob McGrath read a letter from the Society to the government defendants, calling on them to end the litigation and agree to a study and preservation plan.

This wasn't going to happen. The developers had been consistent in refusing to discuss the case, let alone negotiate with us on it. William Esseks, a lawyer who represented some of the biggest and baddest developers and did it in the nastiest way, said, "We're not going to sit down and negotiate with somebody who sits down at the end of the table and says, `Here's how you're going to run Long Island.'" Of course, we knew that the developers wouldn't agree to a study and preservation plan; we just created the letter to paint the developers as the ones who were standing in the way of peace!

The news conference was not without a blemish. Without my knowledge, Vincent Cioci, the self-promoting Director of the Long Island Neighborhood Network, had purchased a bottle of Champagne—or more exactly, put it on the Pine Barrens Society's hotel tab—and appeared out of nowhere toasting the occasion. The cameras flashed. The next day, the photo was in *Newsday*, provoking the developers like few other public scenes. They lamented "environmentalists toasting with champagne the destruction of Long Island's economy." This was just the latest case of Cioci trying to get himself noticed and compromising the campaign in the process. He had to go.

The gaffe could not spoil the long sought, hard-fought victory. The next day's *New York Times* headlined, "Court Halts Projects Planned for Pine Barrens." The story read:

> *A divided State Appellate Court has ordered a sweeping environmental review of the last large tracts of undeveloped pine forest on Long Island, overturning hundreds of zoning decisions by local governments.*
>
> *In the decision, the State Appellate Division in Brooklyn barred any development in the environmentally-sensitive Pine Barrens, an area of almost 200 square miles, until a study has examined the cumulative effects of hundreds of developments planned there.*
>
> *Environmentalists said the decision would force the creation of a master plan that would save much of the unusual woodland, with its rare species of plant and animal life, and preserve some of the purest water in the region, which lies thousands of feet beneath the Pine Barrens. The vote, which overturned a lower court decision, was 3-2. "*

The developers were devastated. Charles Mancini said the decision "cast a pall" over Long Island's economy. *Newsday* quoted him as saying, "What the message has been and will continue to be because of this decision to companies looking to relocate to Long Island is: Go someplace else."

It seemed certain that the decision would be appealed. But Southampton Supervisor Fred Thiele, the guy who had championed preservation as a Suffolk County legislator, announced that Southampton would not join any appeal to the state's highest court. He took heat for the decision, from officials of other towns and Suffolk County—more heat than from any other action he took as Supervisor. "Pulling out of the litigation was the thing I got the most heat on from the county and other towns," Thiele says. "But I figured we had already started doing a generic environmental impact statement for the Pine Barrens in Southampton, so why should we fight in court to prevent having one done?"

The developers' loss in the Appellate Division triggered the first signs of desperation. The builders convened a secret April 7, 1992 meeting where they devised an ill-considered plan to lobby for repeal of state environmental protection law. They created an organization called the Society for Environmental-Economic Balance, an industry group with a name almost as high-sounding as the Association for a Better Long Island. "A developer by any other name is still a developer," Deering opined.

In the midst of the anti-jetport fight, which by now was generating thousands of dollars from a mail campaign, aimed at residents of towns surrounding the jetport, we were suddenly and dramatically reminded of the ongoing Pine Barrens campaign by one of the "Phone Voices." Most Long Islanders supported our clean water/protect the environment message, so it came as no surprise that frequently unidentified Long Islanders would call us up with "tips" on what the bad guys were up to.

Some "Phone Voice" tips were more important and more credible than others information. This Phone Voice message was more important and more incredible than any other. A soft spoken, middle-aged woman called one Tuesday. In deliberately hushed tones she told me that 60 of the very top Long Island power brokers were planning to meet April 7, 1992 at the Huntington Hilton to mount an ominous public relations and legislative assault on the Pine Barrens Preservation Initiative. She warned that the room assignment would not be posted and refused to supply the names of the attendees, except to say, "Let's put it this way, if a bomb went off in that meeting, Long Island would be a finer place in which to live." She abruptly hung up.

It sounded far-fetched. However, by this time I had heard Gayle Brovetto's tale of Brookhaven shenanigans and Steve Englebright's vast conspiracy theory about Pine Valley. Both had proven true. Vinny Scandole had been a cop and admitted to having taken on some private investigations. I called him.

"Sounds like fun," he responded offhandedly. "I'll check it out."

Scandole arrived at the Huntington Hilton and, as promised, could find no meeting on the computerized monitor, nor information from the reception desk. Undeterred, he waited for a familiar face. It was Buzz Schwenk's. He followed at a discreet distance and found Long Island leaders in a first-floor conference room. The bad guys left both the front and back doors of the meeting room open, so Scandole picked up some literature that was set out for a meeting in the adjacent room and pretended to be early for that meeting. He could easily eavesdrop on the bad guys chatting about golf, politics and the lousy state of the economy over their drinks. (Over the years Scandole's story got better and better. At one time he was one of the servers buttling cocktails.)

The meeting involved not merely developers but business and labor leaders, as well. There was Robert Reid, the failed Lake Panamoka developer; Jack Kennedy, a labor leader; Desmond Ryan of the Association for a Better Long Island and dozens of others, presumably equally senior but unknown by face to Scandole. He wrote furiously as those in attendance introduced themselves: "Buzz" Schwenk, the Long Island Association's President James Larocca, developer Wilbur Breslin and his P.R. man Howard Blankman, and so on. "I listened for names and I.D.'d everyone I could," Scandole explained, "but most of all, I was awestruck by the extent that we had them spooked," he remembers.

"They're killing us," mega-developer Wilbur Breslin kept saying over and over, again.

Scandole took down *Newsday* publisher Robert Johnson's statement word for word. "You can't count on *Newsday* alone to do it all. Letters to the editor and Viewpoints are not enough. We must have stories in the main body of the paper to educate people."

In the end they decided to launch a campaign in the state legislature to strip the cumulative impact requirement from the Environmental Quality Review Act. This would moot the Pine

Barrens lawsuit before it came to the Court of Appeals. They called the plan by the catchy name, "Campaign in Support of Effort to Modify State Legislation Concerning Pine Barrens." Former Long Island Assemblyman Jerry Kremer agreed to handle the Albany lobbying effort. The overall campaign would be managed by Thomas McAteer, the pro-jetport lobbyist with whom I had had the debates.

Long Island's business leaders, and not just developers, were setting out on a $250,000 campaign to change state law to allow development in the Pine Barrens and the Island's eight other state-designated Special Groundwater Protection Areas. The plan called for "an aggressive lobbying effort to effect the necessary changes in state legislation that would allow orderly economic development" and promised "to initiate a massive public information campaign intended to educate and influence the voting public of rational solutions to sound economic development."

James Larocca, president of the Long Island Association, didn't know what the meeting was to be about. "Willy [Breslin] was sort of acting as emcee," Larocca recalled, "and he called on me to talk about how we were going to pass this legislation, and I was furious. Not only had I been resisting this, but now I'm in this cheap set-up to put me on the spot in front of a roomful of people to make it look like I was somehow heading some effort to pass a bill. So, I got up and spoke for less than a minute and did nothing more than give my name, rank and serial number. On the way out, I told Blankman that if he ever did that to me again, I wouldn't speak to him."

Scandole was torn between revulsion at the plan for proposed legislation and ecstasy at having uncovered it. As the meeting adjourned, he heard a voice he couldn't identify caution, "It is essential that you keep the document describing this campaign absolutely confidential. You understand the effects on our efforts of its disclosure."

Scandole had to have the document. But how? First, he ducked into the room as soon as it was empty, but found no copy left behind. Picking up his pace, he raced to the nearest men's room and entered unassumingly. Sure enough, the volume of drinking executives ensured more urinators than urinals. There, stacked among other possessions on the corner of a sink was a copy of the "Campaign in Support of Efforts to Modify State Legislation Concerning Pine Barrens."

Without hesitation, he absconded with it, driving directly to Lake Panamoka and laughing all the way. The document was to appear only one more time.

I tried unsuccessfully to persuade the *New York Times* or *Newsday*'s news division to write about Bob Johnson's inappropriate attempt to influence his paper's news accounts for a special interest. The *Times* admitted that Johnson's effort was indeed journalistically unethical but thought the Times' reporting of it would seem competitively motivated. *Newsday*'s news editors found it too "sensational." In the end, the first journalist to cover the conspiracy to undermine state environmental law was East End syndicated columnist and environmental advocate Karl

Grossman. He described the secret meeting in detail and shared his story with national media monitoring organizations—a credit to his professionalism.

Then there was public broadcasting. I decided to confront Tom McAteer in public in the biggest forum I could find.

On May 8, 1992 I arrived at the Plainview studios of WLIW-TV, Channel 21, the Public Broadcasting System channel for Long Island. A UHF station might otherwise not have the reach of a commercial station, but Channel 21 was broadcast on cable as well and enjoyed a large audience of educated and influential viewers. Long Island's opinion shapers regularly watched WLIW for news and information, and a favorite program of those interested in Long Island matters was "21 Edition," hosted by newswoman Dara Welles.

The topic of the broadcast was the jetport proposal. In addition to Tom McAteer and me, Southampton Supervisor Fred Thiele added the "credibility" touch for which broadcasters regularly turn to elected officials. I deliberately pulled Supervisor Thiele aside to give him a "heads up" on the exposure I contemplated, asking him if he had any objections. "Do whatever you want," he said.

For the first 20 minutes of the program, I focused intently on debunking the myths of the jetport promises and warned of the threats to tourism, fishing and farming—the staples of the East End economy. I pointed out the threat to air and water quality represented by the jetport proposal. And I warned against the impact on quality of life to anyone within "a fifty-mile noise footprint" surrounding the Calverton site. The very first five minutes of the broadcast were dominated by segments of our Plimpton anti-jetport video. After a final, nervous look at the studio clock, I decided to strike.

"I think Mr. McAteer has not been very forthcoming about his real motivations in this process. He has said on this program and throughout the last couple of months that he represents the Eastern Long Island executives, and that he, in fact, only wants to see a feasibility study done and that he's very concerned about the Pine Barrens area. In fact, what Mr. McAteer is encouraging is a campaign on behalf of many highly paid developers and western business interests that are in fact designed not just to do a jetport but to promote the malls and the other developments that have been on hold in the Pine Barrens by actually going out and changing state environmental law in all of the Special Groundwater Protection Areas in Nassau and Suffolk Counties, and he's not leveling with us about who he represents and what he is really up to, and I think we should talk to him about it."

When I finally took a breath, McAteer looked thunder-struck. His mouth went dry as he struggled to make a response. Incredibly, Thiele ignored the confrontation and began talking instead about Suffolk County Executive Robert Gaffney's support for the jetport. Dara Welles quickly stopped him. "Some very serious charges were made at this table," Welles said, "and I would like Tom to get a chance to respond. Do you have a hidden agenda?"

Because of the delay Thiele had produced, I had a chance to interject the thrust of my charge before McAteer had a chance to reply. "Very simply, though, I want it very clear that it is appropriate for us to be involved, and Mr. McAteer and I have been involved in a public forum for months debating the jetport, but the jetport is the tip of the iceberg, and his true agenda needs to be addressed and admitted to by Mr. McAteer in the interest of promoting it."

McAteer stammered, "First of all, let me speak about the Calverton project. I got involved in the Calverton project, and Dick and I have talked about this a number of times. The reason I did it is that I believe our economy is in serious, serious trouble. I do not believe intuitively as Mr. Amper does—and it is intuitive at this point, there are not facts to support what he is saying—that it could possibly be a good thing for this economy, and we ought to study it and we ought to look at it. In terms of the Eastern Long Island Executives, I was hired as the Executive Director to take this project on. As to your other issue, there are people on Long Island, and I know that from time to time you have said you think you speak for everyone on Long Island as it relates to environmental concerns."

"That's not the case," I interrupted.

"Well, you've said it. I am very much concerned with a balance between business and the economy—a true balance. You've said many, many times that you should never pit the economy against business or business against the economy. And, Dick, we do agree on that, but, Dick, that's what`s been going on for the last few years, particularly here in Suffolk County. That's got to stop. I've said that to you consistently. I am very much interested in seeing a balanced view to economic issues and environmental issues."

I bored in. Reaching into my suit pocket, I unfolded the copy of McAteer's proposal to the secret meeting and challenged, "Tom, you need to be honest about this and we need to face it down. If in fact that's your position, I don't know why it's been done behind closed doors and not in the public eye. I am telling you that on a meeting on the 7th of April, you actually proposed to Long Island's executives, a plan, a building plan to develop the Pine Barrens in the hopes that you would obtain legislation to change the laws that protect Long Island's drinking water from developers. I ask you to address yourself to that."

McAteer was desperate. "[I'm trying] to bring clarity to the law, to bring clarity to the law so that people will understand what this is, this generic impact statement and what it is that the State Legislature was asking for when they passed the law because in the Courts as you know the lawsuit—the Appellate Court in particular indicated a real vagueness in this. As a matter of fact, introduced a piece to it that it is reasonable to assume was never intended. So this, the idea here is to find out from the State Legislature, is this what they meant?"

The tension in the studio was real as the confrontation continued. I said pointedly, "You are not proposing to support a feasibility study for the jetport on land in the Pine Barrens for the eastern Long Island executives. You have an agenda. The feasibility study has been paid for, it's moving ahead. You are pressing ahead with another agenda that you haven't been discussing in public forums and I think public broadcasting is the time to get that agenda aired."

"Absolutely," McAteer admitted, "and I have been in discussions with people on this very subject. Those discussions are ongoing. They are not concluded."

"What people," I asked?

"If there is an effort in that direction..." he began.

I cut him off. "Who are you working for? And what's the agenda, Tom?"

"I'm not working for anyone on this issue. One is working when one is retained as you know in the business that you work. And I have not been retained. However, as I have stated here, there is a belief that there is a need to seek clarification of what the intent of the legislature was and you may be hearing more about that in the future," he said.

"No," I pressed, "if Long Islanders are to participate in a referendum, then I think we ought to all have our cards on the table and we ought to see what interests are being advanced. Basically, the question Mr. Thiele has asked regularly is if we do a jetport, if we build malls, if we do over-development in the Pine Barrens and other special groundwater protection areas, who benefits and who pays? And I suggest that the builders benefit and the rest of us pay and that you are a part of that process."

McAteer was now furious. He blurted, "And I suggest that you have for the last years you have been using hysterical tactics and in the case of the jetport misuse of information consistently and I believe that your approach is absolutely wrong for what we need here on Long Island and we disagree on that. We absolutely disagree. The fact that I, as a private business person, now make a proposal to a group of people, [which] happens to be proprietary as you know. The fact that you have come into your hands a copy of that proposal..." I interrupted, "Makes you a little uncomfortable."

Sputtering, McAteer continued, "You know, you've leveled charges. You've talked about putting the cards on the table. Do you disclose every proposal you make to every individual?"

"I want to answer that. When we sit in public forums like the one we're engaged in now, we tell the public what we've found out and what we believe is right and why we're doing it. You haven't done that," I concluded.

"That is an absolutely absurd thing to say," he snapped. "It's absolutely absurd. If I am retained by an organization for a subject like this, that will be a matter of public record at that point. But only at that point."

Dara Welles tried to calm the debate, but I concluded, "What we're doing in these forums is that we're trying to come forward and say, 'Here are the people that are trying to do this for a particular reason.' When you've got 84% of the people in Suffolk County saying we want to buy up land in the Pine Barrens, and we say we're out here trying to protect the Pine Barrens, we're leveling. When Mr. McAteer says that he's devoted to protecting the Pine Barrens when he's in fact trying to permit development in these Special Groundwater Protection areas, he's not leveling."

As the program ended, McAteer tore off his lapel microphone and bounded from the set. I never laid eyes on him again. He did not appear at succeeding scheduled jetport debates. To my knowledge, he never had anything to do with the Pine Barrens from that day forward. He certainly never again appeared in public on this or any related issue.

Of course, this was not about beating McAteer in a debate but exposing a massive conspiracy to resume development as usual and put an end to the Society's legal strategy to protect the Pine Barrens.

But, after we exposed the clandestine meeting and savaged the devious plan, the developers discovered reason—they had to negotiate. Warned years earlier by Bob Wieboldt against the notion that the Society lacked the wherewithal to bring the successive series of legal actions that comprised the over-arching Pine Barrens lawsuit, the developers finally realized he was right. They now sought the advice of Larocca. It was clear that Larocca had deliberately determined not to take sides.

Although many environmentalists distrusted the Long Island Association as too "establishment" and too "pro-development," the LIA, under Larocca, sought some form of balance for, among other reasons, a desire to make Long Island an attractive place to live and work. The commercial developers didn't consider Larocca sufficiently pro-building, so they created the Association for a Better Long Island. Nevertheless, ABLI and other developers pressed Larocca to take their part in the Pine Barrens issue.

In addition, *Newsday's* Robert Johnson was actively supporting Wilbur Breslin's "Willy World" project and wanted LIA's support. Larocca says that given his goal of balancing the economy and the environment, "It was ironic that the first pressure on me came from the developers who created the problem in the first place." Larocca contends that he warned Breslin, a man he barely knew, and Johnson that he was absolutely convinced that they would lose the struggle because "any half-assed lawyer can tie you up again and again." An attorney himself, he recalled how when he served as New York State Commissioner of Transportation, "The state won battle after battle in court over the proposed Westway highway in Manhattan, only to lose the war to the activists."

Larocca vowed to maintain neutrality. He wanted to be in a position to bring the parties together at a propitious moment. He expressed hurt and annoyance at environmentalists who lumped him in with the developers, whose pressure he was regularly resisting within his organization. A few months after the Society's Appellate Division victory, Larocca decided the time for his intervention had come.

On a hot day that summer, he met with Bob McGrath, Mike Deering and me at the Wind Watch hotel in Hauppauge. Larocca wondered whether we were open to talks he might convene and whether we thought there was any chance of a negotiated settlement. We said yes. This was a watershed, because for years the developers had dismissed us as out-of-control environmental ideologues. They were now either willing to consider us as reasonable people or persuaded that we had, for the first time, the upper hand and, however wacko we might be, they should at least engage us in a forum other than a court of law. Larocca welcomed the role of peacemaker.

Thanks to Larocca's efforts, a meeting between the environmentalists and developers was scheduled to be held at the Long Island Association on July 28, 1992. We were playing for high stakes, and a major tenet of our strategy was to prepare fully. I acquired more than a dozen books on negotiating, development and real estate finance from the library and bookstore and holed up in the Shawangunk Mountains at the Mohonk Mountain House, another Pine Barrens area. For three days, I studied the books and reviewed scores of Society position papers. Mike Gerard would be there for legal representation, but I needed a clear objective and an understanding of how to negotiate. The future of Long Island hung in the balance. We were, after all, representing the environmental needs of everyone on Long Island and across the table would be some pretty shrewd businesspeople. We wanted to do right by our supporters and neighbors. Or maybe I just didn't want to blow it.

The basic premise, I concluded, was to know our objective going in, keep focused on it and negotiate from strength. I understood what environmentalists wanted but needed to understand what the developers did. That helped me decide what we had to offer our opponents, even as we pressed our own agenda. The individual developers were not really champions of real estate development—they were only concerned about their own projects. Their focus on their own development project allowed us to advance our broader "save land and water" campaign. We wanted to save Long Island. The public found no favor with more and more development. They supported controlled development with a focus on preservation.

We returned to the Island for the first-ever meeting between Wilbur Breslin and me. Both sides promoted their own positions, while voicing hope for compromise. The media was out in force. *Newsday* had previewed the showdown that morning in a story titled "Going Face-to-Face." It quoted Breslin as saying, "In taking care of the environment, you have to consider another endangered species, which is the Long Island woman and man, so they have the ability to pay taxes and purchase goods," Breslin said, "We want to convince Amper we have the ability to do both. *Newsday* quoted me as saying, "The developers are worried because they can't build, but we're worried because the Pine Barrens aren't permanently preserved, either, so maybe there's something for both sides." LaRocca, however, had the best quote in the article, "We're going to check their guns at the door and see what happens," he said.

I arrived at LIA headquarters in Commack in my Mazda Miata. Breslin showed up in a stretch limousine bearing the vanity license plate "Realty 1." He was huddled with one of his two attorneys, Armand D'Amato, brother of New York's long-time Republican United States Senator Alphonse D'Amato. When D'Amato walked away, I introduced myself to Breslin, though he obviously recognized the face. I had been to a recent environmental meeting at the Breslin Building at Hofstra University and complimented him on his philanthropic efforts. Neither of us said anything negative. The media snapped their pictures and were told to leave.

"The atmosphere was intense and distrustful," the Society's Michael Deering remembers. Everyone was very cautious, and first two hours of the three-hour session were spent agreeing on how the proceedings would be dealt with in public. It was clear that the first thing that the developers sought from the "War of the Woods" was how to handle the war of words. They wanted a press blackout, with no one talking until a settlement had been worked out or negotiations abandoned. Our advocacy for the public interest and my devotion to First Amendment free speech imperatives made that impossible. I would not shut out the press. Our first negotiation had produced a sensible compromise. We agreed to agree at the end of each meeting how each side would characterize the sessions.

In attendance were Larocca, his second-in-command Mitchell Pally, Charles Mancini, Wilbur Breslin and his lawyers Herb Balin and Armand D'Amato, public relations consultant Howard Blankman and technical consultant Vincent Donnelly of the engineering firm Nelson and Pope. The Society fielded its president Michael Deering, Jennifer Miller, attorneys Michael Gerard and Lawrence Ceriello, and me. The Society made the demand for a cumulative environmental assessment non-negotiable, so before we adjourned the first session, the developers, led by Breslin, agreed to consider conducting and paying for such a study, as long as the scope and duration of it were agreed upon. In exchange, the developers also wanted some projects to move ahead concurrently. We balked at the last demand but agreed to re-visit the matter. To be honest, we never intended for any projects to proceed. With us, it was all or nothing.

At the next meeting, the parties agreed to the collective environmental review we wanted and proposed technical meetings with ecologists to define the extent and nature of the study. This demonstrated that we were making progress and that the developers at least were listening for the first time. I had played a dominant role in the first meeting, so I deferred in the second. Deering suggested mechanisms and Gerard established our legal position. I remained silent. At the end of the meeting, Larocca quipped, "This may be the first time any of us have ever attended a meeting at which Dick Amper didn't say anything with which we disagreed." Actually, Larocca was a very funny guy.

The technical meetings were held at Armand D'Amato's law office. Breslin brought his consultants, Donnelly and Ronald Abrams of Dru Associates. We sent Sarah Meyland on hydrology, John Turner, Ray Corwin and no less than John Cryan on biology. As usual, they had done their homework.

In the time between the technical meetings, we set out to do the impossible: to create the scoping document—the list of goals, deliverables, tasks, costs and deadlines—for the entire Cumulative Environmental Impact Statement. We were convinced that if we could lay out a solid outline of what the impact statement should include, we would again be negotiating from our position, and the burden of the opposition would be to prove our position incorrect. Louise Harrison, the environmentalist who worked at the county health department, had helped us before. Now, she threw herself heart and soul into her contribution to history.

Night and day we worked to bang out a massive document, comprehensive and environmentally defensible. Louise was difficult, in the way environmentalists can be. She split hairs and complained about the long-hours and pressure. She and I fought endlessly when her science and my common sense conflicted. I even resorted to adopting positions that were the opposite of what I really thought. Louise would automatically disagree, taking the position I really believed, and I would let her win. It worked. As difficult as the marathon was and as contentious as the experience, Louise produced a stellar document that was at once reflective of the developers' position but environmentally sound and irrefutable.

Ron Abrams led the assault on our document. Trained by years of preparing Environmental Impact Statements for developers that basically said whatever the developers wanted, minimizing environmental impacts and encouraging their projects, Abrams missed the point of this exercise. Of course, the purpose was to reach agreement on the scope of the environmental study. Instead, with a pompous attitude, Abrams bitched and complained about everything, however minor. Abrams had two problems. He seemed either to know only how to write building-oriented impact statements or only how to throw up roadblocks and didn't understand that the group was actually trying to reach agreement. You could tell that Breslin's representatives were not impressed.

Finally, in an effort to make him completely lose it, I deliberately began misstating his name. For "Ron," I substituted "Rob." An admittedly cheesy gimmick, it ultimately accomplished its intended goal. "There's no need for that kind of analysis," he stood up and screamed, "And my Goddam name is Ron!" Breslin's team thanked him and excused him. Then we all got back to work.

Apparently dissatisfied with Larocca's even-handedness during negotiations, in advance of the final meeting, at least one lawyer representing the developers admonished him to butt out of the negotiations. "It's none of your affair," Larocca was told. "We get paid to do this stuff."

Despite our having largely agreed on a framework for a preservation and development plan, the negotiations hit a snag. We were insisting that the agreement be codified in state law, binding on all parties. This would require the State Legislature to write and pass a bill that both permanently preserved land and allowed reasonable development. That was asking a lot, to say the least but it was essential to Pine Barrens preservation. This shouldn't have been news to the developers— we'd been saying it all along. The developers refused. "There's no way we're going to bet the future of our industry on the improbable passage in one session of an Act of the New York State Legislature," Breslin insisted, "It's just not realistic."

He had a point. Was the famously dysfunctional New York State Legislature actually going to do something? But we had already thought this through and had figured it out.

"Wait a minute," I said. "If environmentalists and developers agree on the matter, surely the elected officials will be forced to pen the legislation required. The Legislature can't say 'No' to all of us." Complete silence. They didn't get it. For all their wheeling and dealing with politicians, they couldn't see that of course the Legislature would pass a bill if everyone agreed to it. It wouldn't even require a bribe. I looked around the room incredulously and saw the negotiations collapse before my eyes.

We were terribly disappointed at all the wasted effort, shocked by the position that state legislation was hopeless, yet hopeful that the Court of Appeals could still affirm the decision of the Appellate Division. We abandoned settlement talks reluctantly, convinced that we could not accept a settlement based only on the promises of the developers, absent the force of law.

The developers and Larocca mischaracterized the breakdown. Breslin said, "Richard Amper has really shown his hand and wants to set himself up as the czar of the Pine Barrens." Larocca told the press that negotiations had failed "because the Pine Barrens Society kept escalating its demands." He later apologized, saying that *Newsday* reporter Dan Fagin had overstated his position, and that as a result of the Society's tough negotiating position, he felt we needed "a spritzing." In fact, by this time there were so many disparate developers in the room that agreement on anything seemed impossible. Some long-time builders resented Johnny-come-lately Breslin and the dominant role he was playing, and others were either convinced they would win at the high court or that prompt legislation really wasn't possible.

Six days later, we were in Albany at New York State's highest court, the Court of Appeals. We chartered a bus for our friends and were ready for oral arguments on October 20. Bob McGrath and Nina Leonhardt represented the Society's Board. Carolyn Zenk of Group for the South Fork and Neal Lewis of Neighborhood Network were joined by Adriana Brako, Jennifer Miller, Michael Deering, Ray Corwin and his companion Mindy Block and others as we journeyed to our date with history.

When we arrived, we were greeted by a News 12 satellite truck parked outside the Court of Appeals waiting to beam the proceedings back to Long Island on the part of Patti Ann Browne. "This is it," McGrath said as he alighted from the bus. "Our ultimate 'day in court,'" said Deering.

Judgment Day

"It's not over 'til it's over."—Yogi Berra

The Court of Appeals chamber exudes a sense of history and moment. Fine oil portraits of the chief judges adorn the walls, and the room contains a marble fireplace large enough to walk into.

It had taken almost three years to reach this place of decision. Desmond Ryan, Executive Director of the big builder's lobby, the Association for a Better Long Island, said flatly, "This is a lawsuit that will determine the future course and direction of Long Island's economy. This is all the marbles."

We had edited and re-edited the Society's brief and held mock oral argument sessions with some of our appellate counsels' associates. Michael Gerard and Philip Weinberg had done their homework. Their arguments supporting the need for a cumulative environmental assessment were based on previous court rulings. Gerard had designed a chart-like argument, pointing out the circumstances where the courts had required cumulative impact consideration and those where they had not. He argued that our case squarely fit circumstances mirroring those where consideration of cumulative impacts had been found necessary.

Leon Lazer, representing Breslin, made most of the arguments for the government, too. He said that the environmental review would be a de facto moratorium on significant development activity on Long Island, was not required by law and was simply impractical, with devastating economic implications.

We listened intently to the questions posed by the seven judges, for clues as to which way they were leaning. Chief Judge Sol Wachtler provided the first hint. "Mr. Lazer," he began "it seems very clear that under specifically Article 55 of the Environmental Conservation Law, they [the drafters of the State Environmental Quality Review Act] thought it necessary to have some kind of cumulative impact analysis. Do you think that the functionally-unrelated projects should be able to go their own way despite the fact that they would have an impact cumulatively on this very sensitive area?" I wanted to cheer. We were off to a good start. But Lazer and other attorneys representing the bad guys were swift to discount the requirement for a cumulative impact assessment of the 234 projects pending in the Pine Barrens.

The justices created what lawyers term "a hot bench," meaning they asked all of the attorneys tough questions, When the County Attorney Robert Cabble appeared, Wachtler didn't even give him a chance to begin. He boomed, "So, why doesn't the county undertake to do this study? What a magnificent gesture that would be." Cabble averred that the county was neither required to do it, nor had the resources.

We hung on every word. Oral arguments lasted an hour with judges addressing concern about protecting drinking water and "balancing" economic concerns "against" environmental ones. Gerard's strategy was to compare our case to others where courts required consideration of cumulative impacts and contrast it with those that did not. Alas, the judges interrupted him and posed an endless stream of questions as to who would do the study and how it would ultimately impact project approval. So, Gerard never got the opportunity to compare this case with those requiring a cumulative impact. Still, his reasoned responses reflected a deep understanding of state environmental law and plenty of preparation for oral arguments, so when we left the courtroom, our team was satisfied with Gerard's performance and cautiously optimistic that our side would prevail.

Standing in front of the Court of Appeals, Patti Ann Browne reported for News 12: "Now that the judges have heard the arguments and read the briefs, they'll take about a month before reaching a decision that could have wide-ranging implications for Long Island, for years to come."

We piled back on the bus and spent the five-hour return trip to Long Island eating, drinking and sharing observations. The longer we talked and the more we drank, the more confident we were that we'd win the case.

Not yet. There was to be one, final bizarre event before the Court of Appeals rendered its historic decision. Robin and I decided this was the best time to get away for a much-needed vacation. We traveled to the island of Anguilla in the Caribbean in November, 1992. Since the beginning of the war, we had restricted our travel to places where communication was instant and dependable. Jennifer kept me informed about anything I needed to know, including a fax of a *Newsday* bombshell, just two weeks after our day in court.

We were expecting news from the Court and instead we got a weird scandal. "Wachtler Arrested," the front-page headline blared. The sub-head: "State's Chief Judge is Accused of Harassing Ex-Lover." Kevin McCoy wrote the story: "Sol Wachtler, New York's influential chief judge and a powerhouse in state politics for more than two decades, was arraigned last night on a federal conspiracy charge that he harassed his ex-lover, tried to extort money from her and threatened her 14-year-old daughter." The story described Wachtler as a married multimillionaire, obsessed with a socially prominent political woman who was later identified as Joy Silverman, a Republican fundraiser as well. Wachtler resigned from the bench, pleaded guilty to charges and served 13 of a 15-month sentence.

Incredibly, the Pine Barrens case was the last one he ever heard. To this day, it seems impossible to believe that the Court of Appeals was not influenced in any way by the events surrounding Wachtler. Historically, the high Court shunned institutional publicity of any kind. A few lawyers suggested that the Court's decision might have been influenced by the Wachtler scandal. We didn't agree.

The Court announced its decision on November 24, 1992. I was in bed with a 103-degree fever when Robin awakened me. She said Mike Gerard was on the phone. We had received what he termed "an adverse ruling."
"We lost?" I abbreviated.

Gerard was deeply disappointed; I was crushed. He reviewed the opinion with me, describing the Court's clear understanding of the importance of the issue and even our arguments, while rejecting a requirement that cumulative impacts must be considered. The unanimous ruling concluded that there was, indeed, a "policy" regarding the Pine Barrens, but not a "plan" grounded in statute. The Court said only the State Legislature could order a preservation plan.

I interrupted the conversation to give Jennifer an assignment. The decision was coming in on the fax machine. I asked her to find and highlight all of the parts that were favorable to us. The press would be on us in minutes and I wanted to put the best blush on the disaster.

We had long understood that even if we won, the study was simply a means to an end; that a preservation plan, codified in law was the ultimate goal. A court victory would have compelled that process, but we were prepared to shift the battle to the State Legislature immediately, so we were looking for any language in the opinion that could be used to support our next move. It was there.

The ruling came in. Unanimous against us. This was devastating. How could they reach this decision? I'm thinking, what are we going to do? How am I going to spin this for the press? More important, what can we do in the face of this ruling to save the Pine Barrens? So, we're reading the opinion and I'm thinking, "We need to hang this on the politicians who refused to consider legislation. Part of the Court's decision admonishes government to solve the conflict legislatively. Let's take this issue directly to the State Legislature where the laws are supposed to be made."

In fact, the language of the Court decision specifically pointed that way. It said, "The cumulative impact assessment that petitioners envision would be, in essence, a vehicle for the many involved `lead agencies' to engage in comprehensive and long-range planning for the development of this vast area of land which has been designated for special protection...[S]uch an exhaustive and thorough approach to evaluating projects affecting this region is unquestionably desirable and, indeed, may well be essential to its preservation," the Court opined, but they would not order it. Instead, they gave us entree to the next phase of the Pine Barrens Preservation Initiative: "The solution must be devised by the Legislature, which is responsible for crafting sensible deadlines and mandate prompt action by the designated planning bodies to address this matter of urgent public concern," the decision said.

And, in a parting shot to the past efforts of the towns, the county, and especially Lee Koppelman, the Court concluded, "There currently exists no legislatively-prescribed mechanism for agencies to pool their information or share their respective decision-making prerogatives. The existing system of land use planning in the region is plainly not equal to the massive undertaking that effective long-range planning would require." When Patti Ann Browne filed her satellite feed that night, she added, "There is a centralized agency, the Long Island Regional Planning Board. The Court decision says the Planning Board has been slow in preparing a comprehensive management plan for the region." Koppelman was quoted as saying, "The Court's comments are totally fallacious and erroneous." The News 12 story concluded, "Although this round in the fight clearly went to the developers, the environmentalists insist that they've lost the battle, not the war. They say the only change is that the battleground has shifted from the court rooms to the halls of the Legislature."

I thought, "Exactly. The path to resolution of the Pine Barrens issue is the New York State Legislature. Even the Court agrees with that."

When courts decide matters of law limiting the reach of a statute, they frequently defer responsibility to the legislative branch, but it is rarely a requirement for action. In a television report on WCBS-TV, Channel 2, Lisa Castleman concluded simply, "The Legislature has no obligation to take any action at all." Still, we spun the decision to say that the Court had "admonished" the Legislature to act, so maybe the Court decision will lead us to the long-sought objective.

When I got off the phone, I called my brother. He shared our shock. What's more, he disagreed with our strategy, at least for today. "This is a disaster," he said. "Your credibility depends on your treating it as such. People don't understand your indefatigable capacity to charge ahead despite adversity. They won't accept that this is just a bump in the road." He advised that the ruling be described as the disaster that it was and that I demonstrate an attitude of "shock and dismay." "It may not be the end of the world for you, but at least it's a period of mourning," he concluded. He was right. By describing the decision as the disaster it was, it would goad the public to pressure the Legislature to fix it.

Next, I called the Board Members. Before I could complete the calls, the press began their inquiries. Slowly, the house began filling up with Board Members, volunteers, and reporters. It felt like a wake.

The Society's president, Bob McGrath arrived first. He was distraught. I warned Jennifer and Robin to keep him away from the press. The Society had a policy that nobody besides me talked to reporters. But, given his mood, he might break that rule and say almost anything. He did. Sometime during hours of interviews that endless day, Bob escaped from the back office and was immediately accosted by one of three *Newsday* reporters assigned to cover the big story. When we discovered this, we went after him. The next day, the President of the Long Island Pine Barrens Society was quoted as having said that the loss of the court decision was worse than the recent death of his father! Just the kind of comment we were trying to avoid.

Even as Jennifer began working language of the Court of Appeals decision into a white paper proposing a legislative solution, I began the public eulogies. I told the *Times,* "It's a dark day for the drinking water needs of 2.7 million Long Islanders. The Court is saying we have no laws to protect the Pine Barrens, however important they are. It's an environmental disaster of the highest order of magnitude."

At the same time, Breslin was telling *Newsday* he was "delighted." "This is not the ultimate conclusion to all our problems, but I believe it's the biggest hurdle we had to go over."

Schwenk was more conciliatory. He told the *Times*, "Now we are bringing some balance into the picture. Now we and the environmental community can get together and do some things that are good for all concerned." _

As the media deadlines passed, we ruminated over the decision, speculating on what we might have done differently. Mike Gerard minimized the effects of the Wachtler affair, saying it was increasingly clear that the Court of Appeals was not eager to expand the implications of the State Environmental Quality Review Act. Leon Lazer later told his law students and others that his strategy to largely avoid the environmental arguments, focusing instead on economic implications, had won the day.

Cryan was blunter. "The judges just chickened out. They overruled themselves and went back on the Albany Pine Bush decision for fear that this would spread to other ecological areas," he said.

The conversation then returned to the legislative strategy and how we could still turn defeat into victory. Contrary to press accounts that appeared immediately after the decision predicting a dubious strategy to pursue reform of the cumulative impacts provisions of state environmental law, we intended to go just where we would have gone had we won the case. The court opinion had said the Legislature must fashion a preservation plan, and that is precisely what we would seek. The lawmakers were unlikely to do what the court would not—mandate a cumulative impact analysis—but it might create the preservation plan the court recommended. So, my first instinct for the initial quote for the media turned out to be the strategy for the next phase of the Pine Barrens war.

How hopeful was I that the State Legislature would give us the needed bill? It didn't matter how likely—it was the only way.

A couple of cars containing raucous occupants roared past the house late in the evening yelling obscenities. Joe Colao and Vinny Scandole camped out for most of the night "to ensure peace and tranquility," as Vinny put it.

After the day we lost our legal case at New York's highest court, we went to bed beaten and bruised but not the least bit deterred, and maybe even more determined.

Turning Point

At times history and fate meet at a single time in a single place
to shape a turning point in man's unending search for freedom." – Lyndon B. Johnson

All right, publicly we were in a period of mourning. It wasn't difficult to be. Headlines covered *Newsday*'s whole front page. "A Boost for the Builders" it proclaimed in 72-point type. "Court Removes Barrier for Construction Projects," the sub-head continued, "Environmentalists Stunned." The lead story, "A Victory to Build On," featured pictures of an ecstatic Breslin and a disconsolate Amper.

There were follow-up stories for days. Phone calls came in from around the country inquiring about the decision. Letters to the Editor poured into *Newsday*, none of them from the Pine Barrens Society, decrying the decision and calling for new protection for water and habitat. I wasn't the least bit surprised. Throughout the campaign, complete strangers would stop me in the supermarket and praise the Society's work. Add to this, voter approval of funding for preservation ran as high as 84% so there was no question that the Society enjoyed broad support.

The Phone Voices returned. Some were angry, "How could the court do this?" Some were appreciative, "I just wanted to express my thanks for your great effort." Some were consoling, "You couldn't have done more."

Then came the money. For weeks, thousands of dollars in unsolicited donations poured in, some with handwritten notes saying, "I'm sure you'll find another way to beat the f-ing developers." Fundraising had been a constant struggle, and here we had done nothing but lose the lawsuit, yet contributions were pouring in.

Fortunately, we were already segueing into the inevitable legislative phase. The Pine Barrens Society met the week after the Court of Appeals decision. Strategically, we knew we had to demonstrate that despite the devastating defeat, the war was not over. We decided to challenge in court the next major Pine Barrens project approval on site-specific grounds and procedures. Brookhaven could be counted on to make errors in its project review process, giving us grounds for litigation.

Here was another case where fortuitous coincidence or divine intervention won the day. The December Brookhaven Planning Board docket indeed had a major project in the Pine Barrens. Its sponsor was none other than Wilbur Breslin. "If we can't challenge these projects collectively as we think we should, we'll have to challenge them one at a time," we said in our press release. This approach is called, "Not quitting!"

The developers winced. Later Schwenk admitted, "Even when the developers got on a winning streak, I knew that Dick would hang in there and not give up one bit, and that's just what he did."

He said that he and Charles Mancini both recognized immediately that they had won the battle but not the war, and that they could expect plenty more from the Long Island Pine Barrens Society.

But they also pressed their advantage. They focused attention on the Special Groundwater Protection Area Plan produced by Koppelman's Regional Planning Board. The non-binding document went too far, builders said, in advising strictly-controlled development in the Pine Barrens and the Island's eight other state-designated SGPAs. We did not object to the criticism, because, of course, the study report was likely to collect dust and not protect drinking water at all. D.E.C. Commissioner Thomas Jorling understood the study's shortcomings, delaying its acceptance until the dust from the lawsuit decision settled.

At the same time, we began taking the steps to ready the state legislature for a mammoth lobbying effort to make Pine Barrens and drinking water protection the law of the state. We thought it would be useful to discuss our plans with our friends in the legislature—people like Assembly members Englebright and DiNapoli and State Senator Ken LaValle.
On December 3, *Newsday* headlined, "Activists Regroup after Suit Dismissal." With a little help from us, reporter Dan Fagin laid out the options we had adopted for all to see: "Without the lawsuit, environmental and civic groups now face the daunting choice of either trying to convince the Legislature to change state law to mandate an environmental review or trying to fight development proposals on a case-by-case basis."

On December 5, the Long Island Progressive Coalition, an activist group, began a two-day environmental conference which they had been planning long before the court decision. It won larger press attention than such a meeting would ordinarily, because it was the first gathering of the civic community since the court loss. The Regional Plan Association's Robert Yaro introduced himself to me. "Congratulations on your lawsuit," he said. We'd heard many reactions to the court decision but never one like this. "It's been my experience," he went on, "that matters this large are never resolved without a full-blown crisis," he explained. "The Court of Appeals decision now creates the circumstances under which the necessary legislative solution can be sought." At last, somebody besides the Society understood our commitment to pressing on.

Newsday's Johnson pulled a fast one, using an Op-Ed page column to advocate a "Water Summit," a farcical assemblage of pro-development "experts" who would say there was no threat to drinking water on Long Island, preempting legislative remedy. Most every environmental group boycotted the event. Some demonstrated in front of the conference, held at the Stony Brook University. They wore white hats to suggest the nature of the forces on the other side of the debate. Of course, Lee Koppelman happily participated in the conference charade. Years later, the magnitude of contamination of Long Island's groundwater became a multi-billion-dollar clean-up challenge. But the water beneath the Pine Barrens was and is crystal clear.

On December 15 the D.E.C.'s Jorling surprised us by rejecting the SGPA plan. He said it did not go far enough in protecting drinking water. The 208 Study that led to the SGPA Plan was useful inasmuch as it explained the hydrogeology of Long Island as never before, but it was toothless. In returning the study report, Jorling even suggested that the revised document consider assembling Pine Barrens parcels to create a preserve. This went way beyond anything we expected him to say. Environmentalists cheered. The $300,000 ruse—Koppelman's plan—had been rejected, but Koppelman didn't cry for very long. The same day, Brookhaven Town hired him for $175,000 to serve as a special "Planning Czar," as *Newsday* described it. Of course, editorially, *Newsday* hailed the appointment, again calling Koppelman "the Dean of Long Island planners" and describing opponents as opponents, "either parochial, not-in-my-backyard civic groups" or "extreme environmentalists."

Newsday deliberately and repeatedly misused the term "NIMBY." (Not In My Back Yard). A NIMBY attitude or approach involves opposition to a worthwhile project (the siting of a drug treatment facility or half-way house, say.) Neighbors don't fault the facility, but don't want it near them. Here, preservationists were trying to protect Long Island's drinking water recharge area— often miles and miles from their backyards.

The paper also picked up on the developers' charge that supporters of Pine Barrens preservation were advocates of "no growth." This was easy to disprove. More than a million Long Islanders supported Pine Barrens protection; if they were all indifferent to the economy, how was it that polls showed "the economy" as Long Islanders' Number One concern?

The dawn of 1993 saw us in private talks with elected officials at the town, county and state levels. We received cordial, if chilly, responses to our first inquiries about the prospect of winning legislation to protect the Pine Barrens. We saw no reason to press for a law requiring cumulative impact consideration in the Pine Barrens when the Court had suggested the need for a comprehensive preservation plan.

Our cumulative impact consideration was a legal strategy, aimed at boxing the developers into a corner. The Court of Appeals had suggested the need for a comprehensive plan. With this new strategy, we were going for it all.

Deering, Miller and I took trips to visit and learn from the successful Pine Barrens initiatives in New Jersey and Massachusetts. We spent a whole day with Terrence Moore, who had helped lead the effort to preserve the New Jersey Pinelands and then stayed on to run the New Jersey Pinelands Commission. It was obvious that the Pinelands' concept of creating zones for preservation and others for development would have significant applicability on Long Island. We spent January 15 and 16, 1993 on Cape Cod to learn how Armando Carbonell had created the Cape Cod Commission to manage development in the sensitive Pine Barrens watershed there. The establishment of quantifiable standards for development on Cape Cod was to help shape the ultimate Pine Barrens Plan.

On January 28, I met Jim Larocca at the Fox Hollow Restaurant in Woodbury. We discussed what it would take to win buy-in from the developers for state legislation in this session. We had prepared a slick presentation summarizing the need and benefits, comparing and contrasting the New Jersey and Cape Cod preservation scenarios, which he quickly pushed aside. Remembering his days representing Governor Hugh Carey and the Governor's disdain for "folders and stuff," Larocca suggested producing a map showing the area to be preserved and the area where development could occur. "Make it simple and visual," he said.

He underestimated the brilliance of the idea. In fact, most of the land targeted for preservation was in large, contiguous, undeveloped tracts, while most of the proposed building projects lay outside this ecologically important area, near existing infrastructure. We realized that developers, seeing the map, would immediately look for their own projects, and, finding them outside of the no-build zone, would not only approve the map, but browbeat their counterparts with property in the preservation core not to be spoilsports. "The Builders Institute was a loosely-knit group," Schwenk observed. "The members were more concerned with their own current project than in the interest of the industry as a whole."

On Saturday, February 6, the Society assembled its most respected ecologists at a secluded, rustic location and piled the fireplace high with logs as a huge winter storm dumped tons of snow on the scene. We painstakingly mapped what would become a 53,000-acre Core Preservation Area, where development would be barred forever and a 47,000-acre Compatible Growth Area, where development would be permitted under specific provisions. I charged the team with creating a scientifically justifiable map, understanding that its acceptance would be based on its perceived legitimacy. "Get what we need, but don't get piggy," I advised. The marathon session lasted all day and into the night. The result was a masterpiece—a plan based on solid reasons and science that would be hard for the builders to challenge.

Lee Koppelman later charged that the original map was altered to exclude the mall portion of Wilbur Breslin's 2,100-acre "Willy World" proposal, but it was not. To Larocca's credit, among those with whom he shared the map, including the Senate and Assembly sponsors of the Pine Barrens legislation, nobody altered the map for anyone, including the Boy Scouts of America, which wanted their Pine Barrens holdings excluded from the Core. Much of Breslin's 2,100 acres, including hundreds of acres at the headwaters of the Peconic River, were included in the Core Preservation Area over his heated objection.

For a time, Marilyn England of the Open Space Council complained that the Breslin mall site was left out of the preservation area, not so much by map modification but by political considerations on the part of the Society's map makers. I was there. The ecologists viewed the 150-acre mall site as being wedged between two already developed parcels -- a developed racetrack on the west and Brookhaven National Laboratory's (BNL) sprawling campus to the east. While the preservationists fought Breslin for his more sensitive Pine Barrens holdings right up to the start of the state legislature's voting on the ultimate legislation, they couldn't justify the mall site and the already developed BNL site for inclusion in the preservation from the outset. The fact is, that except to translate the map into precise metes and bounds for inclusion in the Pine Barrens Protection Act itself, the Pine Barrens map was never altered from the day it first was drawn.

On February 7, Jennifer Miller colored in what had already become known as "the Larocca Map" on my living room floor. Consistent with Larocca's strategy of showing proposed preservation and development visually, he had circulated it to major developers including Breslin, Mancini and Schwenk. He also showed it to the Department of Environmental Conservation and the LIA leadership. Breslin pressed the LIA to demand boundary changes that would exclude his holdings from the Core, but Larocca concluded that as long as the legislative sponsors (Englebright, DiNapoli and LaValle) were hanging tough, there was no reason for him to step between the combatants. Still, Breslin's efforts to extract all of his holdings from the core represented one of the most contentious battles in the negotiations and one that continued right down to the eve of the Legislature's approval vote.

As February neared the end, the feedback we were getting from Albany suggested that we were likely to see no courageous leadership, absent some formal coming together of the competing interests. Great Neck Assemblyman Tom DiNapoli observed that "the Legislature is certainly not known for stepping into controversial topics." He suggested that obtaining a consensus among the warring parties would have to precede legislation. It was clear that legislation wasn't going to happen unless the two sides hammered out an agreement and came up with a finished plan. Then and only then would the Legislature be happy to rescue Long Island's environment.

To accomplish this, we needed an extraordinary event that would point out to everyone the benefits of a plan that would preserve the Pine Barrens and protect drinking water, even as it expedited the approval of development projects in areas that could sustain them. A major conference would establish how Long Island would get clean water and open space and the developers would see an end to litigation and uncertainty. A land use plan for the Pine Barrens would simultaneously preserve the Island's greatest natural treasure and could reduce a six-year-long approval process for a major development project to less than a year, in some cases.

Jennifer understood well the importance of the conference. Success would propel us toward the elusive goal of Pine Barrens preservation. A defeat would delay a legislative solution for at least a year—a year the Society could not have financially survived. She described the symposium she helped produce as "almost as big a dream as the dream of preservation itself." It was going to be the biggest play of the game!

We began designing an event so important that even antagonists would feel obliged to participate. We wanted an event so big—so prestigious—that anyone who was anyone on Long Island would have to appear there. Rather than to portray a fanciful vision of what Long Island could be if only we brought imagination to the fore, we created a series of presentations on successful Pine Barrens preservation efforts at Cape Cod and the New Jersey Pinelands. Then we went to Larocca and LoGrande and asked them to encourage the coming-together of former combatants to work out a preservation and development plan. They reacted favorably. That's what we needed to give the event credibility with the business community and government. We knew that these leaders had to embrace it, or at least attend it.

Finally, the event was to include the Suffolk County Executive, the three Supervisors of the Pine Barrens towns, a representative of the environmental community (guess who), and Bob Weiboldt, Executive Director of the New York State Builders Association. These people would all speak, thus implicitly endorsing the preservation idea.

Presenters included John Bierwirth and Sara Davison from The Nature Conservancy, Larocca, Terrence Moore, from the New Jersey Pine Barrens Commission, Armando Carbonell from the Cape Cod Commission, David Sampson from the Hudson River Valley Greenways Council, and Bob Yaro from the Regional Plan Association. LoGrande was emcee. We knew that what would make this conference work would be getting all these people to show up and speak their minds. These leaders brought credibility to the event to the point that no one wanted to be left out.

To ensure that we emerged with a positive result from the one-day event, we needed a name for the symposium in the form of a challenge: "Why Can't Long Island?" We used the provocative question in a video presentation that kicked-off the program, explained on camera by WPIX-TV correspondent Drew Scott. He said, "With a new commitment to conciliation and accommodation, Long Island leaders are working with planners who have successfully put together land use strategies that protect sensitive areas, while encouraging needed development. Long Islanders are asking, 'If others can preserve their special places, why can't Long Island?'" We calculated that even the dumbest developer could not answer, "Because we're too greedy, too stupid or too perverse." The rhetorical question could be answered only one way: "Long Island can!"

The concept was easy, the execution overwhelming. All of us understood the importance of the event to our ambitious strategy, without appreciating the enormity of the undertaking. The joke goes that the way you can tell a regular environmental conference from a big environmental conference is that a big environmental conference has those pleated "modesty drapes" around the tables. This alone wouldn't do.

To be credible, this conference had to have the look, feel and promotion of a meeting of business leaders, not of tree-huggers. It had to be impressive in its appearance, in its list of attendees, in its content and in its coverage. We had to change the whole dynamic of the preservation effort from fighting about *whether* it was going to happen to engaging in a process that *needed* to happen and was *going to* happen—the creation of state Pine Barrens legislation. We had a real challenge on our hands.

We needed a location. A school, library or government office wouldn't do. It had to be held in a hotel. Business types love hotels. They're used to hotels. Hotels are credible. A hotel it must be. We chose the Radisson Plaza in Melville because its central location allowed the business community and the press convenient access. Next, the set, audio-visuals and overall content needed to be much slicker than even the business community and politicians were used to.

We needed sponsors. This sucker was going to be expensive. And besides, having sponsors is a big-business thing to do. The room rental, audio-visuals, speaker transportation fees and accommodations all were going to cost money. And we couldn't forget the Danish. WNBC-TV might again send reporter Roger Stern, and we remembered how he judged a public presentation.

We reached out to environmental groups, and they responded. Group for the South Fork, Open Space Council, Cornell Cooperative Extension and Sierra Club quickly signed on as sponsors. Given the skepticism and history of conflict, especially within the development community and government, getting co-sponsors was no easy trick. Repeatedly, prospects required sponsorship by another similar group before they would commit. We had to recruit support, one organization at a time, returning to the reluctant later, to point out the growing support for the conference. Kevin McDonald of Group for the South Fork had good relationships with Long Island University, North Fork Bank and the Suffolk County Water Authority. The Health and Welfare Council also signed on to the "Why Can't Long Island?" conference. In all, we brought in about $10,000, not a lot for a conference of this magnitude and importance. The Society had to make up the difference, and we needed a lot of volunteer help.

The Long Island Community Foundation, a cautious group, initially declined to sponsor the event, unsure of its fairness and objectivity, they said in a letter. We responded that they should send a monitor to the proceedings and decide whether to pay after the event. Instead, they changed their mind and would make that determination in advance. They indeed became a sponsor. They decided they should be part of the conference and didn't want to be left out, and we developed an ongoing relationship with the foundation. Later, we also developed a relationship with the Long Island-based Rauch Foundation that generously supported the Society for 30 years, dramatically advancing preservation in the Pine Barrens and beyond. It was positively exhilarating.

To set the stage, we needed a compelling but non-controversial video that would say, in images and language, something that everybody could subscribe to—exactly what this symposium was about. We produced a broadcast-quality, five-and-a-half-minute video comprised of three elements. First, we interviewed students in Mrs. Hommel's fourth grade class in Shoreham, in which individual children spoke about how nice it would be if the Pine Barrens were protected for various reasons, including drinking water protection, animal habitat, recreation and so forth. Of course, their answers were cut to an instrumental version of the Beach Boys' classic, "Wouldn't It Be Nice." Drew Scott followed with a brief recitation of the history and challenge, punctuated by expressions of support from a builder, an environmentalist and a civic leader. The presentation concluded with a chorus of adorable fourth grade children singing a customized vocal version of "Wouldn't It Be Nice":

> *Wouldn't it be nice to save the Barrens,*
> *Keep a part of Suffolk nice and green?*
> *Way out on the East End of Long Island*
> *It's the nicest place you've ever seen.*

Oh, come on there's really nothing to it;
Say, why can't Long Island do it?
Wouldn't it be nice?
Let's protect our pure, fresh drinking water,
Let's preserve the animals and trees.
We can build some stores and build some houses
Yet take care of all the birds and bees.
Oh, come on there's really nothing to it;
Say, why can't Long Island do it?
Wouldn't it be nice?

The bridge went:

If environmentalists and builders were to find a plan,
The folks who live here on Long Island would give you a hand.
Then we would be happy!
Long Islanders building a better tomorrow.

The piece concluded with:

Oh, come on there's really nothing to it;
Say, why can't Long Island do it?
Let's get to it.
Wouldn't it be nice?

We didn't finish editing the piece until Easter Sunday night, just two days before the conference.

The date and thus the tight deadline were dictated by the machinations of the New York State Legislature. Faced with a legal deadline of April 1 to adopt a state budget—a requirement at the time, universally honored in the breach—we knew that by mid-April the Legislature could be turning to its non-budget agenda. If the conference was to count for anything, we had to be ready to move ahead by then. We picked April 13.

We obtained the generous participation of Armando Carbonell, whose Cape Cod Commission had brought regional planning to the Cape, and Terrence Moore, whose New Jersey Pinelands Commission had oversight across 52 municipalities, covering a million acres. They were key. Larocca and LoGrande agreed to be the key Long Island speakers, and local government officials agreed to sit on a panel responding to the program.

But the builders balked. Buzz Schwenk said publicly that he wasn't about to participate in anything in which he would be "used as cannon fodder." That was completely unreasonable. LoGrande and others appealed to Schwenk for reason, and as the list of prominent attendees grew, so did the pressure to relent. Finally, I called Buzz to ask if he would agree to be included in the video to represent the builder's attitude and he rose to the occasion, as he would time and again in the future. In the video, he said that the builders would gladly support a plan that was fair both to environmentalists and to developers.

158

Other developers and businesspeople also greeted the event suspiciously, and for good cause. We had blown up previous, developer-led forums, including the recent, so-called "Water Summit." They also didn't want to contribute to "another Pine Barrens Society P.R. show," as developer Charles Mancini put it.

We booked professional photographers and videographers and obtained risers to serve as camera locations at the back of the room, with remote audio pick-ups to avoid the distracting aesthetic distance which would have resulted if we had placed the media between the presenters and the audience. We carefully crafted a presentation program that disarmed the skeptical at the outset, then maintained fairness and balance among presenters and responders and concluded with a positive pitch for harmony and constructive engagement for Long Island's sake. This conclusively demonstrated that the Pine Barrens Society could be fair-minded to all parties.

Still, something was missing. It wasn't grand enough. It needed ... a set! Of course, that was it. Something big, impressive, theatrical ... something environmentalists couldn't be expected to think of, let alone produce.

My college roommate, Pete Devens, the general behind the successful ¼-cent referendum, was in the wrong place at the wrong time. By this time, we had moved to a marginal but donated office in Riverhead, which we affectionately called "the hovel." Pete stopped by one day to ask if I had time for lunch. One would have thought he'd have learned by now. Jennifer and I had only just now realized this missing piece. And here was Pete.

"You're supposed to be the engineering mind, aren't you?" Jennifer asked. "How do we build a set?"

"What kind of set?" Pete asked.

"A big set, a beautiful set, an impressive set with a screen for our video built in and a huge version of the newly-created "Why Can't Long Island?" logo displayed."

"Just how big do you have in mind?"

"Really big," she responded. "Tall enough to block off any view of the back end of the room." We didn't know how many people would show up and wanted to be able to end the depth of the room at any point to assure a "full house" and wide enough to hold a raised dais, featuring a podium and seating for six to eight panelists at tables.

"Holy shit!" Pete exclaimed as he began sketching the thing. "You gotta figure that means about 14 feet high and 28 feet wide!"

"Yeah, and it's got to be portable," I jumped in.

"Uh, what do you mean portable?"

"We have to be able to take the set there and set it up in the morning because we can't access the room the night before. And we have to be able to strike it, move it and set it up again in a television studio in Floral Park where we'll be taping two 30-minute television shows on the subject, right after the conference."

"Alright, I'll get right on it," Pete said.

As long as we had the Massachusetts and Cape Cod experts, we might as well do double duty by recording programs, also called "Why Can't Long Island?", to convey our message, unfiltered by the general press, right into the homes of hundreds of thousands of our neighbors. The two-part series would feature Kevin McDonald of Group for the South Fork and Joseph Gergela of the Long Island Farm Bureau, with columnist Karl Grossman hosting.

In just two weeks, Devens had crafted the set in seven fourteen-by-four-foot sections, with the help of an early Pine Barrens supporter and carpenter, Rich Gostic. Jennifer ran down a six-by-eight-foot section of motion picture screen from someone her father knew in the film business. The screen and set design were painted in the basement of one of Joe Colao's rental houses, just three days before the event.

It's important to remember that a key component of the original strategy was to project the Society as larger than it was. The degree of influence we had accumulated, the amount of press coverage we earned and the extent of our capacity to bring off Pine Barrens legislation would have been impossible if the Society was perceived as the understaffed, underfinanced group that we actually were. A key element in the campaign, as designed, was to control perceptions. So, in preparing this elaborate presentation, we were not showing off; we were ensuring the trappings necessary for acceptance of our grand objective.

The Tuesday before the conference, I called News 12 and arranged for a broadcast editorial on News 12 and many other Cablevision channels. Director of Editorials Lisa Allen, asked, "What do the following have in common? The New York State Court of Appeals, the New Jersey Pineland Commission, Massachusetts' Cape Cod Commission and the developers and environmentalists in the LIA-sponsored negotiations about Long Island's Pine Barrens?" Then, she answered her own question, "A recognition that there should be one entity, one commission or agency responsible for overseeing development in the environmentally-sensitive area that crosses different geographic boundaries." This lent important support for the preservation plan we sought. She concluded, "An upcoming conference sponsored by the Long Island Pine Barrens Society would be one forum in which to pursue this. Developers say they want to proceed responsibly. Environmental groups say they are not opposed to all development in the Pine Barrens. Both sides should show they mean what they say. Let's replace Long Island's patchwork quilt of regulation with a seamless plan." This was a great stage-setter for the run-up to "Why Can't Long Island?"

The media blitz continued the next day with an op-ed piece in *Newsday* that Tom and I wrote. Titled, "Look to New Jersey & Cape Cod on Pine Barrens." It called for "conciliation and accommodation aimed at determining what Pine Barrens land must be preserved and what can be developed." It advanced the concept of a "Core Preservation Area" surrounded by a "Compatible Growth Area" and pointed to the successful strategies adopted in New Jersey and Massachusetts. The piece expressed high hopes for the "Why Can't Long Island?" symposium. The next day, the paper ran an in-depth feature on the preservation plan for the New Jersey Pinelands. It quoted some builders, including Mancini, as expressing grave doubts about its lesson for Long Island. But the conference was positioned as a high-stakes, high-drama gathering, a real "don't miss " for Long Island leaders. It was also a media tour de force. News 12 did a special "Focus 12" segment on the eve of the news conference, and we did endless radio interviews to set the stage for the big event.

Even as we were advancing the run-up to the conference, we were planning follow-up media. At one taping of Joel Martin's cable television show, we asked when the videotaped program would air. It turned out that the program would be shown both before and after the conference. Kevin McDonald, who would appear on the show with me, turned and asked, "What am I supposed to say? `It was a great conference; I can't wait to go?'"

Production began at 5:00 A.M. on April 13. We picked up the set in Riverhead, installed audio-visual equipment, set tables, and rehearsed presentations. Preparations started badly. The eight-person team responsible for setting up the room discovered that the ceiling at what would be the back of the room was only 12 feet high. Like the proverbial boat builder in his basement who can't get it out when finished, Pete Devens' crew of bird lovers had committed a cardinal sin. They hadn't "measured twice and cut once."

"Amper may be a communications mastermind," Pete yelled for everyone to hear, "but an engineer he ain't." They contemplated cutting the set down from the top and lowering the painter's tape they had striped the set with at top and bottom. Then the non-engineer pointed to recessed sections of the ceiling further into the room, containing cove lighting and a chandelier. We simply moved it ten feet from the back of the room and up it went. And despite our earlier fears, the extra space was fully filled by the huge audience!

Volunteers greeted participants, answered questions, stroked egos, and assisted presenters, who turned in historic performances. Larocca emphasized his confidence that Long Island's environmental and economic communities could find common ground. Yaro said, "This could be the beginning of a tremendous opportunity for you to become one of the places that have discovered themselves." Carbonell and Moore calmly and precisely described the processes leading to the Cape Cod and New Jersey meetings of minds. Their presentations made overcoming conflict and preserving the Pine Barrens seem more doable, if only because they had been there, and done it. And Michael LoGrande entreated participants to imagine how good they would feel pointing to a Pine Barrens preserve while telling their grandchildren that they had had a hand in accomplishing it. It was clear that he genuinely meant it.

During a panel discussion at the end of the conference, County Executive Gaffney said, "A vehicle has to be found to preserve the Pine Barrens." Brookhaven Supervisor LaMura demanded state dollars for planning and acquisition. Riverhead Supervisor Janoski called the session "a good first step." And Southampton Supervisor Fred Thiele called the conference "an unqualified success." He added, "Not to preserve the Pine Barrens would be crazy."

Bob Wieboldt of the New York State Builders Association and I spoke respectfully and optimistically about the process of negotiating legislation that would produce a preservation plan everyone could live with.

Jennifer was ebullient. Everyone who should have been there was there. The tenseness that had marked everyone's arrival had lifted by program's end. Media coverage exceeded even the launch of the Pine Barrens Preservation Initiative. And Larocca and LoGrande seemed re-invested in helping to pull the players together for an assault on the summit. "I'm not exactly impartial, but I think we just may have pulled this off," Jennifer suggested.

The taping went well, and within days the television version of the conference was airing across the Island. "'Why Can't Long Island?' was a watershed," Deering remembers. "That the perceived power players had come together and acknowledged the need for action, elevated the issue to government's attention. The conference convinced a lot of people that a combination preservation/development plan could be done, because it had been done. Increasingly, folks were agreeing that it needed to be done."

The Society's conference was a pivotal event in the effort to save the Pine Barrens. The answer to the question "Why Can't Long Island," certainly seemed to be "Long Island can." Even the tone of negotiations changed. The conversations became more about what could be done than why it couldn't. As negotiations continued on Long Island, the focus soon began to shift to the legislative halls of the State Capitol in Albany.

Legislation

"A good politician is quite as unthinkable as an honest burglar."—H.L. Mencken

Negotiations for the Pine Barrens Protection Act began in January 1993 and ended in July of that year. In fact, we had been laying the groundwork for legislation since the first of the year. Apart from the visits to Cape Cod and New Jersey, we had met with and sought input from Citizens Campaign for the Environment and Nassau-Suffolk Neighborhood Network, two canvassing organizations that competed bitterly with each other and shared bad blood. We simply refused requests from each that would exclude the other. We also regularly briefed and solicited input from the Affiliated Brookhaven Civic Organizations, an umbrella group of civic associations; Group for the South Fork; North Fork Environmental Council; and the Open Space Council.

The Long Island Association's chairman James Larocca and the Suffolk County Water Authority's chairman Michael LoGrande played active roles in advancing the preservation plan on Long Island. New York State Assemblyman Tom DiNapoli and State Senator Ken LaValle presided over discussions in Albany. Bob Weiboldt and "Buzz" Schwenk represented developers' interests. I represented the environmentalists.

Our strategy was to identify the most sensitive Pine Barrens parcels and preserve them completely while allowing development in a less sensitive area of the Pine Barrens located closer to previously developed land. Negotiations were guided by the "Larocca map," which was produced mostly by the Pine Barrens Society's founders.

For their part, the developers wanted assurances that they could build with limited interference, especially in areas close to existing development. Of course, the builders wanted a majority of the Pine Barrens land, and that included significant parcels in the most environmentally sensitive areas.

At the beginning of negotiations, the developers demanded the right to develop most of the land they had targeted for 234 proposed projects all over the undeveloped Pine Barrens. As discussions moved on, the developers grew more and more impatient to start construction. The longer the process proceeded, the more willing they were to yield to our demands.

We talked with *Newsday*, the *Times* and News 12 on background, so that they would be ready to report the story when events warranted it. We asked Democrat Tom DiNapoli to sponsor a bill in the Assembly. While Assemblyman Steve Englebright had been involved in Pine Barrens preservation for years, the more moderate DiNapoli had seniority and Chairmanship of the Assembly's Water Commission. He also represented Nassau County, making Pine Barrens preservation a regional issue. Perhaps most important of all, he enjoyed a close relationship with Republican Ken LaValle, in whose State Senate district the Pine Barrens lay and who was certain to be the Senate sponsor, if we could talk him into it. We had met with DiNapoli on January 22 and LaValle on January 25 in 1993. They made no promises but laid out the bottom line: get consensus with the developers or fuhgeddaboudit.

Despite knowing that approval of a Pine Barrens law would be decided by the legislative leadership, egos required that our proposal be taken to Long Island members of the State Senate and Assembly. To avoid any optimism that sought-after legislation would be enacted, legislators regularly characterized even routine bills, as "a heavy lift." By mid-February we had met with Assembly Members Beehan, Sweeney, Cochrane, Bianchi, Sawicki and Environmental Conservation Chairman Richard Brodsky, as well as Senators Skelos, Trunzo, Johnson and Lack. Brodsky was a partisan Democrat, bright but very partisan; Skelos a self-satisfied Republican with ambition—he eventually became Senate Majority Leader and, years later, was sentenced to jail; and Lack, a pompous buffoon. He sat in front of us with the fingertips of both hands pressing together to form a tepee. He was the model of the politician who expects you to be grateful that he has deigned to grant you an audience. Public servant? He never heard the term. In the only truly negative prognostication we heard from anyone except *Newsday*'s Dan Fagin and Lee Koppelman, Senator Lack assured us that a Pine Barrens bill had "less than zero chance of passage." Upon exiting the Lack meeting, I said, "The name says it all."

Albany sucks. It's a dull, gray town during the legislative session, from January to June, supposedly. In effect, it's full of self-important windbags who take their direction from the Governor, the Assembly Speaker and the Senate Majority Leader. State Senator Caesar Trunzo made his contribution to history when asked his expected vote on the Environmental Protection Fund. "We haven't been notified yet," he said candidly. The good news is we didn't have to convince 150 legislators how to vote; they were all getting their voting instructions from on high.

It was clear that we would be spending a lot of time in New York's capital. And it was equally clear that the developers would be doing the same. The drive took five hours from the East End of Long Island, and we would need to spend dozens of days up there between January and the end of the session. U.S. Air flew the route from Islip MacArthur Airport in less than an hour, but in 1993 charged more than $400 for a ticket during the session. As a result, only lobbyists with big bucks could easily press their agendas.

We were going to need our own plane. Given our success fighting Governor Cuomo's jetport scheme, we thought there was just a chance that a grateful pilot of a small plane, eager to avoid jet traffic, might give us a cut-rate deal. We put up notices on bulletin boards in the pilots' ready rooms at Brookhaven and East Hampton Airports. "Keep eastern Long Island jet free. Help us obtain the necessary legislation. Regular trips to Albany needed. Signed Long Island Pine Barrens Society." To our amazement, it worked.

An amiable fellow with a good heart but often a blank expression called to introduce himself. A part-time radio reporter who taught flying lessons, Don Lewis generously offered to fly three of us to Albany anytime we wanted, for the cost of the fuel. He had a Piper Cherokee available. He didn't have a commercial pilot's license, but then we weren't paying. What a windfall. Since Don had nothing to do while we were meeting with the politicians, he decided to tag along. That didn't last very long because he kept injecting himself into meeting conversations with incomprehensible comments. Very odd. So, we gave him errands that didn't require interaction with the pols.

Week in and week out, we hopped up to Albany in an hour-and-a-half. Sometimes Jennifer Miller went, sometimes Pete Devens, sometimes a civic leader, but always Mike Deering, Society leader and aide to Assembly bill sponsor Tom DiNapoli, and me. At first, we tried staying at the Econo Lodge, because of the reasonable rates. By June, it had become clear that a lot of lobbying involved being seen with politicians in the "right" places. It was disgusting, but we did it anyway, taking them to dinner at places like Ogden's, Jake's and Lombardo's and staying at the Omni. Another fundraising challenge, but we were not to be outdone by the developers.

I couldn't stand the endless plying of the corridors of the airless Legislative Office Building, the flattering of egos and the ceaseless "hurry up and wait." Mike Deering loved it. "It's called process," he regularly reminded us.

It became clear that Albany featured three distinct casts of characters. In category one, there were the lobbyists—in this case the developers. The second category consisted of us and the third— the rest of the environmental lobby, most of whom were based in Albany for the session.

The environmental lobbyists were a class unto themselves. They rushed about the Capitol talking on cell phones and acting as though they were making a big difference. When they stopped to talk, they invariably asked, "What are you hearing?" By this they meant, "What have you learned the legislature is going to do?" Of course, the proper approach would be to say, "Are we making progress in getting them to do what we want them to do?" The idea that it was their job to tell the legislators what to do seemed to elude them. We, on the other hand, treated the elected officials as public servants who worked for us, and we behaved as though government functioned as it should. Eventually, and amazingly, it did!

Once Buzz and I reached agreement, we began visiting legislators whose egos required that they be read in personally on what we were asking for; we called it "ring-kissing." Because Buzz was the former Suffolk County Republican Chairman, he had relationships with many legislators, especially those in the Republican-controlled Senate. Time after time after we had pitched some State Senator, they would ask me to give Buzz some time alone together since they were past personal friends. After about the third time agreeing to this request, I asked Buzz what conversation transpired after my departure from these sessions. Buzz said, "Well, they all say they've heard that you're smart, but they can't believe that you're so naïve as to keep saying in public that the bill will pass because when the people are for something, it gets done--as though you were still in seventh grade civics class."

"What do you tell them?" I asked.

"I tell them, 'Dick doesn't believe it for a minute, but he knows you can't say, "That's not how it works in real life." By pretending that democracy works, the Pine Barrens Society is succeeding because you have to pay lip service to what the public wants, and once you do that, they've got you in a box.'"

We convened the Albany-based environmental lobbyists at a luncheon held in a conference room at the Legislative Office Building to ask these organizations from around the state to support our Pine Barrens bill. It was actually in their interest to do so, even though it was a local bill, because passing it would require passage of the Environmental Protection Fund, a pool of money that was supposed to be allotted annually for environmental purposes, but which the legislature hadn't passed for years. So, if we won, environmentalists across the state would win. Sharp people like Shelly Kath, the Sierra Club lobbyist, got it. Lee Wasserman, the dean of environmental lobbyists with the Environmental Protection Lobby, now Environmental Advocates, dismissed our efforts as "an inconsequential regional bill" and dissed our meeting with environmental lobbyists. He later emerged as one of the state's most astute environmental activists and served with me on the Board of Environmental Advocates of New York, one of the most effective environmental groups in New York State. But in this case, he got it wrong.

The environmental lobbyists were a dispirited lot. The Nature Conservancy's lobbyist, Andy Beers, seemed to understand the process, but acted like he wanted out of it as fast as he could find another job. Who could blame him? The Albany environmental lobby was not enjoying a string of wins and often seemed reconciled to inevitable defeat. The attitude and atmosphere made Albany even more depressing. Still, the Albany environmental lobbyists took themselves very seriously. One time, Kevin McDonald of Group for the South Fork pointed to two of them standing several yards apart in the quad between the Legislative Office Building and the Capitol, talking with animation on cell phones during a lunch break. "They're trying to look important," he explained to Jennifer Miller. "Actually, they're probably talking to each other." Jennifer labeled the environmental lobbyists "dweebs," and the name stuck.

Then, she said, there were the "grunts." That would be the staff of legislators, who did the grunt work of running the legislators' offices, producing memos, conference schedules, press releases, correspondence and occasionally moving legislation from sponsors to committees, to Assembly and Senate program staff, etc. We wouldn't meet with them. It was a routine practice of the Albany politicians to foist you off on staff, some of them decidedly more knowledgeable than the elected officials themselves. But we determined early on that such brush-offs were not consistent with appreciation of the importance of the Pine Barrens legislation, so we canceled meetings for which the elected official himself or herself did not appear.

This policy was important to elevating the Pine Barrens issue but need not be a general rule. For most issues, legislative staff may be the most useful way to get your position and agenda understood and advanced by an elected official. In our case, that was left to the dedicated and savvy Mike Deering, to diplomatically deal with his counterparts among legislative staff.

So, in fact, there was a third category—the elected officials themselves. This was the most important category. These were the men and women who intoned earnestly about the need for economic and environmental balance, then admitted they had nothing to say about whether our bill passed or lost. Jennifer's name for them was "assholes." With the characters now named, communication became easier. "Until the grunts get back to the dweebs, we're not going to have a clue as to what the assholes are really up to," she summed it up.

Thank God for Mike Deering. His understanding of Albany's ways, and unflappable patience despite all the bullshit, truly saved us. Schwenk said, "Mike Deering showed a hell of a lot of talent in shaping that legislation." He forged a close relationship with his counterpart in Senator LaValle's office, a cautious attorney named Brian Murphy. Many times, especially late in the process, they would overcome procedural bottlenecks and difficult wordsmithing with bill-drafting staff. As winter segued to spring, the real negotiation of the bill began in earnest.

One cold spring night after a mind-numbing day at the Capitol, Mike clambered into the back of the Piper Cherokee and immediately fell asleep next to a jovial civic leader, Desiree Passantino, who headed an organization called "Act Now." I sat next to the pilot, Don. He dutifully ran the pre-flight check list, and the next thing we knew we were at 3,000 feet and heading back toward a very welcome Long Island.

Though I had only been at the controls of a plane a few times, I've always been interested in aviation and I paid attention during the short flights. So, I reacted immediately when I heard Air Traffic Control repeat an instruction for Don to climb to 8,000 feet. He didn't answer. "Cherokee 4372 climb to 8,000 feet on a heading of one-eight-zero." Still no response. I glanced over at Don. He was clutching the yoke with white knuckles. Suspecting the problem, I pulled a flashlight from the glove box and shined it out the window. Sure enough, a thin coat of ice had formed on the wings. The small plane simply wouldn't climb.

"Come on, Don," I urged. "Respond to ATC and get us permission to descend to warmer air." We were shoulder-to-shoulder in the cramped compartment of the small plane. "Come on, Don," I pressed. Still, he sat frozen silently at the controls.

There were many eloquent speeches during the legislative campaign and many pithy sound bites. But the most memorable statement came from the back of the plane as Desiree leaned over and tapped Mike on the shoulder. She said unemotionally, "You might want to wake up for this!"

I realized that giving Don orders wasn't working. I kept thinking, "You're supposed to be the master of communication. Try another approach." I put my left arm around the big man and said quietly, "Don, anyone can fly a plane. We fly with you because we know you can handle yourself in an emergency. How about if we declare an emergency and ask Air Traffic Control for the nearest airport?"

Amazingly, it worked. "There's no emergency, we just have to get down," he snapped back, reaching for the radio. "Departure Control, this is Cherokee 4372. We have an icing condition and the plane won't climb. Where is the nearest airport?" The radio crackled about some county airport just two miles away and Don fumbled with the charts for information.

"I can't do it," he concluded. "The tower isn't manned."

"So what?" I replied, calmly so as not to lose him again.

"Forget it," he replied. "I was out last night practicing my instrument landings, and I just can't do it."

It was then that I realized an important oversight. As brilliant as the idea of finding a plane to take us to Albany may have been, it dawned on me for the first time that there was nobody at the Pine Barrens Society charged with checking out the credentials of pilots. I suggested that we reduce altitude and return to Albany. The air traffic controller balked. We were sufficiently far south that any descent would put us off radar. I negotiated with Air Traffic Control for 500 feet in reduced altitude for every five minutes flying time north and the plane turned back for Albany.

The cabin was very quiet. By the time we reached Albany, worse weather had closed in. I told Don that between us we could execute the required instrument landing. I said I would read out distance, altitude and air speed for the last two miles to the runway. He would keep the plane in the proper attitude for landing. He agreed. There wasn't much choice.

A mile out, at 700 feet up, we dropped below the ceiling. There before us, was the fully illuminated runway, clearly in sight for our final approach. "Visual flight rules," I yelled, "There's the runway, Don." His head buried in the instruments, he kept muttering "IFR (Instrument Flight Rules) all the way, IFR all the way."

We needed a new approach to communicating. Tapping him on his right shoulder I shouted, "My God, Don, what's that?" pointing up out of the cockpit windshield. He looked up for the first time. "My God, it's the runway!" he shouted. "Visual Flight Rules, Visual Flight Rules, all the way!"

He touched down and pulled the plane onto a taxiway. He then climbed over me to the exit. and ran for the terminal bathroom. "I'll be right back," he yelled. The tower radio invited us to taxi to the terminal, but we were in no hurry. We sat looking at each other in disbelief. I turned to Deering, using his favorite quote, " I know everything in Albany is a 'heavy lift,' but this takes the cake." "Yeah, with icing on top," Mike allowed.

Don returned in about ten minutes. He told us we'd have to spring for some de-icing fluid and that we'd soon be on our way. "We're going to that motel we passed on the way to the airport," I replied. "This is too much excitement for one day in the capital." The next day he tried to negotiate for "just a few gallons" of de-icing chemicals, even though the day was warmer. Aviation services explained that they had to use enough to de-ice the plane. You had to be able to afford both wings. We sprung for the de-icing and the return flight to Long Island was our last with Don Lewis. Sadly, months later, Don and two students died in a training crash.

Back on Long Island, the two peacemakers were hard at work. The Long Island business community was increasingly embracing the "Larocca map." And LoGrande's follow up to the "Why Can't Long Island?" conference made the chances for preservation legislation real. By mid-April Larocca and LoGrande were each in high gear. Immediately following the conference, LoGrande invited a large stakeholder group to lunch at the Culinary Institute of New York Institute of Technology's Central Islip campus. For his part, LoGrande wanted to demonstrate that he was a true environmentalist. It was the first of a series of "LoGrande Lunches," as they became known. Kevin McDonald enjoyed a much better relationship with LoGrande than I did, because he had not dueled with him during LoGrande's years at ABLI. So, Kevin went to more LoGrande meetings and I went to more Larocca meetings. For his part, Larocca saw himself as Long Island's leading businessman. He wanted to use his skills to work out a deal that would satisfy environmentalists and developers alike.

LoGrande saw the obvious drinking water implications of a Pine Barrens bill for the Suffolk County Water Authority he chaired, and was carrying on the tradition begun when, as Acting County Executive, he proposed Suffolk's Drinking Water Protection Program to fund land acquisitions. While LoGrande admitted that his approach to government favored "benevolent dictatorship," his surprising inclusiveness in a series of negotiating sessions at the Water Authority and later at the Pine Barrens Commission headquarters in Great River was unexpectedly democratic. Across town, parallel but more corporate talks under Larocca's leadership were underway at the Long Island Association headquarters in Commack. "LoGrande focused on the technical details needed to draft the law and involved a broad range of stakeholders," Deering remembered. "Larocca saw the LIA as a bridge between developers, especially Breslin, and the Pine Barrens Society, so the talks there were aimed principally at resolving policy differences." Mike pointed out that once again the Pine Barrens Society worked extremely hard between what became weekly meetings to prepare documents from which terms of the bill were hammered out. We had learned from the earlier negotiations that it was a great advantage to have everyone working from our documents, and we continued that practice at the Water Authority and the LIA talks.

As the end of June approached, we were running out of time, since the state legislature usually adjourned before July. Senator LaValle and Assemblyman DiNapoli both wanted to see the Pine Barrens Act adopted. They had from the very beginning.

One of the few truly nice guys in politics was New York State Assemblyman Thomas DiNapoli, then the Democratic Assemblyman from Great Neck and later New York State Comptroller.

169

Understated but big in intellect and decency, DiNapoli enjoyed being called "Tommy" by his colleagues, an informality few of them would have tolerated for themselves.

He was perfectly suited to co-sponsor the Pine Barrens Act with State Senator Ken LaValle, Republican of Port Jefferson. Both were low key, serious-minded legislators, possessed of keen political insight. Cautious and conservative in approach, LaValle, a meticulous dresser, was prone to private emotional outbursts, like the time he exploded over a Pine Barrens Society newsletter article celebrating his sponsorship of the bill. (He complained that he had not yet announced his support for the measure.) He also expected hierarchical deference, if not reverence, in ways DiNapoli never did.

Still, LaValle and DiNapoli worked very well together. Their greatest achievement began in downtown Albany. As Tom DiNapoli remembered it, the beginning of their partnership commenced coincidentally at Albany's Lombardo's restaurant, a hangout for a lot of legislators. "In going to our seats that night, we literally just crossed paths," DiNapoli explained. "I said, `What about this Pine Barrens stuff? I hear somebody else may be putting in a bill in the Senate' and he said, `Well, I hear maybe somebody else may be putting it in, in the Assembly' and I kind of said, `Well, given my role and interest in protecting groundwater and chairing the Water Commission, and your interest in being Mr. East End, maybe this is something that we could be constructively engaged in.'" They did.

As June 30th approached, timing was tight…the final details had to be worked out or the Legislature would simply walk away. Troubles grew, and tempers flared.

Gathered in Senator LaValle's well-appointed quarters in the Legislative Office Building (affectionately referred to as the "LOB"), were the Pine Barrens bill's sponsors, LaValle and State Assemblyman Tom DiNapoli. Bob Wieboldt and I were told to meet the sponsors for an important meeting. We were not told in advance of the day's special guest.

Faced with the unpopular prospect of his town's diminished power in land use decisions, Brookhaven Supervisor John LaMura was waiting for us. It was instantly clear that LaMura was being granted a last-minute appeal to limit the power of the new state commission which the bill would create. "Don't you think these land use decisions should be made by the elected officials of Brookhaven?" LaMura asked. Bob Wieboldt calmly observed that, had the towns acted responsibly in the first place, this confrontation would never have occurred, and the need for regional management would not now be necessary. With reference to the McNamara and other land use scandals swirling and as yet unresolved in Brookhaven, I snapped, "Maybe we can provide some role for Brookhaven's elected officials if they're not actually in jail at the time." Senator LaValle who regarded my irreverence as disrespectful, threw a copy of the draft Pine Barrens bill down on the table and stormed out of the room in anger. DiNapoli shrugged his shoulders and said, "I guess not, John."

In fact, State Senator Caesar Trunzo and Assemblyman Steven Englebright were prepared to introduce legislation—especially if LaValle and DiNapoli did not. As much as we appreciated Englebright's dedication to the environment, we preferred the DiNapoli/LaValle approach because it covered Long Island from West to East in terms of representation and mingled water protection with habitat preservation in terms of issues important to the respective legislators.

DiNapoli and LaValle limited their roles, leaving negotiation of the legislation to the stakeholders, principally the Pine Barrens Society and the developers—"a Zen approach," Wieboldt called it. "They basically said, `Make a deal and we'll write it into law,'" he explained. Only where impasse actually threatened the process did they step in to directly intervene in negotiations. For example, one day we got word that developer Wilbur Breslin and the Boy Scouts of America wanted changes to the Pine Barrens Act we were negotiating with the builders' lobby. Breslin wanted the buildable boundaries of his developable property expanded and the Boy Scouts wanted their land in the Pine Barrens excluded from the legislation. Wieboldt pulled me aside and warned, "If the sponsors start negotiating boundary changes, we're both screwed." We asked LaValle and DiNapoli to reject all boundary changes requested by people other the parties seeking the legislation. They agreed.

Later, the bill sponsors accepted developers' demands that the South Setauket Woods Pine Barrens (a separate 2,500-acre tract outside the Central Pine Barrens) be excluded from the Act. Schwenk pointed out that this boundary change was a demand of the builders who were obviously parties to the negotiations. "Englebright was mad," DiNapoli remembers, "but while I understood the legitimacy of his environmental arguments for inclusion, I was persuaded that it wasn't worth losing protection of the entire Central Pine Barrens over the matter." Later, Schwenk admitted that excluding South Setauket Woods from the legislation was a builders' mistake which left that area vulnerable to continuing litigation. Whatever the minimum area for Pine Barrens viability was, South Setauket Woods was smaller and not contiguous with the rest of the map, so we did not make its inclusion a big issue. In fact, we simply pretended it was a big deal, only to win other concessions. (In any case, a few South Setauket parcels were acquired later.)

Wieboldt used his intelligence and expertise to help manage the players. At one meeting, he stood up and pounded his fist on the table in response to one example of over-reaching by the Long Island builders, in the person of LIBI President David Scro. His uncharacteristic and unexpected anger and booming voice startled everyone in the room. "I've been trying to save you guys from yourselves for three years, now!" he hollered at Scro and LIBI attorney Phil Sanderman. "Try not to self-destruct at the eleventh hour." And in a statesman-like voice Senator LaValle, who mostly stayed out of the direct negotiations, interjected calmly, "The last five yards are always the toughest." Everyone calmed down and went back to work.

In fact, Wieboldt had reason for confidence. He had arranged for a "stopper"—a couple of key senators who had the power to kill the bill if the builders didn't like it. "Our first strategy," Wieboldt explained, "was to assure the capacity to kill it, but I worried that with support from other business interests we might have a problem. Besides, I viewed the Court of Appeals 'win' as a pyrrhic victory. I didn't want a situation where for 200 subdivisions, we'd have a new lawsuit in every case. The industry was in the doldrums and we were in a no-win situation. It was clear that the answer was to agree to a core area where our members did not have significant holdings, at least at that moment, and maybe sell off some of our future, but at the same time gain four or five years of immediate production. To me, it was a deal."

"What's your best alternative to a negotiated agreement?" Wieboldt asked the Long Island builders. Mancini understood the issues and opportunities. He supported Wieboldt's focus on "grandfathering" previously approved projects.

The process was dominated by suspicions and personalities. There was little trust. "Nobody before had ever been involved in a complex negotiation on the Island," Wieboldt explained. "Buzz and I had to assure the builders that between us we had 70 years of experience and weren't going to let the industry get hurt." He said the developers kept complaining, "What those environmentalists really want is to stop development and preserve everything," and Wieboldt kept replying, "Maybe they do, but the proposed legislation doesn't say that." Often, Weibolt was the voice of reason that kept reconciliation on track.

On one occasion, LIBI President David Scro came in with a list of five things the builders had to have. "Give me 30 minutes," Wieboldt told him. An hour later, his concerns had been addressed. The demands didn't threaten the environment, and Wieboldt had convinced him that the issues that most terrified Scro had been handled, so he felt better about his participation in continuing negotiations. "The only builder who got the big picture, though, was Mancini," Wieboldt said.

"Once the developers accepted the fact that the environmentalists were barracudas and weren't going to let go once they'd bit, they realized that either we carry a barracuda with us constantly nibbling at us all along or pay a certain price and face up to the barracuda, saying, `This is your turf and this is ours and we'll fight again later," Wieboldt recalled. "I kept telling them, `Don't worry, there is no such thing as permanent alliances, only a coming together on certain points.'"

As the legislative process neared an end, LaValle began prodding all sides to reach agreement. "My motivation was to build a sense that this was going to happen. Once people understand that something is going to happen, the nature of negotiations changes because everyone knows they have to cut the best deal they can," LaValle explained. LaValle said he made it clear to everyone that "I was going to get this done one way or another."

Throughout the process, Deering appeared cool and deliberate. Underneath, he was sweating bullets. DiNapoli had given him wide latitude to negotiate the bill, and he worked hand-in-glove with his counterpart Brian Murphy at LaValle's office. As much as he cared about obtaining Pine Barrens legislation, Deering demonstrated strict impartiality when the developers and environmentalists were at odds. I don't know how he avoided giving me the impression that he was not on our side, while playing the honest broker, but I never doubted his commitment.

On some things we just couldn't move him. Fortunately, they were really inconsequential. I repeatedly urged that the measure be called the Pine Barrens Preservation Act because preservation seemed so much grander than protection. Ray Corwin eschewed the term Central Pine Barrens Joint Planning and Policy Commission, preferring New York State Pine Barrens Commission. There must have been a hundred drafts. Each new version came back with the nomenclature unchanged. To this day, the Commission is burdened with the clumsy moniker, "Central Pine Barrens Joint Planning and Policy Commission."

Even as the final touches were being put on the Pine Barrens legislation in Albany, Lee Koppelman convened a bizarre meeting on Long Island, on June 10, 1993, of what he called a "Pine Barrens Council," chaired by an eccentric Suffolk County Community College Professor, John Black. As usual, Koppelman controlled the forum, which was ostensibly to work on a preservation plan. Deputy County Executive George Gatta urged us to send a representative to the meeting "to humor Koppelman," Gatta explained. "He's so far out of the loop, he doesn't even know the meeting is irrelevant," Gatta added. I called from Albany to ask Bob McGrath to attend the meeting. He recalls answering a two-part question from Regional D.E.C. Director Ray Cowan, "What are we doing here? Doesn't he know it's all done?" "No," McGrath answered, "he's clueless. You're watching the last desperate gasps of a guy, who if he'd had anything to do with it, would have killed Pine Barrens protection for good, years ago."

We flew back to Long Island on Northwest Airlink, a new service running trial flights from Republic Airport in Farmingdale. I went to meet with Nassau-Suffolk Neighborhood Network's Vincent Cioci. The group had reneged on a $10,000 support pledge from their canvass, so they owed us something. I asked Cioci to conduct a town-by-town petition campaign to place a referendum on the November ballot that would preclude the Suffolk County Department of Health Services from granting any septic system approvals (essential to a development's approval) in the absence of a cumulative impact study, which the courts had rejected. The intent was to scare the developers into negotiating the bill, so that they would not face the likely antipathy of the voters and a new law to halt construction. It was an extension of our strategy to make the developers prefer the bill to the alternatives.

In fairness, we never thought the Neighborhood Network had the capacity to mount such a campaign, and they didn't—but the publicity surrounding the effort provided exactly the pressure we wanted. Schwenk repeatedly asked me to order Neighborhood Network to stop the petition drive, but I assured him it would die a natural death with passage of the Pine Barrens Act. We weren't seen as negotiating in bad faith because it was the Neighborhood Network's initiative, but the petitioners were a visible presence in the community, and Neighborhood Network also used the canvas to increase the organization's coffers through contributions from those who signed.

Concurrent with negotiations of the Pine Barrens bill were negotiations on the Environmental Protection Fund. "Don't bother passing the Pine Barrens Act if it's not backed up by funds to pay property owners in the Core," Schwenk told Republican colleagues in the Senate. As the session wore on and on, and differences between developers and environmentalists dwindled, a strange sense of camaraderie developed as we worked the halls of the Capitol. Assemblyman DiNapoli was struck by the metamorphosis of Buzz Schwenk. "Buzz started off influenced by the limited horizons of some of his more extreme members, but discovered, somewhere along the way, being a born and bred East Ender, that this really had significance for the entire future definition of Long Island, and he became increasingly engaged in the possibility of this becoming a reality." DiNapoli said he saw Schwenk evolve in his relationship with me "as something other than a studied adversary at every turn, to really being someone who, although he could point out the excesses better than anybody, recognized that a lot of what was driving environmentalists made sense for the broad interests of all Long Islanders."

For his part, Schwenk credited my honesty and candor as "refreshing" and said that "it contributed to confidence in the honor and integrity of my negotiating partner." He and I later became fast friends when he quit the Long Island Builders Institute because it would not support the creation of a Community Preservation Fund for land protection on the East End of Long Island generally, but particularly in his home town of Southampton.

During dinner recesses, environmentalists and developers dined together at local restaurants. Bob Wieboldt was the instigator. He asked Schwenk and Scro of the Long Island builders to join him, without telling them he had asked Englebright, DiNapoli, Deering, Turner and me as well. He didn't tell us the developers were coming. "It was amazing," Wieboldt recalled, "All of a sudden they saw Dick Amper as a guy who could tell funny stories and was a human being and Dick and Buzz hit it off real well because Buzz appreciates the dry wit and good tales—that Rockefeller Republican kind of humor. Even Englebright wasn't such an asshole. The only one they were never sure of was Turner, because he kept looking at everybody with such distaste." Both Wieboldt and Englebright were huge men, and I never saw two men eat so much food at dinner in my entire life. Wieboldt ordered multiple entrees at once and Englebright simply waited to finish one before ordering second and third helpings. Schwenk behaved as though he had newfound friends in the environmental community. He demonstrated real pride at what we were collectively doing. Jennifer Miller described him as "a man transformed."

June ended. Still deadlocked on a budget, the legislature was struggling to finish its business by the Fourth of July weekend. Even as Senator LaValle prepared to introduce his bill on the floor of the Senate, there was more trouble. Governor Cuomo's office called Mike Deering and Brian Murphy to say that the Governor was objecting to provisions of the bill which said the state would indemnify the Pine Barrens towns from damages resulting from enforcement of the new law. The proposed bill said that the State Attorney General's office would defend lawsuits against the Act. Deering and Murphy demonstrated how minimal was the risk of successful "takings" litigation, where a landowner might claim he had lost all value in his land because of the new law. There was plenty of compensation to assure constitutionality, they pointed out, and they made it clear that without indemnification, the towns would reject the bill. Cuomo relented, but only temporarily. The New York State Department of Environmental Conservation also filed a memo in opposition to the Pine Barrens Act, probably at Cuomo's "request." Its action was inexplicable—unless the Governor was retaining an excuse to veto the bill.

We spent the endless days and nights plying the Legislative Office Building from DiNapoli's office to LaValle's and back. Then we would visit with program and counsel staff or press our agenda in the lobbies outside the Senate and Assembly chambers. Not a coffee drinker, I could be seen drinking Pepsi when DiNapoli arrived at his office early in the morning. We often ended the day with Cognac at the Omni Hotel or somewhere else. Later, DiNapoli observed that he thought that I sustained myself on cola and Cognac alone—the former to start me in the morning and the latter to stop me at night!

There were occasional moments of levity as when Senator LaValle, usually serious and often humorless, did a hysterical impression of Long Island Farm Bureau lobbyist Joseph Gergela. His mannerisms were perfect. I'd heard of but never saw LaValle's purported impression of me. And one morning after another night of battling to keep Wilbur "Willy" Breslin's Core Preservation Area property out of the Core Preservation Area, we came into DiNapoli's office to see a theater-size poster for the new movie, "Free Willy!"

In fact, DiNapoli's and LaValle's defense of the Core Area boundaries was one of their finest hours. The Pine Barrens Act "grandfathered" projects which had received their approvals before it was enacted, so Breslin was free to build his mall, even if his expansive other holdings were off limits. The Society and the bill's sponsors stood their ground against enormous pressure from Breslin, his lawyers and *Newsday* publisher Robert Johnson, all of whom threatened to scuttle the negotiations and kill the bill if Breslin's Core Area properties were not removed from the preservation map. In a late-night moment of high drama, we stood in LaValle's office and heard him courageously tell Breslin and Johnson, "This is bigger than any of us, now. I hope you'll support a good bill, but we're not changing the boundaries for anyone." It was Lavalle's finest hour.

Then there were the Boy Scouts. LaValle remembers, "In the closing hours, we had the [Nassau County Council of the] Boy Scouts of America march in and say they were going to oppose this [because some of their property was in the Core Preservation Area.] So, I said, `Great. I'm going to get on the phone to *Newsday* and there will be a headline: Boy Scouts Oppose Pine Barrens. You will look very, very foolish.'" LaValle then called Johnson, who promised to "take care of the problem." "An hour later," LaValle recalls, "I got a call from the Boy Scouts telling me they were on board."

DiNapoli and LaValle were getting along famously. The Senate jealously guards its prerogatives to introduce legislation and pass it before the Assembly. However, when the committee process moved more smoothly in the Assembly and the opportunity arose for DiNapoli to pass the bill first, LaValle urged him to do it. For his part, DiNapoli deferred.

LaValle was eloquent on the floor of the Senate as he debated the bill. He said, "Unchecked growth in the Pine Barrens could have caused the extinction of one of the last and most beautiful natural resources in our region." In a rare sight, there on the Senate floor behind him, stood

Assemblyman Tom DiNapoli. There was no dissent. The State Senate approved the measure 58-0 on July 2.

DiNapoli was not as fortunate. Republican Assemblyman Thomas Barraga and State Senator John Flanagan, both from Suffolk County, questioned the bill, especially the funding. Barraga was about as prescient as Custer when he said he was going to surround all the Indians. Barraga said to his colleagues, "I will tell you what will happen with this bill. It will pass unanimously, but the money will dry up. It will not come. In a couple of years there will be squabbling where I live as to who is at fault, and they will point to Albany and this chamber...You have the cherry, whipped cream, the nuts and you left out the ice cream. It is not here."

Despite a lengthy briefing in his office the day before, Assemblyman Flanagan questioned stakeholder support for the bill and some of its provisions on the floor of the Assembly. He dismissed it as "motherhood and apple pie." DiNapoli, with LaValle at his side, responded in the calm, deliberate demeanor of the understated gentleman DiNapoli is. "This is not motherhood and apple pie, John. This bill is about planning; it is about decision-making. You denigrate the bill when you call it motherhood and apple pie. This is about a very innovative, a very new way of thinking. This is about blood, sweat and tears, anger, breakdown of negotiations, hard deliberations, giving on points that had never been given before, committing funds that never happened before." DiNapoli concluded, "When we think of the Pine Barrens, when we think of our legacy, of the natural heritage we enjoy, we know that there are forces at work greater than us. Call it nature, call it God. By voting in favor of this legislation, you will be helping to ensure for Long Island's future and for the historic and environmental legacy of all New Yorkers that we, indeed, have a bright future and a future that we can walk in together, arm-in-arm." Assembly Environmental Conservation Chairman Richard Brodsky praised the legislation as a model of collaboration and pledged his support for the needed funding. Long Island Assembly Members Bianchi, Beehan, Cochrane and Sidikman spoke in favor, as did Steven Englebright, who was obviously moved by this moment in history. He said, "Born out of the crucible of conflict, the Pine Barrens Preserve is a gift to our children, a test of our capacity for wisdom, to protect our most precious land and water resources, a bold experiment in regional planning and a new partnership between state, county and local governments."

In the end, nobody dissented, and the Assembly approved the bill, on July 4, 148-0. When Assemblyman John Flanagan came across to shake hands with those of us who had been invited to the Assembly floor for the historic vote, Jennifer declined to shake his hand, angry at his words of opposition, despite the time spent resolving his concerns the day before. "Shaking someone's hand doesn't mean you necessarily like or respect him," I explained to Jennifer, "It just means you don't have a knife in your hand." She responded tersely, "If it weren't for those metal detectors in the lobby, I would have."

Now there remained only the matter of the Environmental Protection Fund—a huge matter! The Republicans pressured Senate Majority Leader Ralph Marino of Nassau County and the Democrats did likewise with Assembly Speaker Saul Weprin. The July 4 adjournment deadline missed, we all sat on the Capitol Mall watching fireworks, while the leadership struggled with its ambitious agenda. Day after day, Buzz Schwenk and I would check out of the Omni, hoping that closure would come today, only to check back in at night for the extended marathon. The Environmental Protection Fund was essential to assure that we had a funding source for the land we needed to preserve.

One night after 2:00 A.M., Buzz and I were walking together down a seemingly deserted corridor in the Capitol. As we came around the corner, we encountered the three most powerful people in the state, the Governor, Assembly Speaker and Senate Majority Leader, taking a break from their late-night negotiations. "If that isn't the odd couple," Senator Marino said of Schwenk and me. "I guess we can't say no to everyone on Long Island," Cuomo observed. And Speaker Saul Weprin added, "Don't worry about it, boys." It was the first hint that our optimism might be justified.

But what Mike Deering called "process" and I called "politics" continued. In the political deal that had made Ralph Marino Senate Majority Leader, a competitor, State Senator Ronald Stafford received something close to veto power over a fund to purchase the needed land. The silver-haired Plattsburgh Republican was on record as saying enough land had been preserved in the Adirondacks, and he wanted no more. For the past three years, the Senate had refused even to bring an environmental trust fund to the floor.

"There would not be an EPF today if there had not been a Pine Barrens Protection Act," DiNapoli asserted, "The Pine Barrens bill was as important to the EPF as the EPF was essential to the Pine Barrens Act."

"This year it's going to be different," promised Brodsky, the Westchester Democrat. "The Pine Barrens bill is so important to Marino that he'll overrule Stafford, and the Senate will pass the trust fund," he predicted.

At 2:30 A.M. on July 8, Cuomo, Weprin and Marino agreed. They approved a $100 million environmental trust fund, of which $10 million a year would be earmarked for state land acquisition in the Pine Barrens. At long last, we had won!

Or had we? By 3:00 A.M. rumors reached us that state environmental lobbyists were meeting secretly over a controversial provision of the agreed upon Environmental Protection Fund. They termed it a "deal breaker." Senator Stafford had slipped into the bill a requirement that before lands could be purchased with the state money, local government had to give its approval. This would effectively allow Adirondack towns to kill preservation. Worse still, the environmental lobbyists had Assembly members threatening to kill the trust fund if the offending provision were not removed.

Because the trust fund had given us what we wanted, no one from Long Island was invited to the meeting of environmental lobbyists, including the environment's greatest advocate in the Legislature, Assemblyman Steve Englebright. We found the meeting and crashed it.

It's understandable why the dweebs would exclude us from their deliberations. They didn't want to see legal obstruction of land acquisition in the Adirondack Park. Also, some of them had given the Pine Barrens bill short shrift, before they came to understand its passage was linked to approval of the trust fund. Still, we wanted to stand with the entire state environmental community, so we agreed to fight the veto provision with them. We suggested eliminating the local veto power over any parcels already listed on the state Open Space Plan, thus "grandfathering" the preservation sites, just as the developers had insisted previously-approved building sites must be exempt from the new law.

Cuomo, who had left the Capitol for the Governor's Mansion, conferred by phone with Weprin, Marino and Stafford. As the sun came up on the morning of July 8, the leadership agreed to the compromise, and the weary legislators waited for the language changes to be incorporated into the EPF, then approved the revised bill. The state environmental community, ecstatic over passage of the Environmental Protection Fund, if not necessarily the Pine Barrens Protection Act, prepared for an 8:00 A.M. news conference. They had, for the first time, a dedicated fund for the environment and we had the dollars to make the Pine Barrens Act work. The next day, I received a warm letter from Eric Sieve, a founder of Environmental Advocates, then the Environmental Planning Lobby, praising the Society for "the most courageous, decent act I have ever seen in Albany" for sticking with the state environmentalists at great risk to landmark legislation for Long Island.

There was no news conference for me. I rushed to Albany Airport and caught an empty Northwest Airlinks turboprop back to Farmingdale, where Robin was to pick me up. I walked to the back of the otherwise empty plane where a row of four contiguous seats could become a bed and stretched out. The pilots waived the usual safety announcements and said simply, "Good night!" I looked out the window briefly, hoping unreasonably never to see Albany again, and flew home. This time surely, we had finally won.

Nope. Even as I worked with Governor Cuomo's Long Island lieutenant Mark Grossman to prepare a rousing bill-signing ceremony, one at which the Governor insisted that I must not be the one to introduce him, there was more trouble. Joseph Martens, Deputy Secretary to the Governor for Energy and the Environment, called Mike Deering and Brian Murphy and told them to alert Senator LaValle and Assemblyman DiNapoli that Cuomo had, in the end, decided to veto the Pine Barrens bill.

Still trying to punish the Society for opposing his absurd Jetport plan, the Governor had returned to the issue of indemnification and was asking the Department of Environmental Conservation to help prepare the rationale for a veto message. The man who had, only days before, stayed up all night to the last minute of the six-month legislative session to fight for an Environmental Protection Fund and who was scheduled to sign the Pine Barrens Act with enormous fanfare, was having a temper tantrum.

Deering and Murphy stayed calm. They suggested amended language for the indemnification section to be adopted next session. Then they went to their bosses and explained the problem. To their credit, DiNapoli and LaValle stood their ground. Meanwhile Cuomo was being told of the political implications for him if he dumped on both the environmental and business communities of Long Island, a region with a population of 2.7 million people who regularly decide state-wide elections, the most important of which he currently faced.

Deering and Murphy went out of their ways to sound conciliatory as they advanced the indemnification alterative, a Chapter Amendment to the Pine Barrens Act, then expressed their hope that the Governor and his staff would change their minds. DiNapoli recalled, "There's no doubt that at nine o'clock on the morning of the bill signing, we were in the Water Authority office when the last telephone calls were exchanged, and we thought, `We're going to get in the cars and go out to the ceremony, and we don't know what the hell is going to happen when we get there.'"

Governor Cuomo arrived at Southaven County Park that day with the same Dixieland band we had recruited for the Lake Panamoka acquisition celebration seemingly hundreds of years earlier, playing "Happy Days Are Here Again" and with Mrs. Hommel's Fourth Grade Class from Shoreham, presenting a rousing rendition of "Wouldn't It Be Nice" from the "Why Can't Long Island" program.

There was one incredibly sour note sounded. Vincent Cioci, whose Long Island Neighborhood Network had been gathering petitions to keep pressure on the developers to negotiate the Pine Barrens legislation, showed up to denounce the bill and promised to press his petition drive. The entire environmental community ignored him, and Governor Cuomo told News 12's Bill Zimmerman, "Any jackass can kick down a barn; it takes a good man or woman to build one." Not surprisingly, the petitions were defective and the number of signatures inadequate, so our strategy worked despite Cioci's having betrayed us.

The environmentalists, civic leaders, developers, politicians, and volunteers were there by the hundreds, in a festive mood. All of the founders except McGrath (who was on a teaching trip abroad) were on hand for the achievement of their long-held dream. We took pictures in the woods for what seemed like forever, and especially in front of the Big Board we had used when we announced the lawsuit to visualize the preservation plan. I was a tired but exuberant man as I walked to the Governor's podium.

"The "War of the Woods" is over, and the people of Long Island have won," I proclaimed. "Today, Long Island obtains a first-rate, national park-quality nature preserve and a progressive new plan for future development that will serve as a model for this nation. The Long Island Pine Barrens thus joins the Adirondacks and the Catskills among New York State's greatest natural treasures. The statewide significance of our Pine Barrens is acknowledged with the creation of a 50,000-acre greenbelt that will protect our most important drinking water supply while we preserve a globally important habitat boasting the greatest biodiversity anywhere in New York State."

The Governor was eloquent, bringing some of the environmentalists to tears. He said, "This is an environmental state and the Pine Barrens now is its latest, most glorious expression. We're always looking for something bigger than we are, something more beautiful, something we can throw our arms around and wrap our souls around and say, `This is right, this is good; this is something I can believe in with passion, this is something I can give myself to.' And you find this truly barren land if you're looking for something larger than yourself and then it occurs to you— Niagara Falls, the Adirondacks, the Pine Barrens, the water under Long Island, the rivers, the chestnut tree in the park in South Jamaica, Queens—the environment, ecology, preserving it, saving it, fighting for it. I won't save a single fish in a single lake for me to catch with all that we do for clean water, but somebody will have a fish, some child ten generations from now who doesn't remember our name or even the place as it used to be will benefit from this. I've found it! Eureka! Something larger than me. Something beautiful. Something better than I am. Something to believe in. Something to give myself to, selflessly—not because I'll be able to build a house or make a dollar. Not because it will make me richer. Not because they'll pin a medal on me but because it's good, it's right and no quarrel and no dispute and no equivocation, with sureness, I go to bed tonight having signed a bill and made it a law knowing that I did the right thing. Thank you for that."

When he was done speaking, the Governor retired to a table and signed the Pine Barrens Protection Act of 1993. At that moment, more than 50,000 acres of pristine, watershed land, critical habitat—one of the world's "Last Great Places"—was off limits to development and preserved for the people, for all time. Then, Cuomo climbed into his limousine, remarking to his aide Mark Grossman, "That Amper is a genius, but I still hate his f---g guts," and drove off.

I was thrilled beyond belief.

The Plan

"Winning isn't everything, it's the only thing."—Vince Lombardi

In the end, the Pine Barrens Protection Act of 1993 emerged as a tremendous victory for the environment. At the bill signing ceremony for the Pine Barrens Protection Act, Michael Deering remembers thinking, "We've done something no one thought we could ever do: we'd won state legislation that would preserve huge portions of the Pine Barrens, but there's an enormous job still ahead to design and win town approval of the plan by which the remaining land will be developed." He was right. A key provision of the new law was ratification by the town boards of Brookhaven, Riverhead and Southampton. But as difficult as that challenge would prove, the environmentalists were increasingly driving the preservation/development agenda.

The new agency of government met for the first time August 6, 1993. Its cumbersome name, the Central Pine Barrens Joint Planning and Policy Commission, couldn't disguise the familiar cast of characters. Supervisors John LaMura of Brookhaven, Joseph Janoski of Riverhead and Fred Thiele of Southampton were seated with Suffolk County Executive Robert Gaffney and a man unknown to most, Ulric Haynes, Jr., the Dean of the Hofstra University School of Business, who was to represent the Governor.

The first meeting started almost an hour late as the new commissioners wrestled in a back room at the County Center in Riverhead over who would be named Chairman. Senator LaValle had urged Gaffney to take the leadership role, despite early doubts on the part of the County Executive. But LaMura wanted it too. The out-of-sight wrangling presaged too much of the Commission's work, which was to be conducted behind closed doors. I believe that the people's work should be done in public, and New York State has an open meetings law that lists such exceptions as confidential personnel and litigation matters as exemptions. The man who would ultimately be selected as Executive Director of the Commission, Ray Corwin, insisted that these provisions not be used or abused to hold regular Executive Sessions for no other purpose than to keep the people they represented from knowing what they were up to. So, the Commission renamed the secret meetings "Advisory Sessions," ostensibly limited to providing advice of counsel, but a secret session, by any other name, is a secret session.

At the outset, I think the commissioners saw themselves as the decision-makers. We and the developers saw it differently. We knew what we had agreed to do during negotiations, and we were now setting out to do it. Between meetings, the environmentalists and developers met and decided how we wanted the Commission to act on these matters. Thus, we went into the Commission's monthly meetings with a punch list of things we wanted done. This made it difficult for the Commission to act in conflict with both sides.

The Pine Barrens Act created a Core Preservation Area where development was largely prohibited. So, the Commission quickly began trying to develop the plan by which the

Compatible Growth Area, about 47,000 acres, was to be developed. This less sensitive property, much of it partially developed, was the land that mattered most to the developers. The Pine Barrens Act called for adoption of interim standards for acceptable development—things like how much of a parcel could be cleared, how much nitrogen discharge would be permitted, what slopes were too steep to build on, and so forth. A final plan had to be adopted within 18 months, though later this was extended by six months. At that point, the Town Boards of the Pine Barrens towns would vote to ratify the plan, or the Pine Barrens Act would self-destruct. Neither the environmentalists nor the developers wanted the plan to fail, so the commissioners were unlikely to piss everyone off.

The tight timetable was designed to keep the process of completing Pine Barrens planning moving, and it did just that. Deadlines force action. For the Society's part, we had won more than the territory we had sought initially for protection in the Core Preservation Area, and we now turned to ensuring that the area where development was permitted was not overrun. For this purpose, we had carefully crafted into the law the creation of an Advisory Committee of stakeholders who would help the Commission create and adopt a Comprehensive Land Use Plan. Unlike most government Advisory Committees which are appointed by politicians and are often little more than window dressing, this body was created by statute, with specific organizations represented from the business, environmental and civic communities. The developers, realtors, farmers, and Long Island Association were balanced by organizations like the Society, Group for the South Fork, North Fork Environmental Council, Long Island Greenbelt Trail Conference, Open Space Council and The Nature Conservancy along with civic leaders. Ultimately there were 26 in all. James Tripp of the Environmental Defense Fund and I nominated Michael LoGrande to Chair the Advisory Committee because he had the best relations with all of the stakeholders and had done well in chairing the LoGrande Lunches during negotiations. I served as Vice-Chair. In fairness, I think the developers saw LoGrande as sympathetic to them because of his role as a town planner and his involvement in the builders' lobby, A.B.L.I., so my subordinate role was O.K. with the developers.

The Advisory Committee established three sub-committees: one each for Land Management, Ecology and the Transfer of Development Rights Program. The TDR sub-committee was abolished when the quasi-independent Pine Barrens Credit Clearinghouse was established to manage the TDR program.

The TDR Program was designed to supplement acquisition of Pine Barrens land for preservation. Property owners of land in the development-prohibited Core Preservation Area could obtain TDRs, called Pine Barrens Credits, that would permit them to develop at greater density than permitted under zoning in areas outside the Core, or to obtain extra sewage discharge (to expand a restaurant, for example). These credits thus had monetary value both to the landowner and to a developer who would purchase them from the landowner. In fact, most of the credits were used for extra sewage discharge, mostly in sewered areas where groundwater impacts were less of a concern. Although 2,000 acres of Core Preservation Area land was protected through the use of

TDRs, the three Pine Barrens towns demanded that 75 percent of preserved land be paid for without TDRs.

TDRs thus served to re-direct development out of the most sensitive water recharge areas to less-sensitive land elsewhere. It further assured property owners of just compensation for land they could no longer develop.

Buzz Schwenk and I then agreed to nominate Ray Corwin, the former Society Board Member and current Water Authority employee, to be Executive Director of the Pine Barrens Commission because he was transparently fair and chose to remain outside of politics. Corwin was calm, dry, and deductive. He did not engage in politics and was unflappable. With an undergraduate degree in math and a Master's in computer science, Corwin was working in the Suffolk County Water Authority's Watershed Division when LoGrande charged it with a key professional role in negotiating the Pine Barrens bill and plan. An enthusiastic Water Authority attorney, Timothy Hopkins, was part of the early Corwin team, working tirelessly with Natural Resources Defense Council leader Jim Tripp on the Pine Barrens Credit Clearinghouse. Later, another SCWA lawyer, John Milazzo, became the Commission's legal counsel after a stint by James Rigano.

Ray Corwin was a perfect fit for the job of day-to-day management of the Pine Barrens Commission staff. His matter-of-fact style gave the developers and environmentalists comfort that he wouldn't give any side an advantage. "I tried not to turn issues that we had to solve into issues that were confrontational," he said. "That is not to say that there doesn't need to be confrontation. It's just that at that particular time, I didn't need to create controversy or confrontation, because there was already plenty of it out there. I agree that strategically, some confrontation is necessary and good. Sometimes it takes crisis to create the environment for action. There were plenty of people out there engaged in controversy, so I didn't think it my role to engage in it." Corwin assiduously sought to keep the process of plan development open and inclusive. "We accepted input from everyone," Corwin said.

"Corwin was a key guy who didn't have any baggage, was respected and unfettered," Suffolk planner Steve Jones observed. "He knew the land, had enthusiasm but a low-key personality and was very well organized—just what was needed."

Even those groups which had been on the periphery during negotiations were now included, with one notable exception. The law made no provision for the seating of any groups solely concerned with property rights. This was deliberate. While we recognized that owners of private property in the Pine Barrens were indeed stakeholders, we felt that their interests were not readily distinguishable from those of the developers (and to a large extent the Long Island Farm Bureau). We were concerned that such a group could be expected to fail the primary test for inclusion in the Pine Barrens preservation debate—namely a commitment to Pine Barrens preservation. We weren't wrong.

From the very first meetings, a few strident owners of private property declared themselves victims of the new law, charging that it was an unconstitutional taking of private property and generally whining about everything. "Their concerns were bogus," Michael LoGrande concluded. "Most of them have never seen the property they owned and couldn't get to it if they wanted to," he added. He was right. There were thousands of tiny parcels, most of them landlocked by surrounding undeveloped property. Before the "War of the Woods", this land was nearly worthless. It would have cost a fortune to bring in roads and utilities, even to build a modest home. Many property owners had gotten their deeds for free as part of a bank promotion years earlier. That's how little this land was worth. But now that government was preserving Pine Barrens, suddenly this land was priceless, owners argued.

New Jersey's Terrence Moore had established the tenet, "No windfalls; no wipeouts," to describe the intended effects of Pine Barrens legislation. Nobody should get rich quick, and nobody should be economically hurt. In fact, most of the private property owners benefited from having a willing buyer prepared to pay fair market value for their land. Some were better off as a result of a program that supplemented the state, county and town land purchase programs.

Then, by using Transferable Development Rights, owners could sell it to someone who was developing property somewhere else on the island and could use it to build slightly more than the zoning would otherwise allow. The value of that development right would be set by the market and by its worth in the "receiving area," where an extra house that might be built would be worth more than it would have been in the middle of the woods—the "sending area." Still, the malcontents created a Civil Property Rights (CPR) group, which filed a lawsuit against New York State for approving the Pine Barrens Act. We think CPR would better have served owners of private property by advising them of opportunities to sell their land or development rights instead. The value of a development right, at one point, exceeded $100,000. In any case, they lost at both the state and federal levels.

The Pine Barrens Commission was new, but the behavior of its Commissioners was old hat. They declined to meet with the Advisory Committee for many months and basically behaved like politicians. County Executive Gaffney made a genuine effort to be even-handed and pressed the Commission to meet difficult deadlines. A mid-level but knowledgeable deputy, George Proios, sat in for him regularly and was goal-oriented. Ulrich Haynes rarely attended meetings representing the Governor and was soon replaced by Ray Cowan, the Regional Director of the New York State Department of Environmental Conservation for Long Island. Cowan actually behaved as though he was supposed to implement the Pine Barrens Act, which they were all supposed to do but frequently didn't. His was the only consistent voice of reason on the Commission, with the exception of that of Fred Thiele, Supervisor of Southampton, who was a goal-oriented leader from the outset. Supervisors James Stark of Riverhead, who succeeded Joseph Janoski, and John LaMura of Brookhaven were not regularly helpful.

It quickly became clear that decision-making was falling back into the hands of politicians and out of the hands of stakeholders. For example, Riverhead Supervisor Stark threatened that if his town didn't get funding and permits from the New York State Department of Environmental Conservation, his town board would disapprove and thus kill the Pine Barrens Act. This wouldn't do. The negotiation process taught us that we could get what we wanted from the politicians most times simply by agreeing together with businesspeople on what we both wanted.

The deadline for the approval of the Pine Barrens Act and plan was nearing. So, frustrated by the arbitrariness of the Commission, often at the hands of lawyers and planning department staff, I created the "Consensus Group," a coalition of stakeholders. Our plan was to take the job out of the bureaucrats' hands by doing it ourselves, as we had done with the legislation. I asked the Long Island Association to convene a small group of major players from the economic and environmental communities to discuss objectives. There was Jim Tripp from Environmental Defense Fund, Sara Davison from The Nature Conservancy and I representing environmental interests; Mitch Pally, from the Long Island Association; Herbert Balin, the attorney representing Breslin Realty; and Don Eversoll from the Long Island Builders Institute, representing business interests. Eversoll, one of the Island's leading home builders, did not officially represent LIBI, and his presence undercut "Buzz" Schwenk's avoidance of the Consensus Group. "Don Eversoll's involvement in the Consensus Group compromised LIBI," Schwenk said. He was still smarting from LIBI's poor end-game performance in negotiations and would be further hampered by the ideological rantings of new LIBI president James Zizzi, a zealot if I ever met one. LIBI debated internally whether or not to join the forum but decided against it. With Breslin and Eversoll representing the perceived needs of developers, the Builders Institute was marginalized at a time when many of the issues most important to them were coming to the fore.

Michael LoGrande represented the Water Authority on the Consensus Group, Mike Deering sat in for Assemblyman DiNapoli, and Ann Libassi represented Senator LaValle. We simply continued the negotiating process begun a year earlier, deciding on this matter and that, then appeared before the Commission to tell them what we had agreed upon.

"Who appointed you?" one Brookhaven bureaucrat said during our first presentation. "We appointed ourselves," I replied. "We're supposed to make the decisions around here," he retorted. "And we're telling you what decisions you're supposed to make," I shrugged. Through solidarity, we were able to reinforce our view that public officials have no legitimate stake different from those who will be affected by the decision-making. Thus, the process continued to be driven by the agreed-upon interests of the stakeholders. The Consensus Group recommended that the new Pine Barrens Commission abolish the superseded Suffolk County Pine Barrens Review Commission to reduce the red-tape for the developers and called for expedited funding for acquisitions—essential to environmental preservation. Then, we moved on to specific standards and guidelines. After a while, the politicians gave up their resentment of this self-created ad hoc group which made monthly pronouncements. The bureaucrats decided to look on the bright side: at least they wouldn't have to make any decisions they could be faulted for later.

We had fought for and won good legislation to preserve the Pine Barrens, but we did even better negotiating the Management Plan–the rules prescribing what the developers could do and what they couldn't. LIBI's James Zizzi was a right-wing ideologue who "saw the Pine Barrens Society as radical, fringe, elitist environmentalists representing only a handful of people who were taking over 50,000 acres as a part of a much larger plot," Bob Wieboldt explained. "Zizzi thought the whole thing was a Communist plot and was really down on it. To this day he doesn't think it was a good deal."

The developers hired consultants to advise them on the creation of the Management Plan. They included Theresa Elkowitz, an environmental aide to industry; Philip Sanderman, the former Brookhaven Town Attorney; and Vincent Donnelly of the engineering firm Nelson & Pope. They didn't help much. Wieboldt agreed. "Our consultants kept telling the builders, who were their clients in real life, that this thing was a real threat. They thought they had to act more right-wing than the builders did," Wieboldt explained, "The paranoid three were like the Macbeth witches," he said "They saw evil under every rock."

Wieboldt thought the legislation was fair and served the builders as well as the environmentalists. Still, he had some regrets, "Retrospectively, the core area line was poorly drawn for industry," he said. "It went down the middle of roads and should have permitted development on both sides before the core began. We should have hung in for that, but the environmentalists had better people on the ground who knew the land better and had a way of articulating the need."

But once negotiations returned to Long Island, largely outside Wiebolt's influence, the developers' position grew more contentious. Key provisions of the land use plan were negotiated at the Long Island Association, while the majority of the plan was created at the Suffolk County Water Authority. Elements agreed to one week were reneged on by the builders at the next. The developers' paid consultants kept issuing new demands if only to keep them on the payroll. The new LIA President, Mathew Crosson, who had succeeded Larocca, grew more and more impatient with the bad faith. Repeatedly, negotiations ended with solid agreements. Then, Zizzi would renounce them and instruct Buzz Schwenk to go back and renegotiate the same points. "Buzz could not make it look like the environmentalists were getting what they wanted week to week without making the builders feel like they were losing the war," Wieboldt explained. "Buzz was hamstrung because of this. He had some real hard-liners who were very irrational about the whole thing. Others were rational but paranoid, and the consultants enhanced the paranoia."

As a result of all this, the developers negotiated badly. Wieboldt explained, "The builders should have understood the deal and focused on what was important to them, but they missed the point. For example, there was a major failure to grasp the Transfer of Development Rights potential, and we gave it over to Jim Tripp and the planning types with their Dutch auctions and Socialist horseshit and ended up with nothing. Buzz thought that TDR was some kind of far-out concept. The real issue for us was how many units that would otherwise have been built in the Core could be built elsewhere." Ultimately, the builders agreed to town demands that at least 75 percent of the Core Preservation Area would be preserved by acquisition. This was, in part, because towns were giving away extra density anyway, without requiring the redemption of Pine Barrens credits.

Instead of focusing on this key area of interest, LIBI spent months haggling over special protection for something called Critical Resource Areas. These were environmentally-significant parts of the Compatible Growth Area, many of them already publicly owned, but the builders simplistically fought them stubbornly as an invasion of their territory. Wieboldt says, "The CRAs were obviously very environmentally important spots—wetlands, lakes and so forth—and we didn't really have to be building there. We could have given away literally dozens of them as long as they weren't in private hands or ripe for development. Meanwhile, we let the TDR thing get in the hands of the planners and get completely blown away and not made useful."

As the planning process neared the ratification deadline, LIBI erupted again. The Pine Barrens Commission was quietly suppressing a badly executed analysis of the economic impacts of the plan, and Jim Zizzi smelled a rat. "What are you hiding?" the paranoid president asked. "I told them it was a lousy study that they were trying to bury, which could show nothing of any use to us," Wieboldt remembered. "What are they hiding and why are they hiding it?" Wieboldt says Zizzi repeated. The developers' group sued and won access to the document which contained nothing harmful to the builders. "It was just a bad study," Schwenk agreed. But the developers' paranoid behavior undercut their credibility and undermined their negotiating strength.

Meanwhile, the process of completing the Management Plan neared the end. Fred Thiele praised Suffolk County's role in developing the Pine Barrens Plan. "Gaffney and his people were very good," he said. "At first, the state seemed indifferent, uncommitted, but after Ray Cowan replaced Ulrich Haynes, the state participation was much better."

Remarkably, despite disparate interests and tough deadlines, the Land Use Plan was falling into place. Nevertheless, the Commissioners couldn't resist the urge to push through their pet projects, regardless of the new Pine Barrens Act. As predicted during the drafting of the legislation, the Supervisors could be counted on to support their fellow supervisors when one wanted something for his own town. For example, just months after passage of the Pine Barrens law, Supervisor LaMura proposed clear-cutting 30 acres of Pine Barrens core in town-owned parkland for the construction of soccer fields for the Longwood Youth Soccer Association. Preposterous. The law said clearing constituted development and that development was prohibited in the core. Developers were being told by government that they could not do something that the government itself was trying to do as soon as the law was passed. The Commission went along by a vote of 3-2.

The first test of the new law was at hand. This could not be allowed to stand. It would mean that anything a Town Supervisor decided to do would be pushed through with the three supervisors' votes. The Pine Barrens Protection Act would be a meaningless piece of paper.
We had painstakingly built into the statute specific language that governed what could be done and what could not be done. Both environmentalists and developers had sought certainty on matters important to them and wanted local discretion to be strictly limited. The Society immediately challenged the soccer field approval in court, charging that the Commission had no authority to approve something now prohibited by law, regardless of their vote. The Court

agreed. State Supreme Court Justice R. Bromley Hall concluded, "Just as it is difficult to have the Clean Water Act without water or the Clean Air Act without air, so it is to have a Pine Barrens Reserve Act without pine trees."

It was during the soccer field litigation that Corwin resigned from the Pine Barrens Society's Board of Directors. "I didn't want to be in the position of sitting on the Board of Directors of an organization that was suing the people who were paying me," Corwin explained. This was a rare case where Corwin was wrong. The people who were paying him were Long Islanders, not politicians.

The first court defeat didn't stop Brookhaven. Three years later, the Town approved a million-cubic-yard sand mining operation on the border of the Core Preservation and Compatible Growth Area at the Marando Nursery in Manorville. The acting Commissioners were warned by the Commission's counsel in Executive Session that the plan violated the tree-clearing standards contained in the Pine Barrens plan. The meeting adjourned temporarily while new Brookhaven Supervisor Felix Grucci called Riverhead Supervisor James Stark and new Southampton Supervisor Vincent Cannuscio to the Commission meeting. The three marched into the meeting room in lockstep. They sat down, Grucci moved the Marando proposal, Stark seconded it and Cannuscio called the question. The sand mine, termed "nursery expansion" was approved 3-2, in two minutes flat. Then they marched out, almost knocking over petite Lauren Terrazano, a reporter for *Newsday*. On their way out the door, Grucci deputy Jesse Garcia leaned over and whispered to me, "So much for your f--ing Pine Barrens law. We make the law in Brookhaven."

Suffolk Chief Judge Mary Werner disagreed. We sued again, and in her opinion, she declared: "The proposal which provides for 72.85 percent clearance is violative of the [Pine Barrens] plan which allows for only 65 percent clearance. The Commission violated [the Pine Barrens Act] by approving this project which is not in conformity with the plan. The approval is thus arbitrary and capricious and must be annulled." Our effort to limit discretion by the town supervisors was paying off.

The Pine Barrens law was working. The politicians were trying to have their way, despite the Pine Barrens Act but the courts were saying, "you can't do that." Next, Riverhead Supervisor Stark had a dirty deal he wanted his fellow Supervisors to support. The Nassau County Council of the Boy Scouts of America, which owned 550 acres surrounding Lake Wauwepex in Wading River, had sought to have the land excluded from the Core Preservation Area when the Pine Barrens Act was before the Legislature, but their efforts had proven no more successful than Breslin's. The boundary lines weren't changed, but Scout attorney Donald Pupke had assurances built into the law that recreational use by the scouts would not be infringed upon.

Now, a friend of Stark's was proposing to build a golf course on 147 acres of the Boy Scout property. It seemed the Nassau County Council had fallen on hard times—its coffers lower than low. The Scouts wanted to sell a huge swath of their camp for as much as two million dollars. It looked like Stark figured he was due his payoff for supporting Brookhaven's Grucci over the sand mine. We quickly blasted the move all over television and the press, charging that clear-cutting a Boy Scout camp was "like Smokey the Bear setting fire to the forest."

Public outrage was tremendous. Letters to the editor poured in, contributors to the Boy Scouts threatened to stop giving, articles appeared about bad management at the Nassau County Council and young scouts lectured their leaders. More important, Ray Cowan of the Department of Environmental Conservation, now representing the Governor on the Pine Barrens Commission, moved to bring off one of the fastest land-acquisition deals in the history of Pine Barrens preservation. Seeing that the scout leaders were hurting themselves, the Governor's representative was looking for a quick way out. He made it clear to the scout leaders who had applied to the Commission for a hardship exemption that they should "think acquisition." The quick availability of funds and the firestorm of opposition to the golf course plan put a quick end to this latest effort to thwart the Pine Barrens law through cronyism.

The confrontation ended not with a bang, but with a good laugh. At the Commission meeting following the preservation of the camp (which the Scouts continue to use today), we took turns making jokes about the absurdity of converting a scout camp into a golf course. We suggested that had the plan been approved, yuppy Nassau scouts would soon trade their khaki uniforms for plaid pants and polo shirts…they would stop cooking hot dogs and marshmallows over campfires, turning instead to eating sushi at the club house … they would stop helping elderly ladies across the street but would instead allow seniors to "play through."

Equally funny was the Society's Awards Gala in honor of Ray Corwin's increasingly successful work. When, in 1995, Corwin won the Society's award for "Outstanding Contribution to Long Island's Environment," Commission Counsel James Rigano barred him from attending the ceremony. "The Commission members didn't think it was a big deal one way or the other," Corwin recalled. "but Rigano said I couldn't go."

Always avoiding confrontation, Corwin went to the movies that night. He was represented by a life-sized cardboard cut-out of him accompanied by a video which showed Corwin in his various unemotional paper-pushing functions, cut to the music of the rock classic "Wild Thing." Here again, the hilarity broke the tension of petty politics, to the enjoyment of the 17th Anniversary Dinner Dance audience.

As the final review of the plan approached, Riverhead town officials used their capacity to kill it as a weapon to obtain concessions on the re-use of the Navy-owned airfield at Calverton, which had been the site of the infamous proposed jetport. Outspoken Riverhead Councilman Victor Prusinowski told reporters that the Pine Barrens plan was "dead on arrival" in Riverhead and told News 12 that the vaunted Pine Barrens bill had "now reached the lowest form of government there is." Had it not been for the existence of Brookhaven, we would have been forced to agree.

By now, we were nearing the end of the two-year period that followed the approval of the Pine Barrens Protection Act. Commission activity was fundamentally focused on how the new law would work, how local government would be impacted and how environmentalists and developers would complete the complicated process.

Apart from negotiating the rules and regulations for preservation and development, the Pine Barrens Society campaigned non-stop for public appreciation and support. We spoke in front of scores of community groups, maintained good relations with most public officials, especially the town boards in Brookhaven, Riverhead and Southampton, and ensured that an ecosystem known to less than 3% of the Island's population in 1989 was appreciated as an environmental treasure Island-wide by 1995.

Because the law provided that the towns had to ratify the Pine Barrens Act for it to take effect, we had to maintain positive relations with Brookhaven, Southampton and Riverhead. As 1995 emerged, there were a couple of pro-development council members in Brookhaven who were still not in love with the Pine Barrens. We knew Riverhead was demanding favors from New York State in exchange for ratifying the Act. Only Southampton was a sure friend as we approached the end game.

"There was a lot of posturing," Fred Thiele observed. "Once the Pine Barrens Act was approved in '93, nobody who ever again had to run for office wanted to be the guy who blew up the Pine Barrens Plan. It took a long time for everybody to see their enlightened self-interest," Thiele continued, "I was in the trenches in the '80s as a planning board attorney dealing with developers every day. Nobody wanted to sell their land; everybody wanted to 'max out.' The developers' mentality was against clustering, against acquisition, against everything. It was all black and white."

"What turned the situation around," he concluded," was that even those developers who didn't like the process at least had to pay heed to it. By now, it was clearly established that the public wanted the Pine Barrens preserved, and anyone who got in the way of it was a bad guy. The elected officials got the message more quickly than the developers got it, but ultimately the business community finally recognized that they had to be a part of the solution."

Because Southampton Town had taken the most environmentally-supportive position, and after checking individually with Thiele and his Town Board members to assure a unanimous vote, we went to town hall with a cake and Champagne to celebrate with our friends in office. To our shock and horror, Councilman Douglas Penny, a bright but volatile councilman, objected loudly. "How dare you presume our vote" he shouted at the top of his lungs. "I won't be a part of any PR show!" he screamed, waving his hands in the air. Everyone was taken aback. To this day, no one knows why he exploded. "It's hard to understand," Thiele noted, " because most of us have this premise that we can expect people to act at least in their own self-interest, but sometimes Doug just liked to be contrary for the sake of being contrary." Penny and the rest of the Town Board later voted unanimously in favor of the Pine Barrens Plan, as expected. However, Penny was not re-elected the following November.

In the week before the deadline for ratification, we went from one town board to the next, first to answer questions, then to watch the vote. The two most pro-development members of the three town boards were Eugene Gerrard and Patricia Strebel. Both were Brookhaven Town Council members. Gerard voted against the Pine Barrens Plan and Strebel arranged to be absent on the day of the vote. The rest voted "yes." Riverhead had no opinion about the Pine Barrens Act at all. But the Town held out to the last day, holding its town board meeting even as Governor George Pataki's plane headed toward Francis Gabreski Airport in Westhampton Beach in the Dwarf Pine Barrens for the plan's signing ceremony.

Riverhead had issues with the D.E.C. over re-development of the Navy-owned Calverton airfield, scheduled to be transferred to the town after Grumman/Northrop abandoned operations there, including required sewage treatment facilities and development within the Peconic River corridor. It was clear that Stark and the Town Board were seeking concessions in return for Plan ratification. The extortion continued to the eleventh hour.

As we waited for Riverhead's vote, a young college student, Christine Chase, who was writing her master's thesis on the Pine Barrens Preservation Initiative, approached me. "Mr. Amper," she said, "no matter how this turns out, you'll have the satisfaction of knowing there was nothing more anyone could have done. It's not whether you win or lose, but how you play the game."

I corrected her gently. "If they don't ratify this, we will have wasted five years of our lives for absolutely nothing. How you play the game is important only in determining whether you win or lose, but thanks anyway." In the end, Riverhead got what it wanted, ratified the plan and everyone headed for Westhampton.

The signing ceremony was set up by the Pine Barrens Commission and the Suffolk County Water Authority, with little or no community involvement. I didn't care about that…we had gotten the job done! Under a huge tent several hundred chairs faced a long dais occupied by public officials, but from which the Society and the other stakeholders were excluded. Sharon Olsen, whose husband co-chaired the so-called Civil Property Rights group of angry private property owners, came up to me and said, "We may not agree with you all the time, but it is undeniable that you and your group made this happen. I think it's outrageous that you're not being recognized."

I replied, "After today, we can turn all of our attention to making sure that you owners of property in the Pine Barrens get paid for your land. When the politicians are made to do it and stage some political show to brag about it, you won't care anymore than we do about recognition."

LIBI President James Zizzi, who had been such a pain during negotiating the plan, opposed it to the end. Buzz Schwenk actually showed up at the signing ceremony dressed as a hobo and carrying a sign which read, "This will be the future of our industry if the plan is approved." For all the lofty speeches about compromise and consensus, in the end, the developers had simply been out-thought, out-worked and out-maneuvered, even if it was impolitic to say it at the time. We had preserved acres of Pine Barrens, far more than anyone had ever expected we could save. More important than the numbers were that we had preserved an ecosystem—a true natural treasure.

Governor Pataki flew in after two passes over the Pine Barrens, suggested by Mike LoGrande so he could get a sense of what was being protected. Senator LaValle, who was on the plane with the Governor, described his appreciation. "The Governor had not been given prepared remarks, so he asked a lot of questions and his enthusiasm was evident as he scribbled notes about the significance of the achievement. His remarks were extemporaneous and from the heart," LaValle said.

In his speech, Governor Pataki said, "In government and in life, there is a very fine and important balance that you have to reach and this legislation—with today, the adoption of the Comprehensive Land Use Plan—we are putting in place a critical element of that balance." Then he signed the Land Use Plan into law. The day was Wednesday, June 28, 1995.

Patti Ann Browne reported on News 12: "Governor Pataki called it a model for the rest of the state and the rest of the country. Others called the Pine Barrens Plan, 'Long Island's greatest success story.' Today, the Pine Barrens Protection Plan was cemented into law, capping years of compromise and consensus-building by former adversaries who put aside their differences to protect the island they love."

Newsday emblazoned "The Pine Barrens Saved" on its Thursday front page over a wrap-around photograph of the Peconic River Pine Barrens. There was page after page of stories and pictures and a pull-out guide to the ecosystem. The veteran land use reporter Tom Morris wrote, "Gathered on the edge of a great watershed forest and on the cutting edge of Long Island history, top local officials and New York's governor yesterday signed an unprecedented pact to preserve the Central Pine Barrens for its water and its wilderness."

The Regional Plan Association's Bob Yaro said, "I think the Pine Barrens plan is a very big deal. It is Long Island shouting out that 'The pavement stops here.'" Barbara Kelly, curator of the Long Island Studies Institute at Hofstra University said, "I'm certain that 50 and 100 years from now, people will look back and admire our foresight in protecting the Pine Barrens." And I was quoted as saying simply, "Congratulations Long Island—we did it."

The following day *Newsday* editorialized, "A lot of Long Islanders have never paid a visit to this uniquely precious ecosystem. But now we'll have plenty of time to explore and savor the Pine Barrens, because a handful of determined leaders were farsighted enough to save them for the rest of us and for generations of Long Islanders to come. We'll also have plenty of time to drink up the bounty under the Pine Barrens: an estimated 15 trillion gallons of water that now should remain pure enough for our great-grandchildren to drink."

Cryan and McGrath attended the ceremony. Regretfully, Turner had been invited to participate in a prestigious environmental conference out west. Jennifer Miller attended, as did Christine Chase, the thesis writer and the woman who succeeded Miller at the Society.

As the afternoon ended, *New York Times* reporter John Rather, who had written often about our years of confrontation with government and the developers, asked, "Does this historic accomplishment prove that the system works?"

"Off the record," I replied, "only if you drag it kicking and screaming against its will."

Epilogue

2022

"Innovations are 10 percent inspiration and 90 percent perspiration."
-Thomas Edison

Almost 30 years have passed since the signing into law of the Pine Barrens Preservation Act. In 2019 we reached our goal of preserving over 100,000 acres of Pine Barrens at a cost of $2 billion dollars…funds that the people of Long Island supported throughout this campaign.

Today, the Society is poised to acquire the last remaining Pine Barrens parcels totaling over 3,500 acres while it serves as a watchdog to ensure that the preserved acres remain forever wild. We encourage Long Islanders to visit the Pine Barrens to appreciate the treasures they have saved. Two of the founders remain Long Islanders and serve on the Society's Board of Directors. The third lives in upstate New York and serves as a constant adviser to us.

As an example of how a region can get something done, the Pine Barrens Preservation Act and resulting plan can serve as a model for doing so. A program officer with the Rockefeller Brothers Fund thought our use of communications might be a model for some of their other grantees. NYS Governors Pataki and Cuomo cited the law and the plan as models for the state and the nation.

Perhaps the leading dedicated champion of Pine Barrens protection is Nancy Rauch Douzinas. The foundation that she leads has contributed significantly to our efforts for more than the last two decades.

The battle to save Long Island's premier ecosystem was a life-changing experience. Starting out as a novice with a passing interest in the environment, I learned what it means to be an environmentalist and to fight to reach a desired public goal. I developed strategies to engage volunteers and the public to achieve what was viewed by many as impossible. A very rewarding process and outcome!

CPSIA information can be obtained
at www.ICGtesting.com
Printed in the USA
BVHW010232110123
656076BV00024B/442